THE GARDEN

An Illustrated History

By the same author:

A History of Flower Arrangement

Flowers and Table Settings

Flowers in Glass

THE GARDEN

An Illustrated History   *by Julia S. Berrall*

A Studio Book

THE VIKING PRESS · NEW YORK

The Library of Congress cataloged the first printing of this title as follows:
Berrall, Julia S
The garden; an illustrated history, by Julia S. Berrall. New York, The Viking Press [1966]
388 p. illus. (part col.) plans. 29 cm. (A Studio book)
Bibliographical references included in "Notes" (p. 382)
1. Gardens—Hist. I. Title.
SB451.B47   712.09   66–18845
ISBN 0-670-33433-2

Designed by Nicolas Ducrot
Printed in the United States of America
Second printing May 1978

Contents

The following plates also appear in color, following page 196:
15, 16, 32, 34, 52, 69, 105, 138, 149, 178, 179, 180, 189, 190.

Foreword

The story of the garden begins in the earliest days of civilization when man not only had learned the worth of plants, fruits, nuts, and grains as a supplement to his diet of meat but had started to cultivate them close to his home. He ceased to be a nomadic hunter and settled down in communal villages to farm the land and care for the animals he had domesticated. With the rapid advance of civilization and its technological achievements, artistic expression gradually developed and time for leisure became available. Two kinds of garden therefore evolved — the truly utilitarian one of fruits and vegetables meant to provide food for a man's family and the restful "pleasure garden" designed to nourish a man's soul. It is with the story of such "pleasure gardens" that this book is concerned.

Gardens have brought beauty, quiet, and repose to those who have sought a retreat from the burdens of daily living. They have also formed the settings for colorful and exciting pageantry. Large or small, grandiose scheme or intimate enclosure, they have all mirrored the cultural achievements of a period in history or expressed a way of life. Most important of all, in their character they have revealed the vagaries of climate and geography.

The practice of gardening has been so nearly universal that it would be impossible to write of all its manifestations, but throughout its long history certain trends have become styles and styles have become "the fashion." Usually the wealthy have been the pace setters, and in this survey we shall see many royal "pleasaunces" and lordly estates, many of them still in existence. Since examples from every country cannot be shown, most of the illustrations are of those gardens that typify a particular style or period or are accessible to today's travelers.

Plates

1. "The Garden of Eden." Primitive American painting by Erastus Salisbury Field, circa 1860. Close by the river which waters Eden, Eve plucks the fruit of the Tree of Knowledge of Good and Evil. (*Courtesy of Webb Gallery of American Art, Shelburne, Vermont. Frohman*)

2. Plan of the garden estate of a wealthy Egyptian official. The approach is from a long canal (at right), and the entrance to the grounds is through an imposing gateway in their surrounding walls. Of particular interest are the two clearly indicated different types of palm trees growing around the garden. The single-trunked tree is the date palm and the bifurcated tree the doum palm. From Ippolito Rosellini's *I Monumenti dell' Egitto e della Nubia. (New York Public Library. Photo: Roche*)

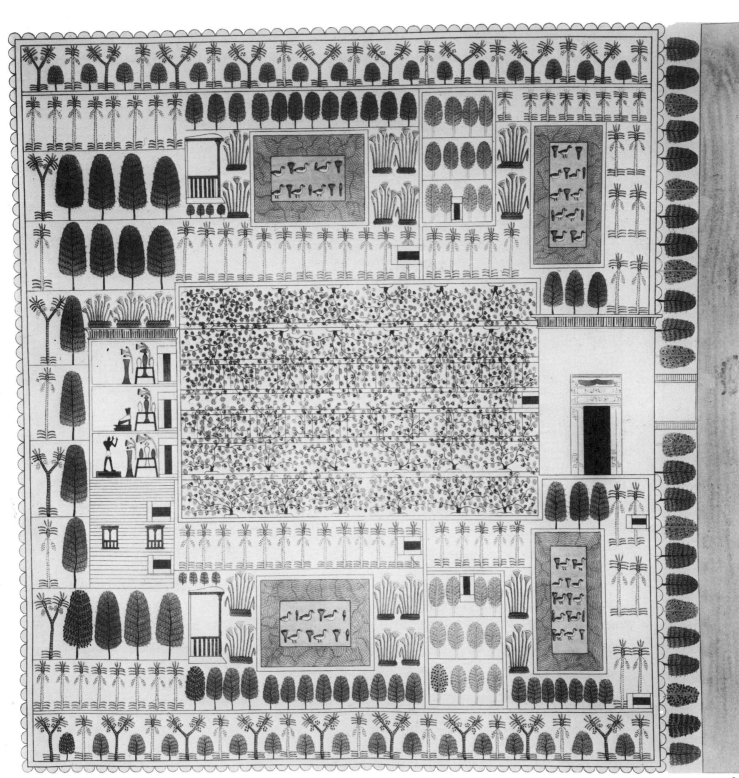

2

I

In the Time of the Pharaohs

Man's earliest cultures developed beside the mighty rivers of the Near East — the Nile, the Tigris, and the Euphrates — where the two life-giving factors of water and hot sunshine enabled man's first civilizations to grow, as seeds grow. Here, we are taught, the first garden was created — the Garden of Eden. Eden, Paradise, Park: the words were synonymous to the old translators. The Old Testament story tells how the Lord planted trees of all kinds, including the Tree of Life and the Tree of Knowledge of Good and Evil, and of how "a river went out of Eden to water the garden." This was the very essence of ancient gardening: shade for comfort and water for irrigation.

We know more about Egyptian gardens than about any others in the ancient world, for they were pictured in the tombs, either in sculptural relief or in painting, and there are many references to gardening, trees, and flowers in hieroglyphics carved on the walls and written on papyri. No ancient home or palace is extant today, as their bricks and timbers have not survived, but the stone temples and the tombs, built as eternal dwellings for the dead, reveal to us the full story of life in ancient Egypt.

Not only the gardens but the whole of Egyptian life and economy were dependent on the great river running the length of the country from its cataracts to the Mediterranean. The Nile has always overflowed with predictable regularity and gentleness, gradually depositing over the land a broad layer of dark, fertile soil which is easy to work and full of nutrients. Its flooding, from mid-July to mid-October, has insured dependable crops for centuries. The Nile Valley is a long casually winding ribbon of greenery, sometimes bordered by the dull brown of arid land and sometimes rimmed with shimmering deserts or rocky cliffs.

Many prosperous Egyptians built their villas outside the limits of towns and cities, and their extensive landholdings supported large households, including slaves. Huge walls were constructed around these country estates to protect them from marauders and wild animals and from the searing desert winds. The estates above the flood lines of the Nile needed irrigation to sustain orchards and vineyards as well as vegetable and flower beds. To achieve this, canals were dug from the river, some deep enough for river boats, others designed as ditches from which water could be carried to the crops or to storage wells and pools. The latter, either T-shaped or rectangular, often became decorative elements in the garden. A simple water hoist was devised, consisting of a pole weighted at one end by a stone and a leather bucket suspended from the other end. Called a *shaduf*, it is still used in Egypt today. Water was also transported by serfs carrying water skins or wearing shoulder yokes from which clay pots were suspended. With constant evaporation under the hot sun, it must have been a continuous chore to keep plants watered and the reservoirs full. Some paintings show trees surrounded with built-up rims of earth to conserve the moisture.

All plans and delineations of Egyptian gardens indicate that they were formal and geometrical and therefore, in design, the prototype of all gardens throughout Europe and the Near East for over three thousand years.

The most complete plan of a villa and its surroundings was discovered in a Theban tomb during the last century by the Italian Egyptologist Ippolito Rosellini. The estate may have belonged to a high official of the reign of Amenhotep III (circa 1411–1375 B.C.), for its mile-long canal, imposing entrance gate, numerous trees, and large vineyard all suggest great wealth. One can imagine arriving there by boat, stepping immediately into the cool protection of the gate, and then walking to the villa under the shelter of the grape arbor. The roof of the villa is shaded by awnings, and small garden pavilions overlooking the storage pools invite relaxation. One is impressed not only by the architectural details, the orderly symmetry, and the loveliness of growing things, but also by the functionalism of the whole plan. The shade-giving trees all bore fruit. We recognize the date palm and the forked doum palm, sometimes called the gingerbread palm. Probably the darker trees are sycamore figs (*Ficus sycomorus*), which, because of their dense, almost evergreen foliage, were desirable as shade trees. The smaller trees beneath the palms were probably the common fig (*Ficus carica*) or pomegranate. The large vineyard of long, trellised arbors gave a bounteous wine harvest and the rectangular, papyrus-bordered pools containing lotus and water fowl also became storage tanks for fish, which were fed and kept for eating.

The wall painting of Neb-Amun's gratitude for his wealth dating from the Eighteenth Dynasty (circa 1415 B.C.), has the same features of shade and water. It shows a T-shaped pool bordered with sycamores and terminated by a gate opening to a vine-covered pergola where servants are gathering grapes. The posts of the pergola were probably painted, and the columns have conventionalized papyrus capitals. A funeral scene found in another tomb of the same period contains a detail of a large garden in which a small summerhouse and a large pond are depicted. The corpse of the owner is being rowed across as a priest offers prayers. On shore, men are burning incense and waiting to honor the dead man with flowers. We see wine jars for the burial feast, covered with vine leaves to keep them cool, and bread and cakes prepared as votive offerings.

Besides the large garden estates there were small city gardens belonging to the middle classes in which a tree-shaded well was probably the most important single feature, with checkerboard vegetable plots and straggling grapevines. Sometimes there may have been a few flowers such as red poppies or blue cornflowers (*Centaurea cyanus*), for we know from their art that the Egyptians loved pure, bright color. These utilitarian gardens were pleasurable only insofar as they also provided restful shade and a few colorful flowers. It also seems possible that acacia and tamarisk trees were sometimes planted, for their blossoms attract bees, and honey was the only known sweetener in those days.

The gardens belonging to the temples and the royal gardens were naturally the largest of all. A wonderfully complete plan of a royal villa and its grounds, including an orchard of trees surrounding a very large pool, was found in the tomb of a high priest at Tell el

13

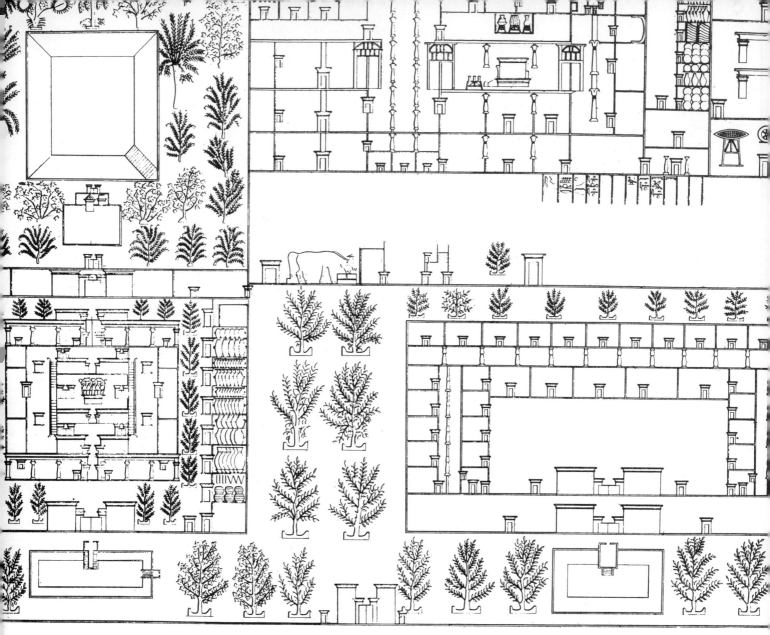

'Amarna, the site of the city built by Ikhnaton in the fourteenth century B.C. Outdoor living space shaded by trees is indicated in the complex of colonnaded courtyards, at the center of which is a high altar reached by ramps. The plan also indicates living quarters for a large number of people, horse stables, and many store rooms.

A temple garden represented in an early scene is believed to be that of Karnak. Large boats on the Nile approach the canal and pool in front of the temple. Inside the temple the high priest is presenting King Neferhotep with a bouquet for his queen, Meryet-Re, who has been awaiting him outside. If this is the Karnak temple, as, from the obelisk standing near the entrance pylon, it appears to be, it was depicted before King Thutmose III (who reigned from circa 1501 to 1496 B.C. and circa 1493 to 1447 B.C.) built the vast hall with its rows of heavy columns. At one time fine gardens spanned the two-mile distance between the temple at Karnak and the one at Luxor. Excavation is still going on along the stone roadway connecting them, where probably as many as fourteen hundred sphinxes, at fifteen-foot intervals, line the sides. A revealing inscription on the base of one of them

14

(LEFT) Plan of the buildings and gardens of a royal or priestly villa at Tell el 'Amarna, drawn from a bas-relief. Pomegranates, figs, and date palms are among the recognizable trees surrounding the very large pool (upper left). In other areas the trees are encircled with built-up mud banks for water retention. (*E. Prisse d'Avennes*, Histoire de l'Art Egyptien)

(RIGHT) Suggested restoration of a portion of the royal villa at Tell el 'Amarna. (*Charles Chipiez*)

tells of the Thirteenth Dynasty pharaoh who started the road: "He built this road in honor of his father and lined it with trees and flowers."

Flowers or herbs must surely have been cultivated in these temple gardens, for the Egyptian priest was skilled in medicine — "more than any of human kind," Homer wrote. The papyri tell us that the following medicinal plants were in common use: acacia, aloe, anise, caraway, colchicum, castor beans, cassia, coriander, cucumber, cumin, dill, elderberry, gentian, lettuce, lotus, mint, myrrh, pomegranate, poppy, squill, saffron, and wormwood. (The word "lotus" is a misnomer. *Nelumbium speciosum* or *nucifera*—the true pink lotus — is not indigenous to Egypt. Blue and white water lilies, *nymphaea caerulea* and *nymphaea lotus*, are the flowers the ancient Egyptians knew.)

There are many references to the sacred groves of trees often planted around temples; in this land where trees were scarce, they were greatly venerated. Some, such as the incense trees of Punt, were acquired as tribute from foreign countries. (The incense tree was probably *Boswellia*. Its dried gum is frankincense.) On one occasion Queen Hatshepsut, who began her reign about 1501 B.C., sent an expedition of five sailing vessels to the land of Punt (now thought to be Somaliland) to obtain myrrh trees for the mortuary temple she built for herself in the western cliffs of Thebes. After its magnificently proportioned triple terraces and colonnades had been planted, the Queen proudly proclaimed that she had made for the god Amon "a Punt in his garden, just as he commanded me. . . . It is large enough for him to walk abroad in it."[1] Within the temple, sculptured relief and hieroglyphics tell the story. The great ships, which sailed over three hundred miles down the Nile and probably through a canal into the Red Sea, are shown being loaded by bearers carrying the incense trees in rope slings. The Queen's half-brother and husband, Thutmose III, who reigned jointly with her for a period of years, became a great empire builder. Yearly campaigns extended his kingdom as far east as the Euphrates River. Recorded for history in relief in one of the great halls at Karnak are all the flowers, plants, and animals he found and brought home from Syria and Palestine.

The Egyptian, firmly believing in a life hereafter, planned his tomb long before old age. By custom, when he died, all the appurtenances which had provided comfort and happiness during his lifetime were placed in the tomb for his future needs. Small-scale models of objects in daily use were often used for this purpose. Wall decorations recalled the happy times of a man's life, his proudest accomplishments, and the activities he wished to continue. Since gardens and flowers had furnished many of the pleasantest moments in life, they were frequently depicted.

The so-called "lotus" which grew in the quiet waters of the Nile appears more often in tomb pictures than any other flower. It was sacred to the goddess Isis, and its form was easily conventionalized. It is laid on banquet tables, worn in the hair or in garlands around the neck, offered as gifts, and placed in vases. Frequently its form became the capital of a column just as the palm and papyrus forms did. Other flowers and blossoming trees were popular, but since their complex forms were difficult to depict they rarely appear in art forms. Preserved funeral garlands found on mummies show us that the following plants existed: cornflower (*Centaurea cyanus*), false saffron (*Carthamus tinctorius*), mallow (*Malva alcea*), and corn poppy (*Papaver Rhoeas*), as well as the small flowering trees acacia and tamarisk. *Lawsonia inermis*, which provided henna for use as a cosmetic dye, has also been identified. Many more flowers were introduced to Egypt during the Graeco-Roman period and became easily acclimatized. Perfume recipes mention sweet flag (*Acorus calamus*), white jasmine, and a morning-glory or bindweed. The rose (*Rosa sancta*) dates from the period also. Tombs of the era have revealed *Anemone coronaria*, *Narcissus Tazetta*, *Chrysanthemum coronarium*, *Lupinus Termis*, *Delphinium orientale*, grass pea (*Lathyrus sativus*), and *Celosia argentea*. Pliny, the naturalist, mentioned the opium poppy (*Papaver somniferum*) and cockscomb (*Celosia cristata*).

During the several thousand years of ancient Egyptian civilization, flowers were such an important part of daily living that many gardeners — men, women, and children — were employed to cultivate them. Besides maintenance and watering, it was also the gardeners' responsibility to fashion the garlands and chaplets worn during religious and social festivities. In fact, it was not uncommon for a favored gardener to be commemorated in death

16

by a statue or an impressive tomb. One of the most beautiful tomb interiors of the Theban necropolis is that of a royal gardener, Senufer. The entire ceiling is painted to resemble a grape arbor with stems, foliage, and flowers climbing up the walls.

The people and the gardens they cared for are clearly portrayed in Egyptian writings. An ancient love poem reads:

> I am thy beloved,
> I am for thee like the garden,
> Which I have planted with flowers
> And all sweet-smelling herbs.

And what could make these gardens spring to life more vividly than the touchingly human and realistic agreement between a young woman of the third century and her gardener? She, Talames, says to the gardener, Peftumont: "If you intend to be gardener for me in my garden then you are to give water to it. You are to give drawings of water to it in the proper measure of twenty-eight hins of water to the pot. . . . You are to connect the dyke to my garden . . . and you are not to cause me to compel you to do it. . . ." She asks him to make four baskets of palm fiber in the evenings for transportation of earth, and charges him to protect the garden against sparrows and crows. She gives him his choice of payment: wheat, gold, or bronze, though she will not take on the obligation of milling the wheat. To protect himself against being blamed for injuries, or to lessen her interference by frightening her, he insists that when she comes to the garden, she wear a covering on her head because of the sunshine, and a pair of work shoes because of stones. He charges her to bring a spear in her hand because of the hyena, and a sword because of the wolf![2]

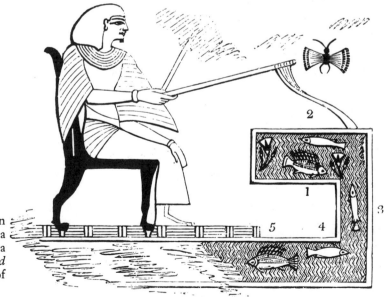

One of the pleasures enjoyed in an Egyptian garden was fishing in a storage pool or reservoir. From a Theban tomb. (*Georges Perrot and Charles Chipiez, 1883*, History of Art in Ancient Egypt)

17

Plates

3. King Neferhotep receiving a bouquet at the temple of Karnak and bestowing it upon his queen. The garden before the temple is tree-bordered, and its pool has a landing stage for boats from the Nile. Papyrus and grapevines grow near the canal. Note the water-hoist, or *shaduf*, at lower left. (*Norman de Garis Davies, "Tomb of Neferhotep at Thebes," Metropolitan Museum Publication*)

4. Neb-Amun's gratitude for his wealth. Tomb painting, circa 1415 B.C. A house is indicated in the upper right corner. Before it lies a tree-lined pool, at the far end of which a gate opens into the grape arbor. (*Metropolitan Museum of Art*)

5. Men and monkeys gathering figs. Wall sculpture at Beni-Hassan. Tomb of Khnemhotep, circa 1920–1900 B.C. (*Nina M. Davies, University of Chicago Press*)

6. Funeral scene in a garden, circa 1450 B.C. A long staircase leads down from the house to the pool, across which the coffin of its former master, Min-nakhte, overseer of the granaries of all Egypt, is being poled. Servants are carrying ceremonial bundles of papyrus reeds. The shape of these staffs inspired Egyptian architects to design columns with papyrus capitals. In the painting, palm trees are seen with suckers at their bases, from which new trees would be propagated. (*Metropolitan Museum of Art*)

7. Girls gathering "lotuses" in the marshes. These flowers were used in many decorative ways at ceremonies and within the home. A painting in the Theban Tomb of Menna, circa 1420–1411 B.C. (*Nina M. Davies, University of Chicago Press*)

8. Men of Punt offering tribute. Wall painting from Tomb of Rekh-mi-Re at Thebes, circa 1450 B.C. The dark-skinned men from Africa's east coast bring incense trees, and ostrich feathers and eggs as gifts. The trees, carried in rope slings, were probably balled with woven date palm fiber. (*Metropolitan Museum of Art*)

9. The high priest Userhet relaxes in his garden. Under the shade of a fig tree in which birds are singing he enjoys a beaker of wine or beer while a servant offers him a selection of fruits — figs, pomegranates, and grapes. A pool can be seen at the lower right of the painting. From a Theban tomb, circa 1313–1292 B.C. (*Nina M. Davies, University of Chicago Press*)

10. Wall painting in the tomb of Khac-em-Weset, Thebes, Eighteenth Dynasty. A scene in a grape arbor, in which serfs are harvesting the grapes and watering the vines. (*Metropolitan Museum of Art*)

11. An ornamental fish pond in the garden of Nebamen, a "scribe who keeps account of the corn of Amen." This painting from a Theban tomb, circa 1400 B.C., suggests a shady oasis and beauty spot in a larger garden scheme. A variety of colorful flowering plants and papyrus border the lotus-filled pool and the surrounding trees include date palms, figs, sycamore figs, and pomegranates. A grapevine is indicated in the lower left corner of the painting. (*British Museum*)

12. Plan of an average-sized house and garden. The irrigation canal is lined with palm trees, and the checkerboard garden was probably meant for vegetables and herbs, with incidental flowers. (*E. Prisse d'Avennes, Histoire de l'Art Egyptien*)

13. Wall painting showing the use of the *shaduf* for drawing water. The large tree is a pomegranate, and beneath it is a pollard willow. The small house or garden pavilion, seen at the left, has steps and a pillared portico. The column represents a bundle of papyrus stems, with tapered buds forming the capital. On the surface of the pool float clearly delineated "lotuses." (*Metropolitan Museum of Art*)

3

4

5

6

7

8

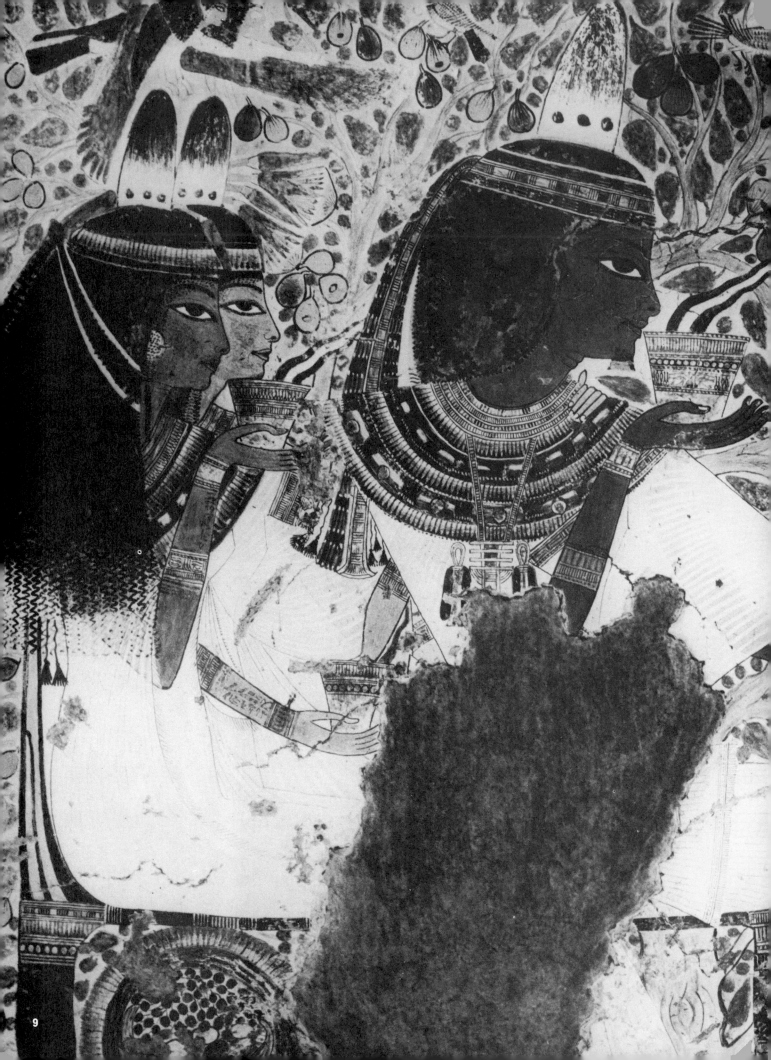

9

10

11

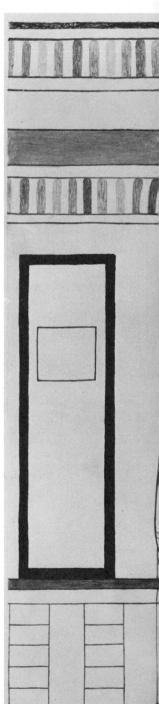

12

13

II

Mesopotamia:
"The Land between the Rivers"

The great Tigris-Euphrates Valley has left no important garden heritage except the establishment of the park. Unlike the Nile, whose gradual flooding and receding enabled the Egyptians to plant in the fall and harvest fully matured crops by March or April, the rivers of Mesopotamia, rising in the Armenian mountains, became violent torrents which deluged the land with water, mud, and rubble. The floods came in May and subsided within a few weeks, after which the lands dried out; by July they were already parched by the scorching sun.

In their efforts to control the floods, irrigationists engineered vast lakes, reservoirs, and, between the two rivers, a network of canals, the maintenance of which was imperative to the country's economy. History tells of forced labor under Hammurabi, and it is also recorded that Nebuchadnezzar, who reigned between 604 and 561 B.C., restored not only the walls of Babylon but the canals and reservoirs as well. In later years these were to be destroyed by the Persian invaders under Cyrus the Great.

Conquerors, floods, and the transient quality of the clay bricks used in the constructions of the buildings have made it difficult to trace the history of the ancient Babylonians and Assyrians. However, archaeologists have skillfully interpreted their lives from excavated seals and tablets covered with cuneiform writing and from the fragmentary remains of old monuments, many of them ornamented with magnificently carved stone reliefs.

14. (OPPOSITE) A nineteenth-century artist's conception of the Hanging Gardens of Babylon. Their grandiose luxuriance is well represented, but the materials of construction are inaccurate, since Babylon was a city of brick, not stone. (*American Museum of Photography, Philadelphia*)

These do not show gardens as such, but details of conventionalized flowers and of roof gardens planted with trees indicate that some gardens did exist, either for a source of food or for relaxation.

Although flowers seldom appear in the arts of these people and apparently had no special place in their religious rituals there is ample indication that trees were greatly venerated. This was not the tree worship which many primitive cultures embraced, but was a significant appreciation of its gifts to man — food, timber, and shade. Some trees, such as the beautiful cedars of Lebanon, were coveted by all the Mediterranean nations. The date palm was important too, for it provided fruit, sap for wine, timber for roofing and furniture, fiber for rope, and leaves for mats, brooms, fans, and baskets. In fact, it was said that the date palm had a use for every day of the year. It is little wonder that one of the more vengeful acts of war was to cut down the enemy's trees.

Much has been written about the large, wooded hunting preserves of the Assyrian kings and their parklike tree plantations. The earliest known ruler to leave a record of his park was Tiglath Pileser I (circa 1100 B.C.). This king brought back cedars and box from the lands he conquered, and he proudly declared them to be trees "that none of the kings, my forefathers, have possessed." Sennacherib (705–681 B.C.) built "a palace that knew no equal" — his own words — and around it planted a park with palms brought from Chaldea, "all the spices from the land of the Hittites," myrrh — which, he asserted, grew better in his gardens than in its native land — cypresses, and "vines from the hills, fruits from every country." For irrigation he had a canal cut in from the Chusur River, "one and a half hours' journey" long, and he "set a pond in the garden" in which reeds were planted. Sennacherib also wrote that "by the grace of the gods the gardens prospered . . . they grew tall and flourished greatly." One of the most impressive aspects of this record is the warrior king's claim that he did it all for the benefit of his people. Specifically he mentioned the trees, which, he said, "I have planted for my subjects."

Within the large areas of royal hunting grounds or parks, small temples and outdoor pavilions were built on hilltops. Possibly the hills or mounds were artificially created, the prototypes of the garden mounts of medieval Europe. Feasts were given here in pleasantly cool and shady surroundings. The relaxation that a shaded grove provided is vividly portrayed in the stone carving of King Ashurbanipal enjoying a meal with his wife. Within his garden "paradise" the king finds a welcome retreat after battle; in regal splendor he reclines upon his couch and enjoys the enticements of "wine, women, and song." The ultimate barbaric delight feasts his eyes — the decapitated head of his enemy hanging from the limb of a tree before him.

The most famous gardens of ancient times, other than the legendary Eden, were created on the terraced structure built by Nebuchadnezzar about 605 B.C., one of the seven wonders of the world. Nebuchadnezzar created the Hanging Gardens of Babylon for the pleasure of a Persian wife. Apparently the lady was homesick for the tree-covered mountains of her homeland, and Nebuchadnezzar sought to please her with this most impressive token of his love.

The Hanging Gardens were not a suddenly improvised form of gardening; they were probably developed from the combined influences of a utilitarian style of terraced hillside

28

The Assyrian King Ashurbanipal feasting with his queen in the royal garden after the defeat of Teummann in 660 B.C. (*British Museum*)

gardening and the temple tower or ziggurat. The latter, consisting of seven stories of diminishing size built upon a large foundation platform, was regarded symbolically as a link between heaven and earth. The Hanging Gardens remain to us in legend only, for no remains have ever been found. Babylon, a city of bricks, was at the mercy of earthquakes as well as invaders, but despite the destructions of the city the fame of the gardens was kept alive by word of mouth from generation to generation. By the first century A.D., the Greek historians Strabo and Diodorus wrote down all they could learn of them, possibly guided by what they had seen of similar, later gardens. In some details the accounts of Strabo and Diodorus differ, but both agreed that they covered about three or four acres and that they were set back in ascending terraces "like a theater." Under supporting arches were "many stately rooms of all kinds, and for all purposes." Diodorus also stated that "the highest arch, upon which the platform of the garden was laid, was fifty cubits high, and the garden itself was surrounded with battlements and bulwarks." Within the highest arch were "certain engines" to draw "plenty of water out of the river Euphrates, through certain conduits hid from the spectators, which supplied it to the platform of the garden." Strabo, on the other hand, claimed that slaves drew the water up from the river by means of wheels of buckets or spiral pumps.

The main garden was planted on the uppermost terrace and was waterproofed by a covering of reeds daubed with a native asphalt; on top of them a double layer of tiles or bricks was laid in mortar, and over all this large sheets of lead were placed. In addition to supporting this weight, the structure was sufficiently strong to hold enough soil for large trees to grow in. Many of the supporting brick columns were hollow and filled with earth to provide deep runs for roots. The whole fabrication was compared to a green mountain, and from a distance it could well have seemed so, for all along the ascending ramps grew trees, among them, perhaps, the larch, cypress, cedar, acacia, mimosa, aspen, chestnut, birch, and poplar. All these are possible, for the flora of northern Mesopotamia, with its high elevation, is that of the temperate zone. It seems almost certain that palms were planted there also.

With the cool recesses for entertainment, the lively, splashing fountains, the variety of blossoming and shade-giving trees, and the view over Babylon and the river, the hanging gardens must have presented an incredibly impressive sight.

29

Artist's conception of a "philosopher's garden" in Athens. (*American Museum of Photography, Philadelphia*)

III
Ancient Persian and Greek Gardens

For centuries, conquering armies moved back and forth across frontiers south of the Mediterranean, and some crossed the Mediterranean Sea itself. Egypt overran Assyria, and later the Assyrians attacked Egypt; the Persians conquered Babylon and pushed westward; the Greeks met the Persians on the field of Marathon, and afterward, under Alexander, overran all Asia Minor and reached India. Among the many prizes the conquerors brought home was a greater knowledge of the culture of the nations they had vanquished, and frequently this knowledge included ideas about gardens and gardening.

The Persians particularly admired the parks and hunting preserves of the Assyrians and Babylonians, and in their own country they set about copying and adapting them. We are told that the Persians planted trees with "impressive regularity" and that it became the fashion to surround important tombs with shady groves. In fact, trees became so greatly esteemed in Persia that youths were taught how to plant and cultivate them at the same time that they learned to forge armor.

The word "paradise" is derived from the Greek translation of the Persian word *pardes*, which signifies park. As first used by Xenophon in his account of Cyrus the Great, it refers to a garden scene: "The Persian king is zealously cared for, so that he may find gardens wherever he goes. Their name is Paradise, and they are full of all things fair and good that the earth can bring forth."

When the Persians conquered Egypt in 525 B.C. the Egyptian walled, geometrically laid-out garden undoubtedly inspired the private, secluded enclosures with which they later surrounded their fine homes and palaces. By combining these two divergent expressions of gardening, the park and the enclosure, the Persians laid the basis of a great heritage of garden appreciation which they kept alive for centuries despite wars, invasions, and adverse climatic conditions.

Of Greek gardens we know very little, but it would seem certain that the Greeks made few significant contributions to the development of ornamental horticulture. In Homeric and Archaic times the people were primarily farmers who worked in the valleys and, being isolated by mountain ranges, gradually developed their lands into city states. The soil was poor, and it was only by irrigation and assiduous labor that they managed to cultivate grains and other essential crops. However, as in other nonfertile lands, the vine and the olive bore well. There were many wild flowers in the Greek countryside, which were extolled by their poets. Asphodel, narcissi, violets, cyclamen, hyacinths, lychnis, lilies, iris, a wild celery with flowers similar to Queen Anne's lace, *Gladiolus byzantinus*, crocuses, and roses abounded throughout the land. However, the only flower which we know to have been cultivated for private gardening was the rose. Herodotus, who wrote his *History* in the fifth century B.C., told of the garden of Midas, where "the sixty-petaled roses" grew. This reference would surely have been to *Rosa centifolia*.

Nevertheless, the ideal garden as it had developed elsewhere did take root in the Greek mind, for in Homer's *Odyssey* the regal garden of Alcinous was described as consisting of three parts: an orchard of pears, pomegranates, apples, figs, and olives; a vineyard; and "all manner of garden beds, planted trimly." We are also told that there was a hedge around it all, and two fountains of water, one distributing its streams about the garden, and the other flowing under the threshold of the courtyard to the side of the palace, where the townspeople could draw from it.

Evidently the Greeks also followed a custom similar to the Persian one of making youths plant trees: Odysseus on his return home made himself known to his aged father, Laertes, by pointing out the trees which had been given to him as a child.

By classical times, beginning with the fifth century, it seems that the Athenians were too gregarious a people to retreat into the quiet shelter of private gardens. They preferred to congregate in large meeting places such as the agora and the academy, where they could discuss events and exchange ideas, and even in the gymnasium. However, the use of trees to enhance their public monuments and meeting places became customary, and elms, planes, aspens, yews, and myrtles transformed meeting places into public parks. These became so popular that the philosophers who habitually spoke there eventually retired to their own newly created shady retreats with their followers. Epicurus (342?–270 B.C.), whom Pliny the Elder (23–79 A.D.) called "that connoisseur in the enjoyment of a life at ease," was one of the first to do this. "Up to then," Pliny wrote, "it had never been thought of to dwell in the country in the middle of town." But we learn from the orator Isaeus (c. 420–350 B.C.), who was concerned with questions of inheritance, that the poet Dicaeogenes purchased the house of Theopompus, had it pulled down, and made a garden for his own house on the same site, before Epicurus had created a garden. Soon wealthy home-owners followed suit, and since many city houses were small and crowded together, with little or no room for outdoor gardens, some built country houses in beautiful tree-studded settings.

Religious worship often took place away from the temple, in the rural surroundings of a sacred grove with its altar. Sometimes a single tree was held sacred, and a clear flowing spring or a grotto was usually part of the shrine. Much later, the grotto was adapted to secular use in the garden and became a not unusual adornment in Renaissance gardens and in the landscape gardens of eighteenth-century England.

From Pliny's *Natural History* we also learn that many market gardens in the suburbs of Athens supplied the city with flowers and vegetables. Earlier, Xenophon had stated that these gardens were enriched with the sewage of the city, brought by a main sewer to a reservoir and thence by brick-lined canals into the valley of the River Cephisus. The flowers were raised for, or by, the garland-makers and -sellers, who formed a distinct trade both in Greece and in Rome. Wreaths or garlands were an inseparable part of every festive public occasion; they adorned statues and altars and were awarded to public servants, worn as emblems of office, and bestowed upon military and naval heroes, poets, and athletes; they were exchanged between lovers and worn at weddings and used as funeral decorations. When hung on a doorway a wreath or garland announced the birth of a son. Since perfume-making was also undertaken, there was a continued demand for quantities of flowers, the cultivated wildings of the countryside.

Familiarity with and appreciation of the native plants was fostered by the writings of Greek naturalists. Of greatest importance were the ten books forming *The History of Plants* written by Theophrastus (372? – 287 B.C.), the "father of botany." Later, in the first century A.D., the physician Dioscorides, who served and traveled with the Roman armies, compiled a herbal called *De Materia Medica* in which he described over four hundred European plants. It remained authoritative for fifteen hundred years and was·said to be the most-copied book in all that time, with the exception of the Bible.

It is alleged that we owe pot gardening to the Greeks, whose women planted quick-growing seeds of lettuce, fennel, wheat, or barley in pots or shards for the festival of Adonis. After their quick growth the plants withered rapidly, symbolizing the early death of Aphrodite's young lover. So the custom, which originally signified the reproductive life cycle of all growing things, came to represent impermanence and the fleeting pleasures of life. The potted plants decorated statues of Adonis and were placed on the flat housetops during the period of this summer festival. A natural step was taken when other plants were displayed for their decorative beauty, a custom copied by the Romans when they transplanted Greek culture to their own shores across the Adriatic.

IV   *The Roman Epoch*

Contemporary accounts of the villa gardens of Imperial Rome and the remains of the small city gardens of Pompeii reveal the appearance for the first time of true "ornamental horticulture." Large or small, Roman gardens were laid out with a proper sense of design and scale as well as with a thorough knowledge of the kind of plant materials most suited to the pleasure garden. Previously, in the gardens of the Egyptians, Syrians, and Persians, it was usual for food-bearing trees and useful herbs and plants to be combined with water and shade-giving elements to provide functional beauty. In Roman times there appears to have been little compromise between utilitarianism and aestheticism; herbs and fruit trees became incidental to the over-all plan, and the garden for food crops was most often a separate entity.

Rome began its amazing history as a trading center where, among other things, garden produce could be exchanged; then it became a city-state and eventually developed into a world empire. Essentially Roman people were farmer-soldiers, passionately devoted to the land, whether they were cultivating it or fighting for it. Their orderliness of mind enabled them to formulate and administer a system of laws on which much later jurisprudence has been based. In the arts we know them to have been more adaptive than creative, and their practical genius led them to great structural and engineering feats.

Roman society was an oligarchy unequally divided into four main groups: a few enormously wealthy families; a powerful class of knights, or *equites*, whose position depended upon the possession of at least 400,000 sesterces ($16,000); the great masses (there were well over a million during the reign of Augustus Caesar) made up of shopkeepers, artisans, and craftsmen, some of them freedmen, but all underfed and largely dependent on gov-

Plates

15. Remains of the colonnade of Canopus at Hadrian's Villa. At the opposite end was a marble *nymphaeum* for dining. (*Photo Researchers. Photo: Susan McCartney*)

16. Frescoed wall from the Empress Livia's garden room. Outside the low wall which encloses the garden scene grow a variety of fruit trees, palms, and oleanders. A little path is suggested between the wall and the latticed fence. There are many recognizable flowers in the garden. The room is now installed in the Museo delle Terme, Rome. (*Scala, Milan*)

17. The pedestal in the ivy-bordered pool in the peristyle of the Casa dei Postumi probably supported a marble or bronze statue. Violets, hyacinths, and roses bloomed in such Pompeian gardens. (*Author's photo*)

ernment largesse for grain; and lastly the slaves, who remained the property of their masters, lacking both social and civil rights.

Because of his farming heritage, the Roman had an innate love of the land, and great wealth enabled the favored to acquire it and to own a multitude of slaves to tend it. But because of a lack of artistic originality, the average estate owner laid out his garden in ordered and geometric formality, though not necessarily in the straight-lined patterns of greater antiquity. The most important contribution of the Romans to the development of garden history lay, as stated before, in their recognition of the beauty and worth of ornamental plant material and in making the garden an inseparable extension of the house. Love of the land and growing things was the motivation behind the strong urge to plant.

Rome's narrow, twisting, overcrowded, and dirty streets were interspersed with great open spaces or promenades. Shade, grass, and places of rest surrounded the many public baths and monuments, and parks and gardens were created on the seven hills and along the banks of the Tiber. To gain more room in the city Rome built four- or five-storied "apartment" houses or multiple dwelling units called *insulae*, which outnumbered individual houses by about twenty-six to one. While the *domus* of a wealthy owner might have its interior garden, the majority of people living in the *insulae* had only the public promenade areas, window-sill pot gardens, and trained plants and vines on balconies and pergolas. After the great fire of Nero's time when much of the city was rebuilt, wider tree-lined avenues were laid out, but we are told that the people missed the shade and coolness of the narrow, dark streets of former times.

The gardens and flowers of Rome were frequently extolled. In the first century A.D., Martial described the city as being rich in "the beauty of spring and the charm of fragrant Flora" and as having "ruddy paths twined with roses." He also made fun of one rich homeowner who had so many walks and plantings and so much running water that he had neither a dining room nor a bedroom!

A number of Roman aristocrats built villas outside the city walls to escape the congestion within the city, and the magnificent gardens they planted around their houses lived long in history. The Palatine, the city's birthplace, was the setting for the palaces of Augustus Caesar, Tiberius, Caligula, Nero, and their Flavian successors. Today, because of the diligent work of archaeologists, the foundations of many of the buildings are laid bare, though many are obscured by the remains of Renaissance gardens that were planted over them. However, we know that these buildings were awe-inspiringly beautiful, with their classic colonnades and courtyards and glittering gold roofs. Marble and bronze statuary and garden pools added to their magnificence. When the emperors were not campaigning in distant lands, they frequently used the garden as a place in which to transact the affairs of state, whether it was rendering justice or plotting murder. Pliny the Elder stated that "the kings of Rome indeed cultivated their gardens with their own hands." Gardens were held in such high regard, and their enjoyment was considered so important to the masses, that imperial gardens were opened to the public and Augustus Caesar bequeathed his to the people.

The most famous of the imperial palaces was Nero's Golden House. This was not the Emperor's original dwelling on the Palatine but the one he built after the fire of 64 A.D.

17

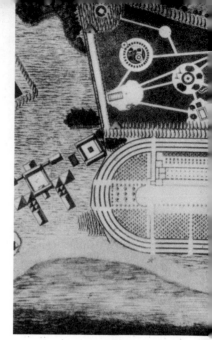

(LEFT) Wall painting from Pompeii of a seashore villa. Its setting resembles Pliny's Laurentinum villa, and the planting recalls his description of ivy-garlanded trees at Tusci. The treetops behind the villa also suggest the tree-encircled hippodrome which he mentioned. (*Sir William Gell*, Pompeiana, *1852*)
(CENTER) Hypothetical restoration of Pliny the Younger's villa and garden at Laurentinum, 62 A.D. The eighteenth-century restorer Robert Castell of London probably suggested the pillared type of

Records state that it covered the equivalent of nearly a square mile, with porticoes three thousand feet long. It was designed by two Greek architects and contained frescos and thousands of Greek sculptures. It was most famous for a colossal statue of Nero himself, one hundred and twenty feet high, which stood before the entrance. Hundreds of people were ousted from their homes to make way for Nero's vineyards, grain fields, woodlands stocked with game, and the large lake and waterfalls created for his own enjoyment. A fearful sidelight on Nero's life in the Golden House is the story that Christians were sometimes made into living torches to light the gardens. After his death every means was taken to obliterate his odious memory, and when Vespasian finished the rebuilding of Rome, Nero's costly fish pond became the site of the Flavian Amphitheater, now known as the Colosseum. It earned its name not because of its great size but because of the colossal statue of Nero which had once stood nearby.

For patricians who wished to develop villa grounds, the Pincian hill and the Janiculum hill across the Tiber became favorite sites. During the first century B.C. on the Pincian hill stood the villas of Sallust the historian and Lucullus, one of Pompey's generals. The hill became known as the *Collis Hortulorum* or hill of gardens. Throughout the gardens and home of Lucullus (now the site of the Medici Villa) the General displayed art objects he had brought home from campaigns. War booty frequently enriched other great places, either in the form of statuary or as money with which the owner could indulge new extravagances and improvements. In time all these properties were bought by a Valerius Asiaticus, whom the jealous Emperor Claudius (41–54 A.D.) subsequently put to death so that he could acquire them as imperial property. Further building was done by Domitian. Then, in 270 A.D., the Emperor Aurelian bequeathed the entire estate to the city as a public park, today called the Pincio.

Of greater fame are the remains of Hadrian's villa at Tivoli (then called Tibur) some twenty miles outside Rome. Hadrian had his architects and builders re-create some of the

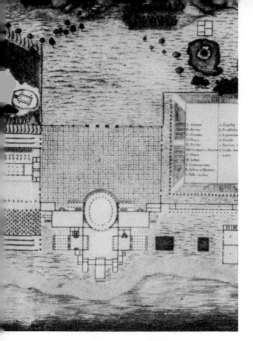
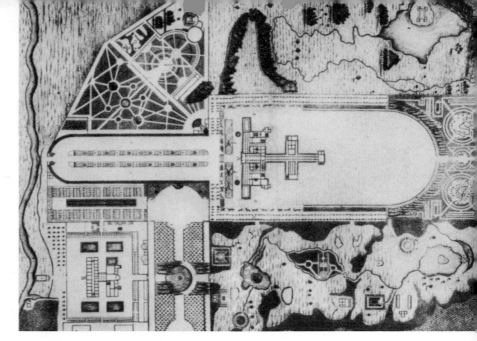

Roman architecture and the classical garden fairly accurately, but he also added a romantic "landscape" garden of his own period, with paths and woodlands dotted with such "classic" details as pyramids and temples of love. (RIGHT) Castell's restoration of Pliny's estate in Tuscany. The formal plantings are all indicated, but again the artist added English "landscape" details. (*Both plans from New York Public Library, Print Department*)

monuments which had most impressed him during eight years of travel throughout his empire. This construction of buildings and gardens lasted from 125 to 136 A.D., by which time the Emperor had only a few years left in which to enjoy them. The Vale of Tempe, a Greek amphitheater, an Academy, a Lyceum, and a colonnade of Canopus were a few parts of the vast complex of arcades, pillared halls, peristyles, baths, terraces, and enclosed gardens. Marvelous mosaic floors and statuary set up in arched niches or forming colonnades of caryatids have been excavated, but little remains architecturally of the original scheme. Soon after Hadrian's death the villa was looted; later the place became the headquarters of foreign invaders and brigands and so dangerous that it was purposely leveled. The most recent excavations have uncovered the beautiful colonnade of Canopus which surrounds an elongated pool, at the far end of which are the remains of the so-called temple of Serapis, a marble nymphaeum. (The *nymphaeum* was a small marble building embellished with water, derived from the outdoor sanctuaries for the nymphs which the Greeks established near natural springs or pools.) A long, narrow pool of water was often called a Nilus, and the name Canopus was appropriate in this connection, for it was the name of an Egyptian town near Alexandria. Recovered statuary includes an Egyptian crocodile.

Wealthy families left Rome during the heat of the summer to enjoy the fresh air and privacy of country estates situated on the slopes of mountains, beside lakes, or at the seashore. Many Romans received income from farm lands, and, like true gentlemen farmers, after attending to business in the city they retired to the luxurious rural establishments where large-scale agriculture was practiced under the supervision of overseers or procurators.

In 62 A.D. Pliny the Younger, in letters to his friend Apollinaris, described two such places, one for vacationing, the other for farming. He writes of garden practices, site planning, plant materials, and the enjoyment of leisure at that time. Pliny owned five hundred slaves divided between his town house and his two country places, a not unusual number which was sometimes exceeded. Pliny's shore home was at Laurentinum near Ostia. He describes it as lying seventeen miles from Rome, "so that having finished the business of the city, one may reach it with ease and safety at the close of day. The road is partly sandy, something heavy and tedious for carriages, but short and easy to those that ride." Today's traveler, arriving at Rome's Leonardo da Vinci Airport, drives into the city over a highway which passes very close to Ostia and through the countryside Pliny knew so well. "My villa is large enough to afford a convenient though not sumptuous reception for my friends," he wrote. Could anything sound more relaxing or more hospitable than the dining room (*triclinium*) that "advances out upon the shore so that the sea is driven in by the Wind Africus, its foundation gently washed by the last, spent and broken waves"? Another winter dining room is described, "where never but in a storm is heard the roaring of the sea." This one overlooked the garden, which was bordered with box. Rosemary was used to fill in damaged spaces, for, as Pliny says, "box where it is sheltered by buildings flourishes much, but withers if exposed to the wind or weather or be in the least subject to the sprinkling of the sea water." Surrounding the garden was a wide exercise area called the *gestatio*, lined on its inner side with a shady arbor of vines. There were also many fig and mulberry trees. Along its inner length (at least as reconstructed by Castell in the eighteenth century) ran a covered and pillared walk, the *cryptoporticus*. There was also a terrace (*xystus*) "fragrant with violets." Pliny speaks too of his private apartment or *diaeta*, overlooking the garden, where he retired for quiet during the Saturnalia winter festival when his young people and servants kept him awake. He refers to it as his "delight."

Pliny's other estate, Tusci, lay among the foothills of the Apennines, where he found the clemency of summer wonderful and the winter cold and frosty, so that myrtle and olive trees did not thrive but laurel grew plentifully. His description of the garden area at Tusci is even more complete than that of Laurentinum, but he tells us nothing of the agricultural areas. Obviously his pleasure gardens were closest to his heart. The house faced south and its entrance portico looked over a terrace. A descending slope (the Romans never had stairways in their hillside gardens) was bordered on each side with clipped animal forms and led down to a flat lawn area planted with "soft" acanthus, a variety used as a ground cover. This was surrounded by a walk (*ambulatio*) enclosed by greenery clipped into a variety of forms. Around this was a *gestatio* "laid out in the form of a circus, ornamented in the middle with box cut in numberless different figures, together with a plantation of shrubs, prevented by the shears from shooting up too high." A fence covered with box divided this from the meadowland. The opposite side of the villa overlooked a large hippodrome toward a garden house shaded by plane trees. Here, water flowing from a marble basin kept everything around it green. The great open space was surrounded by plane trees, with ivy entwined around the trunks and branches and spreading in garlands from tree to tree. The rounded end of the hippodrome was planted with cypresses "to vary the prospect and cast a deeper gloom." The inner walks were sunny and "perfumed with roses."

Many paths are divided from one another by box. In one place you have a little meadow; in another the box is interposed in groups, and cut into a thousand different forms; sometimes into letters expressing the name of the master, or again that of the artificer; whilst here and there little obelisks rise inter-mixed alternately with apple trees, when on a sudden, in the midst of this elegant regularity, you are surprised with an imitation of the negligent beauties of rural nature; in the centre of which lies a spot surrounded with a knot of dwarf plane trees. Beyond these are interspersed clumps of the smooth and twisting acanthus; then come a variety of figures and names cut in box.

At the upper end is a semicircular bench of white marble, shaded with a vine which is trained upon four small pillars of Carystian marble. Water, gushing through several little pipes from under this bench, as if it were pressed out by the weight of the persons who repose themselves upon it, falls into a stone cistern underneath, from whence it is received into a fine polished marble basin, so artfully contrived that it is always full without ever overflowing. When I sup here, the tray of whets and the larger dishes are placed around the margin, while the smaller ones swim about in the form of little ships and waterfowl. Opposite this is a fountain which is incessantly emptying and filling, for the water which it throws up to a great height falling back again into it, is by means of connected openings returned as fast as it is received.

Fronting the bench stands a chamber of lustrous marble, whose doors project and open upon a lawn; from its upper and lower windows the eye ranges upward or downward over other spaces of verdure. In different quarters are disposed several marble seats, which serve as so many reliefs after one is wearied with walking. Next each seat is a little fountain; and throughout the whole hippodrome small rills conveyed through pipes run murmuring along, wheresoever the hand of art has seen proper to conduct them; watering here and there different spots of verdure, and in their progress bathing the whole.

Pliny's full description makes it easier to visualize other large Roman gardens. He tells of the development of the lawn and the advanced stage of the art of topiary. About a hundred years earlier Cicero said that the word *topiarius* belonged to the highest class of slaves. This was the word for the general ornamental gardener, while the *aquarius* was in charge of indoor and outdoor fountains. Gardening had reached a pinnacle of development by Pliny's time, and other writers tell of hothouses or conservatories with windows made of thin talc or mica, where roses were forced into bloom out of season and foreign plants were nurtured.

The *Natural History*, written by Pliny's uncle, Pliny the Elder, is a good source of information concerning trees, shrubs, and plants commonly planted in gardens and promenade areas during the early period of the Empire. Through him we learn that the favorite for the public parks was the vigorous plane tree, or sycamore, still frequently used today for street planting. He quoted Virgil in calling the umbrella pine one of the most beautiful things to see in a garden. The cypress was planted commonly and was sometimes clipped into shapes. Laurel (*Laurus nobilis*) and myrtle (*Myrtus communis*) were garden favorites whose leaves could be woven into crowns. Pliny also mentions box and ivy, ferns and periwinkle (*Vinca Major*), and twelve varieties of roses. There were violets (white, purple, and yellow), hyacinths, lilies, narcissi, irises, anemones, poppies, verbena, rocket, crocuses, and oleanders. Most of these were spring flowers, the Italian summer being too hot to encourage other blooms. Therefore variety of form and texture was always important in the permanent greenery of a garden. Many of the above-mentioned flowers were grown in private gardens and all were bountifully displayed in the market gardens of the campagna.

The more crowded Rome became, the more vacation villas were built in the country and along the shores of the Mediterranean. Pompeii and Herculaneum flourished — Pompeii as a watering place where people came for thermal cures in its adjacent hot springs, and Herculaneum as a much smaller resort. Set in fertile country (before Roman shipbuilding deforested the hillsides), with fishing and navigation industries, and rocky heights for defense, these ancient towns had grown from Greek trading posts. Fought over by native tribes, they did not become settled Roman communities until well after 290 B.C. From what we can reconstruct at Herculaneum, it remained an aristocratic place of fine villas built with pergolas, colonnades, and terraces facing the sea. Native fisher folk and craftsmen formed the proletariat. Pompeii gradually developed into an overcrowded, noisy, and vulgar city whose old families began to go elsewhere as a class of *nouveaux riches* merchants became dominant.

The architecture in both towns was Hellenistic, and in small city homes such as those excavated at Pompeii, the Greek *peristyle* and Roman *atrium* were combined into a typical style of almost windowless dwellings grouped around interior courts. The usual entrance was the *atrium*, which had an opening in the roof for light (originally to let out smoke); underneath was a small pool called the *impluvium*, which trapped rain water. Since guests were received in the *atrium*, it was often splendidly decorated. A connecting hallway led to a large inner courtyard, the *peristyle*, traditionally kept as a private area for the family. This was surrounded by roofed, colonnaded walks, but the whole center was open to the sky and made a natural garden site. If it contained pools and fountains, the purely ornamental garden was called the *viridarium*; otherwise it was called the *peristyle*. The *triclinium*, used for dining, usually opened onto this area.

Excavations made at Pompeii reveal how charming and secluded these courts were. Garden beds in varying patterns and shapes were edged with ivy or box and planted with roses, hyacinths, violets, and other flowers. Small trees, remains of which are calcinated in their original planting holes, have been identified as pear, fig, chestnut, and pomegranate. An elaborate piped water system fed the many fountains, jets, basins, and pools. Bronze and marble statuary were popular decorations.

At several houses, excavated garden areas other than the *peristyle*, reveal what were once vine-covered pergolas. A T-shaped one with a water canal makes the loggia at the rear of Loreio Tiburtino's house one of the most interesting at Pompeii. The small outdoor *triclinium* of another seems a most inviting place for eating an *al fresco* meal. This house also had a small staircase which led to a roof garden. The flat sunny roofs were often planted with trees, shrubs, and potted plants to make attractive solariums. Some had trellised pergolas. A ground plan of the House of Castor and Pollux at Pompeii indicates a home of great wealth and luxury, with several dining areas and three gardens. The large garden within the *peristyle* at the rear had an altar for the *lares* or household gods. The garden near the front of the house had a large pool, almost half the size of the garden, for keeping fish.

It was common practice in Pompeii to decorate the inner walls of a house with painted scenes of mythology, idealized scenery, or religious subjects. The houses were small, and artists became adept at depicting a garden scene or architectural detail with a three-dimensional effect that made the rooms seem larger. These scenes add to our picture of ancient Pompeii by showing the favorite plant materials and the birds that graced the gardens. There are both exotic peacocks and song birds.

The most beautiful garden scene was painted for Augustus Caesar's wife, Livia, at her summer villa — not at Pompeii but at Prima Porta, approximately nine miles from Rome. Her house was built on a plateau with splendid views of the Tiber, the Alban hills, and the Apennines. The most original feature of the villa was a barrel-vaulted underground room without windows and with only one door. Here the four walls were painted in unbroken sequence with trees, shrubs, and flowers, which give one a vivid impression of standing in the middle of a garden enclosure surrounded by a low balustrade. Just beyond the balustrade are oak, pine, and spruce trees, two of each, planted in *trompe l'oeil* recesses in the wall. They are interspersed with fruit trees and shrubs, and peeping over the balustrade are a variety of flowers — roses, poppies, periwinkles, violets, irises, and a rayed daisy-like flower. Birds perch in the trees, and it takes little imagination to hear them singing. The scene is charmingly colorful and full of beauty and repose. Anyone who has ever enjoyed the coolness of a basement cellar on a hot summer's day will appreciate what a welcome retreat this must have been. The painted walls, carefully removed from the site at Prima Porta, are now installed in the Roman National Museum. Pliny the Younger described a similar underground room in his Tuscan villa. It resembled a crypt, "which in the midst of summer retained its pent-up coolness."

The pleasure-loving Romans sought novelty to satisfy appetites long accustomed to the gratification of every luxurious whim. Pliny the Elder wrote of a huge plane tree with a trunk cavity large enough to be made into a shell-covered grotto in which eighteen people could dine. Smaller grottoes were not unusual in the garden, some artificially made of tufa or pumice stone embedded with shells. Another plane tree with a dining platform built in its branches belonged to Caligula, who dined there with fourteen guests. The emperor called it "a regular nest."

One would like to think that garden-making was a civilizing influence on the Romans. This may be hard to prove, but there is much evidence of their enjoyment of horticulture and certainly they made important contributions to the historic development of garden design and maintenance. In the fifth century invading Goths and Vandals sacked Rome. All was ruined and abandoned, as people crowded within the city walls. Centuries of darkness lay ahead.

Plates

18. Garden of Marcus Lucretius, Pompeii. Many small sculptures adorned this garden, which included a small marble staircase down which water flowed into a pool — not unusual in Pompeian gardens. (*Soprintendenza alle Antichita della Campania, Naples*)

19. Peristyle and *viridarium*, House of Meleagre, Pompeii. The beautifully designed pool had a central jet and a fountain stairway at one end. (*Soprintendenza alle Antichita della Campania, Naples*)

20. Pompeian wall painting suggesting a rooftop pergola, House of the Vettii. (*Anderson*)

21. Fruit trees and singing birds appear with such frequency in the Pompeian wall paintings that they must well have been among the most desirable elements of any garden. (*Soprintendenza alle Antichita della Campania, Naples*)

22. Painted marble fountain similar to the real ones within the Pompeian peristyles. A carefully constructed system of lead pipes fed all such fountains and pools. (*Soprintendenza alle Antichita della Campania, Naples*)

23. An arbor for vines and an ivied grotto with a marble fountain are aspects of a garden scene painted on the walls of a villa at Boscoreale. In the right panel a potted plant can be seen on the roof of a little solarium. (*Metropolitan Museum of Art, Rogers Fund, 1903*)

24. At a seaside villa a pleasant walk could be taken to a belvedere which offered a view of ocean and cliffs. Pompeian wall painting of the Fall of Icarus. (*Naples National Museum*)

25. Windows were practically nonexistent in the Pompeian villas, since daylight was furnished by the open courtyards within. Nevertheless, rooms could be dark, and a painted wall such as this gave a very definite impression of looking through a good-sized window into a garden. The garden suggested in this fresco contained an almost life-size marble statue. (*Soprintendenza alle Antichita della Campania, Naples*)

26. View down the long axis of Loreius Tiburtinus' garden. Water adorns its entire length. This villa was among the largest in Pompeii and was built near its outskirts, away from the congestion of the city. (*Soprintendenza alle Antichita della Campania, Naples*)

27. Hadrian's Villa: Nilus and colonnade. (*Alinari*)

19

20

21

22

23

24 25

V   *Gardens of Islam*

PERSIA

The light of culture was rekindled in the seventh century when the Arabs began to spread the cult of Islam in much of the Mediterranean region. For the next thousand years the legacy of gardening was preserved by the great religions, Christianity and Islam.

The Moslems, following the commands of the Koran, spread their faith, but not by religious fervor alone. Most often, they imposed it by the ruthless force of arms. Persia — not present-day Iran but a larger area that included Turkestan and Iraq — was the first to be converted. For centuries, as followers of Zoroaster, her people had worshiped the natural elements of earth, air, fire, and water, and this adoration of nature always remained a fundamental Persian trait even though religious beliefs changed. Like other Orientals, those of the Arab world had a natural disposition to cling to the same manners, customs, and traditions for hundreds of years. Persians always retained their ancient love of tree planting and of gardens, and much of their life was spent among them.

The one aspect of Islam that differed little from the earlier religion of the Persians was the belief that Heaven, or Paradise, was a garden. The Koran states that the Day of Judgment will take place "in gardens of pleasure" where there will be "a crowd of those of yore, and a few of those of the latter day," resting on "gold-weft couches" and served with wine, fruits, and flesh of fowl by "eternal youths and large-eyed maidens." For those on whom judgment is passed favorably there await two gardens, continually verdant, shaded by trees, and cooled by flowing springs and gushing fountains. In each garden grow two

28. (OPPOSITE) This miniature illustrating a famous folk legend, "The Physicians' Duel," depicts a typical sixteenth-century Persian garden. The large sycamore tree and the little pavilion provided shelter from the sun's rays. At the left, the cypress and blossoming fruit tree, usually coupled, appear as symbols of life and death, as do the cypress at the right and the young willow growing from an old stump. Easily recognizable are a poplar tree at the left, a rose bush beneath the sycamore, and flowering clumps of iris, hollyhock, poppy, and narcissus. (*British Museum*)

55

kinds of fruit, dates and pomegranates, and within the gardens are beds with linings of brocade, "the fruit of the two gardens within reach to cull," wherein "are maids of modest glances," virgins like rubies and pearls. Every sensuous delight makes the garden a Paradise for the Mohammedan.

Traditionally in every Persian garden there have been four essentials: water for irrigation, for the serenity of pools, and for soothing sound; shade for coolness and shelter; flowers for color and fragrance; and music to delight the ear. The trees include fruit-bearing, flowering, and evergreen varieties, the latter never being artificially shaped. The flowers are domesticated wildings from the meadows, including roses, lilacs, hawthorn, and other flowering shrubs. A voice singing, a stringed instrument playing, birds twittering, and fountain jets splashing have provided sound.

A number of the old Persian gardens were laid out in four divisions crossed by water channels. This scheme corresponded with the cosmological idea that the universe was divided into quarters by four great rivers, an ancient belief suggested also by the Old Testament description of Eden. Where the water courses intersected there was either a pool or a small hill (surmounted by a pavilion) to represent the mountain sometimes described as occupying the center of the universe. In the gardens of the aristocracy the simple cross plan was elaborated with many subdivisions to bring in additional water.

Fantastic descriptions of Persian gardens occur in the tenth-century stories, brought back by Byzantine ambassadors, concerning the gardens of the caliphs of Baghdad. They told of precious metals decorating marble colonnades and pools, of seats of gold lining the summer houses, of a gold and silver tree in which gold and silver birds whistled as the breezes blew through them. The ambassadors were also impressed by the many dwarf palm trees (introduced by the Arabs), whose unsightly trunks were covered with teakwood bound with gilded rings, and by the large menageries, a legacy to the caliphs from the original Persian hunting parks.

Visitors always marveled at the richness of the Persian royal gardens. In 1587 A.D. the palace of Hasht Bihisht at Tabriz was described by an Italian traveler as set in the middle of a garden and park in which were "a thousand fountains, a thousand rills, a thousand rivulets" — or so it seemed! The garden of Shah Abbas was noted for its huge pools, probably lined with blue tiles to make them seem deeper — and for its flowers and pavilions.

A most charming source of study for the typical Persian garden exists in the painted miniatures of the fifteenth and sixteenth centuries, a period following the great Mongolian invasion. After a ruthless conquest the Mongols superimposed a veneer of their own culture over the Persian traditions and then absorbed much of the latter in their own way of life. The colorful miniatures illustrate legends and princely occupations. Idealized visions of lovers in gardens, outdoor feasts, entertainments, and affairs of state were the typical themes for the artists' brushwork.

Outdoor shelters were many and varied, some being merely colorful tents or awnings with rugs placed beneath to sit on. Often the *chabutra*, or railed platform, is set under a tree, or covered with a canopy, called a *baldaquin*, supported by poles. Usually these small structures were permanent, the balustrades and miniature towers of the roofs being not only decorative but functional as well, for they provided ventilation. Some pavilions are depicted as two-storied. Miniatures nearly always show these attractive shelters set in green-tiled areas overlooking a pool, with a painted railed fence often of Chinese inspiration enclosing them.

Pool shapes also make an interesting study. Some are rectangular or square, some are cross-shaped, others are more elaborately formed into lacy-edged medallions or ogees; all of these seem to have been more popular than the simple circular pond. All have tiled borders, are connected with channels, and contain delicately designed fountainheads for a central water jet. There are never any of the elaborately carved stone fountains with figures, so popular in European gardens, nor do we find any representational topiary work. The Koran strictly forbade the making of images, so the art of sculpture did not flourish among the Moslems.

Frequently the paintings include the combination of two trees particularly significant to the Moslems, the cypress, which symbolized death (it never sprouts after being cut down), and the blossoming plum or almond, which symbolized life and hope. Greatly revered was the sycamore tree, so generous with its shade. Poplars, elms, oaks, maples, willows, ash, sweet myrtle, and mastics are all native to Persia and all found their way into gardens. These shade trees, planted thickly along garden walls and in avenues, were interspersed with the smaller fruit trees such as apricot, apple, peach, pear, pomegranate, cherry, almond, and fig, or with nut trees. Grapevines grew on garden walls or pergolas.

Flowers were very dear to the Persian heart, for their precious period of bloom was all too brief. Spring on the high tableland becomes a miracle of but a few weeks' duration. As the snow melts, blossoms appear on fruit trees and beneath them rise the native bulbs — narcissi, tulips, scillas, grape hyacinth, crown imperials, and the smaller fritillarias. Shortly afterward come lilacs, jasmine, pinks and carnations, violets, primroses, irises, larkspur, anemones, wallflowers, cyclamen, poppies, hollyhocks, lilies, and roses.

With a last rush of color, and with a mass of bloom, the roses take over. The Persians have known many varieties — China, noisette, hundred-petaled, moss, damask, and the unusual rose with red petals reversing to yellow. No flower has ever ranked with the rose in universal popularity. Pagan Romans made revelry with roses, and devout Christians adored them as a symbol of divine love, but no one appreciated the flower's contributions to the sensuous delight of a garden more than the nature-loving Persians. In season they held rose fetes outdoors, with merriment and wine-drinking. As one poet wrote: "In the rose season one should drink large bowls of wine, for the rose is a guest for only forty days."

The poets extolled the rose, and there are at least eight references to it in the *Rubáiyát* of Omar Khayyám. The lines, "Each Morn a thousand Roses brings . . ." and, "I sometimes think that never blows so red/ The rose as where some buried Caesar bled" are familiar to everyone; so too the sigh of regret "that Spring should vanish with the rose." Another poet, Hafiz, wrote of the Persian spring, "Earth rivals the Immortal Garden during the rose and lily's reign."

This queen of flowers, as Sappho named it, was also perpetuated in faïence by the designers of pottery plates, bowls, and tiles. In Shiraz the interior of a magnificent tiled mosque was completely covered with a design of roses, with every shade of pink in the blooms and green malachite and emeralds forming the leaves.

Plates

29. Sixteenth-century Persian miniature painting of a sultan holding audience in his garden. The four-quartered garden design is divided by shallow water channels issuing from the tiled pool. In many of these painted manuscripts it is seen that a paving of green tiles is substituted for grass. Typical of all these garden scenes are the shelter or *chabutra*, the rail fence, and the paired cypress and blossoming fruit tree. (*Metropolitan Museum of Art, Hewitt Fund*)

30. Portion of a Persian garden carpet. Trees are planted by the octagonal pools, and beneath their leafy boughs a checkerboard of flower beds is displayed. Bordering the wide central channel are cypress trees alternately planted with small flowering varieties. Many birds dwell in this garden. (*Metropolitan Museum of Art, Theodore M. Davis Collection*)

31. The garden called Eram in the southern Persian city of Shiraz. Its perspective reveals the actual size of the gardens shown in the miniature paintings. (Life. *Photo: Ralph Crane*)

32. A golden throne sheltered by a carpet canopy made a sumptuous and princely setting for the activities within this enclosed garden. The round pool with its arabesque design emphasizes man-made formality in contrast with the starkly barren mountain in the background and the informality of a meandering meadow stream. Miniature painting illustrating one of the poems of Nizami, sixteenth century. (*British Museum*)

33. Detail from an early Persian manuscript painting, "The Sage Buzurjmihr discoursing to King Anushirvan." The king is seated on a *chabutra*. (*British Museum*)

58

30

32

Because the garden provided so many of the comforts and delights of living the Persian sought to remind himself of those joys during the long cold winter through the use of garden carpets. In geometric stylizations, many early and carefully preserved carpets depict pools and water channels, often enlivened with fish. Bordering the channels are flowers and rows of trees (usually the cypress because it was the easiest to conventionalize) with birds among the foliage. Square flower beds, sometimes with a tree at the center, usually fill up the rest of the areas. Such carpets helped dispel the dreariness of bleak winters and provided comfort and luxury when tile floors and walls were cold. One remarkable carpet, "The Winter Carpet," or "The Spring of Chosroes," has lived long in legend and history. It is said to have measured no less than one hundred and fifty by seventy-five feet, and was one of the great treasures of the palace of King Chosroes. "On it," we are told, "was represented a beautiful pleasure ground with brooks and interlacing paths, with trees and flowers of the springtime. On the wide borders were represented flower beds in which precious stones, (blue, red, yellow, white and green,) denoted the beauty of the blooms. Gold imitated the yellow-colored soil and defined the borders of the brooks, and water was represented by crystals. Gravel paths were indicated by stones the size of pearls. Trunks of trees were of gold and silver, leaves and flowers of silk, fruits of many colored stones."[1] In the seventh century this carpet of incalculable worth fell into the hands of the Arabs and no one knows what became of it.

While for hundreds of centuries Persians cherished the garden as a source of great beauty, and a setting for entertainment, they also found in it, as have other Orientals, a place of seclusion for meditative thinking. In the springtime when flowering trees, shrubs, and plants burst into bloom almost simultaneously, the Persian must have found in his garden a Paradise on earth.

INDIA

Despite ruthless Mongolian and Tartar invasions in the thirteenth and fourteenth centuries, Persian culture did not perish, nor did her garden heritage. Moreover, within two hundred years, when the Mongols reversed their direction and subjugated northern India, Persian gardens of extreme beauty were created by the conquerors during the reigns of six great emperors from 1483 to 1707.

The first Mogul emperor was Baber, "The Tiger," whose ancestor Tamerlane had subjugated Samarkand. With the help of the Persians themselves, Baber (variously spelled Babur or Babar) tried to recapture the city on three occasions but, failing, raided India instead. In his headquarters at Kabul (now a part of Afghanistan) he created ten gardens, all of which are documented in his own memoirs. Baber's favorite, Bagh-I-Vafa, or "Garden of Felicity," was laid out in 1508. In a color miniature by an artist of that time, the emperor is shown within the four-part garden, where a brick wall and trees surround the flower beds. Here was a directly transplanted Persian garden, altogether different in conception from the naturalistic ones of Buddhist India. The Emperor moved his capital to Agra in 1526 and built the still existing garden of Ram Bagh, which became his body's temporary resting place before it was interred in Kabul.

34. An Indian princess reclines in a jewel-like setting of colorful flower beds, tiled pavilions, and sparkling fountains. Eighteenth-century Rajput miniature. (*Free Library of Philadelphia. Photo: Roche*)   67

The pleasure gardens of these great Moguls were enjoyed thoroughly during their lifetimes and frequently became their resting places in death. Pavilions were often placed in the center of a reservoir, and channels and pools radiated from the various façades. These marble pavilions were used for banqueting and court receptions as well as relaxation; in addition, they were frequently used as tombs for the owners. Smaller pavilions were sometimes attached to shelter other members of the family after their deaths.

The most famous garden mausoleum is, of course, the Taj Mahal in Agra, built by the Emperor Shah Jahan for his favorite Persian wife, who died in childbirth in 1631. The great sheets of water which reflect the beauty of the white marble monument and express the serenity of death also mirror the vitality of moving clouds and growing things. Similarly, while slender cypresses, symbolic of death, add to the architectural quality of the whole design, borders of flowers radiate life in thick carpets of color.

During the hot Indian summers the Mogul emperors and their courts moved to the Vale of Kashmir and in later centuries were followed there by the British ruling class and tourists. In this remote part of the world, guarded by the snow-capped Himalayas, some of the most eulogized gardens of all time are yet to be found. The greatest source of beauty is their setting — lofty mountains descending to a fertile green valley crossed lengthwise by the Jhelum river, which widens occasionally into lakes. Pink lotuses rise above the waters of the shoreline, and on land huge evergreen trees, the chenars, bring man-made things into scale with their magnificent mountain background. Most of the gardens of Kashmir were terraced and used mountain springs to feed the central water chutes that coursed through them. The water was channeled into rectangular pools, where jets in the shape of lotus buds cast it into the air. Sometimes pavilions were built across the pools, so that icy water flowed under as well as around them to keep the marble floors cool.

The most famous garden of Kashmir, Shalimar, on Lake Dal, is reached by boat from a mile-long canal. The garden is walled and developed on four terraces. Leading up to these are velvety lawns shaded by chenar trees and patterned with colorful flower beds. Each terrace had its particular use and was adorned with flowers and trees and a pavilion. On one of these terraces is a black marble throne where the emperor held public audience. Another level formed the emperor's personal garden, with a pavilion reserved for private audiences, and the topmost level or terrace, the "Abode of Love," was used by the empress and her court. At its center stood a black marble pavilion built in a large shallow pool designed with a hundred and forty fountains. The whole of Shalimar is animated by the sound of water rippling down the chutes or ruffling the surfaces of the pools after splashing out of hundreds of fountain jets. Each summer the Emperor Jahangir, fourth in the dynastic line of Baber, moved court, harem, and servants to Shalimar from Delhi by means of elephants, two-wheeled carts, and sedan chairs. The magnificent scenery and high elevation lifted the spirit and brought welcome relief from the torrid Indian heat.

The word *bagh* was used by Persian and Mogul to connote the combination of pleasure garden and dwelling. Those developed along the shores of Lake Dal were often referred to as "water palaces." Long ago numerous *baghs* existed along the lake, but today only a few remain intact. One of the greatest is Nishat Bagh or "Garden of Delight." The tall mountains form a beautiful backdrop for this walled garden, which originally had twelve terraces. Fed by the same source as the Shalimar, its central falls alternate with quiet pools in the descent to the lake. Other channels serve to water flower beds. Here lilacs and roses bloom and the masses of brilliant annuals are a continual delight in the summer. The spectacle is magnificent when the central waters are turned on for Sunday visitors, but the original effect, as developed by Shah Jahan's prime minister, must have been even more entrancing. Colorful clothes are said to have vied with the plumage of the peacocks which strutted about the lawns and with the bright goldfish shimmering in the water-lily pools. As a contrast to the liveliness and excitement of animated water and colorful flowers, that priceless ingredient of shade is ever present in the airy pavilions and under the protecting branches of majestic chenar trees. Their lacy shadows still flicker over velvety green lawns, and among their branches dart hundreds of little birds.

SPAIN

The garden heritage of the Moslems became firmly implanted in every country they conquered. Along the southern shores of the Mediterranean, Lebanon, Morocco, and other such places, their traditional garden art can still be seen in secluded patios shaded with cypress and orange trees, cooled by fountains and pools, and scented with jasmine. Even at the edge of the desert, gardens have been coaxed into being through irrigation. However, the most famous Moslem gardens left to posterity lie in southern Spain, in sunny and colorful Andalusia. Several of these gardens date back to the thirteenth century and have been maintained ever since.

The North African converts to Islam, whom we call the Moors, began to arrive in Spain early in the eighth century, ousting the Visigoths, who had succeeded the Romans. Only in the north did they fail to conquer. Eventually they were pushed back by Christian armies warring against the Infidel, but not until they had established and maintained a prosperous civilization solidly united with the rest of the Arab world, which then reached east to the Indus River. Moslems retained part of Spain until the time of Ferdinand and Isabella in the fifteenth century. All during the period of Moorish ascendancy its civilization far outshone that of Christian people in cultural achievements. Throughout the territory surrounding Córdoba, where the first emirate was established in 756 A.D. by Abd-er-Rahman I, the Moors reintroduced irrigation, a skill forgotten since the Roman occupation, and luxurious vineyards and orchards were developed in the Andalusian plains and along the broad valley of the Guadalquivir River. Sites with impressive views were chosen for their palaces, as well as for hillside terraces, open pavilions, arcades, and miradors. Architects and artisans were brought from the Eastern Empire to plan, build, and decorate not only palaces but whole towns and gardens. Flowers and trees were brought from distant places, water from rivers or mountains nourished them, and sunny skies blessed them.

Córdoba, with its magnificent Mosque, became a center of learning and was known as the Mecca of the West. The courtyard garden of the Mosque, the Patio de los Naranjos or Courtyard of the Orange Trees, was laid out in 976 A.D. and still exists as probably the oldest enclosed garden in Europe. Originally avenues of orange trees were planted as a

Plates

35. Early-eighteenth-century painting of an Indian shah riding in his garden, which resembles those of Persia. Geometric divisions made by the pools, as well as the slender cypress trees and flower-bordered beds, could easily have inspired a carpet design. An elaborate entrance gate pierces one side of the garden wall, and both the corner kiosk and the central pavilion have open-air terraces. (*Museum of Fine Arts, Boston*)

36. The Emperor Baber superintending the making of the Bagh-I-Vafa, or "Garden of Felicity," at Kabul, in 1508. His memoirs tell of collecting plants and trees during military expeditions. (*Victoria and Albert Museum, London*)

37. A pavilion in the Kashmir garden of Shalimar, cooled by water and sheltered by trees. (*Mahatta and Company, Srinagar*)

38. The many-terraced garden of Nishat Bagh has a dramatic background of mountains, and its symmetrical design is softened by majestic chenars. Its flower beds are thickly planted and brilliant with color. (*Mahatta and Company, Srinagar*)

39. The Taj Mahal reflects its beauty in great sheets of water, and the scale of its garden approach adds grandeur. Colorful flower beds repeat the gemlike quality of the interior. (*Government of India Tourist Office*)

70

35

36

37

38   39

continuation of the many aisles of columns, and these directly linked the Mosque and garden, but today some of the archways are blocked by partition walls and the design is not so apparent. The large garden court, measuring four hundred by two hundred feet, holds three fountains, each with a plot of its own in which trees are connected by little runnels for water. Towering palms accent the design.

The largest Spanish garden that retains the Moorish tradition is the Alcazar at Seville. It is actually a series of connected garden areas laid out on level ground beside the fortress-palace; these were begun in 1350, a hundred years after the period of Moorish occupation of Seville, but they retain many typical characteristics. In many instances the arts of the Moors were sufficiently appreciated by Catholic Spaniards to be retained and further developed in the Mudejar style, an intermingling of both Moorish and Christian ideas. Built on the site of the original fortress, though less extensive, the Alcazar today lacks the usual Eastern interrelationship of palace and garden, the one opening into the other. Nor are the gardens arranged with one side open to a view; four walls enclose them on all sides. Furthermore, much of the garden area has been changed into what now resembles a small eighteenth-century English landscape park. However, enclosing walls, raised walks, fountain basins, and, above all, colorful tilework, recall the glories of old Moslem gardens. Cypresses and orange and lemon trees interspersed with palms predominate, and under them grow jasmines, oleanders, roses, blue and purple iris, narcissus, and the spiraea we call "bridal wreath." But here, too, as in the countries south of the Mediterranean, the hot summer sun discourages length of bloom, and the tilework in the form of basins, channels, seats, benches, and step risers provides bright color when the flowering season is over. The color is forceful, yet the effect is subtle, for in the various blues, in yellow, and in the several greens, the tiles repeat the contrast of sunny blue sky and green shade.

A common feature of Spanish gardens has been the garden bower, *glorieta* or "little Paradise." Developed from the Persian pavilion, it sometimes consists merely of a vine-covered arch, but in Moorish gardens it frequently appeared as a circle of cypress trees with their tops bent over or clipped to form arches. These were placed at the crossings of paths. Examples can still be seen in the Alcazar gardens and those of the Convent of San Francisco at the Alhambra. In the past, large gardens which were divided into square plots, as in Persia, incorporated eight *glorietas* to represent the eight pearl pavilions of the Mohammedan paradise.

Seville and Córdoba are both on the Guadalquivir River and in fairly flat country, but Granada, which possesses two of the world's most famous garden treasures, lies high in the foothills of the snowy Sierra Nevada. The Alhambra (meaning Red Castle) crowns the city with its massive walls strung out along a ridge. Across a little valley, and higher still, shining like a jewel in this crown, lies the small white-walled "Lofty Garden," or summer palace of the Generalife. The walls of both enclose a complex series of airy rooms and garden courts which breathe the very essence of the Orient, but they are different in character because the Alhambra was built as a fortified palace and the Generalife as a villa.

In 1238 Mohammed ben Alhamar began developing an old castle into the complex fortress-palace now known as the Alhambra. He succeeded in bringing water by aqueduct from the River Darro, thereby making it habitable and beautiful. The ascent to the

40. (OPPOSITE) Court of the Pool, an original Moorish section of the gardens of the Generalife. The mirador at the far end looks over the city of Granada and beyond to the Vega. (*Rapho-Guillumette*)

Alhambra from Granada is steep and wooded, and the hillside was once the site of a number of private palaces. Some years ago it was famous for its magnificent elm trees, planted under the Duke of Wellington's direction during the Napoleonic wars. Today, however, in this parklike area, the trees are badly mutilated by severe pruning; their height must have begun to obscure the fortress which makes such a handsome and impressive silhouette across the crest of the hill.

Among the complexities of the Alhambra's plan, four of the original garden courts are still to be found. The central and dominating feature of each is water — a pool or a fountain dripping into a basin. The largest and most important court is the Patio de los Arrayanes, the Court of the Myrtles, which is also known as the Court of the Pool. The large green pool has hedges of myrtles and orange trees along its sides, and at each end a loggia with alabaster columns is reflected on its shining surface.

The adjacent Patio de los Leones, or Court of the Lions, is probably the best-known and most photographed example of Moorish architecture, yet the simplicity of its plan and the delicacy of its surrounding arcades fall far short of appearing trite. The twelve stone lions supporting the great central fountain basin are crude in execution because of Moslem religious scruples against creating likenesses, but they have a great air of solemnity. The court is quartered by four runnels of water and the intervening spaces, now graveled, were once planted with orange trees and flowers. It is a pity that the plantings no longer exist, for they would give us a more complete picture of how the court looked when it was a part of the sultan's private domain.

Of a much later date is the Garden of Lindaraja, which belonged to the women's harem. Nestled between the walls of the inner palace, it has flower beds surrounding a central fountain, paths edged with clipped box, and the favored Moslem association of slender cypresses and blossoming orange trees, though in feeling it rather closely recalls a Christian cloister. This patio is directly connected with the small Patio de la Reja, or Court of the Grille, a seventeenth-century creation consisting of a central fountain guarded by four cypress trees. One side of the court opens on a view. The connecting links between the courtyard gardens are the many small rooms of the palace, exquisitely decorated with lacy marble and alabaster, tiled in color and honeycomb-vaulted.

The gardens of the Generalife, so breathtakingly beautiful, have been added to by successive generations, and it takes a little study to separate the original Moorish parts from those created by the conquering Christians. The pleasure garden and small palace owe their existence today to a service done in the fifteenth century by the Moorish owner for the Catholic kings who spared them during the reconquest. Formerly, the private approach from the Alhambra to the Generalife was over a small ravine; the public approach was that used today, a long, narrow avenue bordered by tall cypress trees. Within the oldest building, there is a narrow patio with a central marble-lined canal, over which arching jets form a little tunnel of water. Similar water arches occur in other Spanish gardens, both on the mainland and on the island of Majorca, and some were used as "jests," for the water could be suddenly turned on to surprise an unsuspecting visitor. This caprice was copied by fun-loving garden owners in other countries during the Renaissance and the eighteenth century. Garden beds border the canal of the main court of the Generalife and were planted with cypresses, myrtles, oleanders, and roses. At the far end is a pavilion with a mirador, or look-out, which commands a view of the great panorama unfolding below. Ideally it should be seen in the late afternoon of a spring day when the light is soft and the sky is full of billowy clouds. The great plain or vega would be green with newly sown crops; the orchards would be in blossom and the mountains blue in the distance.

Since Moorish times the gardens of the Generalife have grown and developed into many outdoor rooms and corridors of cypress, but always one long side has been kept open to the view which takes in the Alhambra. New flowers and plants have been imported to beautify them further and now wisteria from China, bougainvillaea from Brazil, calla lilies and geraniums from South Africa seem always to have belonged. They were first introduced to Europe during the great wave of exploration in the nineteenth century. The particular Moorish aspect of the gardens comes from dark cypress hedges against which orange trees, heavy with brilliant fruit, are displayed, and from the rose-bays (native oleanders), the roses, carnations, and jasmine, and most of all from the various ornamental uses of water. In the secluded Court of the Sultana there are a large pool and a miniature waterfall rippling over a small staircase. In the hot summers when the sultan, court, and harem came here for relaxation, it was the languorous flow of channeled water or the sparkling animation of a thrusting jet which gave life to a scene that would otherwise have drowsed continuously under the unremitting sun.

Impressive as all the royal pleasure gardens and palaces are, no greater charm can be found than in the traditional Andalusian home which is built around a court. This Spanish patio is derived from the Roman *atrium*, the ecclesiastical cloister, and the Persian enclosed garden, all sequestered, all having a central water motif. One catches glimpses through open doors of stone-paved courtyards made gay with bright potted plants. In the older sections of cities such as Seville and Córdoba, where rabbit warrens of tiny, narrow streets are lined with two-story houses, balconies flaunt veils of trailing geraniums, and tiled patios are invitingly yet protectively displayed behind doorways of iron grillwork. Many of these patios have furniture and paintings along their arcaded walls. Each patio has ornamental water, potted plants, vines, and small trees. Most popular are acacias, oranges, palms, wisteria, roses, geraniums, and carnations. After a stroll through Andalusian streets, one long remembers the white façades dazzling in the sunlight, the sharply silhouetted black suits and broad-brimmed hats of the men, the black shawls and dresses of the women, and a variety of lacy black grillwork. Dabs of brilliant color from pink and red geraniums in pots on the tiny balconies or within the patios make the scene gay instead of somber.

Plates

41. Patio de los Arrayanes within the Alhambra, Granada. The large expanse of this deep-green pool surrounded by its green myrtle hedges presents, as it always has, a serene welcome to the visitor. (*European Picture Service*)

42. Patio de los Leones, a part of the private quarters of the sultan's palace in the Alhambra. Formerly decked with flowering plants, it now relies solely upon its few orange trees and great fountain basin for its garden effect. (*Spanish National Tourist Department*)

43. Within the gardens of the Alcazar, Seville, tiled benches surround a little fountain court whose pool is reminiscent of those seen in Persian miniature paintings. Shady walks provide inviting shelter from the hot southern sun. (*Spanish National Tourist Department*)

44. Patio de los Naranjos within the walls of the great Mosque-Cathedral in Córdoba. With impressive simplicity the age-old elements of water, stone, sunlight, and shadow combine with the verdure of orange trees and palms to invoke a mood of quiet solemnity before one enters the Mosque. (*A. Campana, Barcelona*)

45. A view of the Alhambra and the gardens of the San Francisco monastery, seen from a mirador in the Generalife. (*Author's photo*)

46. A portion of the new gardens of the Generalife, as they have been developed, between clipped hedges of cypress. The garden beds along the narrow pools are bordered with tree roses. The summer palace can be seen at the far end, beyond the slender cypress trees. (*Spanish National Tourist Department*)

47. A section of the gardens developed along the ramparts of the Alhambra. The beauty of the view is apparent. (*Spanish National Tourist Department*)

48. Many small jets ripple the surface of the pools, which mirror the pink oleanders in the sultana's secluded patio, within the Generalife. (*Torres Molina, Granada*)

49. The small Patio de la Reja, within the private apartments of the Alhambra, has a beautiful view of the countryside outside. An old cypress grows in each corner. (*Eduardo Mulá, Barcelona*)

50. A section of the Maria Luisa park in Seville. This is a twentieth-century creation, but its pools, its tilework, and many of its plant materials are of Moorish inspiration. For ease of maintenance during long hot summers, the Spanish people cultivate many plants in pots. (*Spanish National Tourist Department*)

51. Typical private patio in Seville. The garden court serves as an entrance hall. (*Serrano, Seville*)

52. Within the entrance court of the Generalife, wisteria and Banksia roses adorn the walls. (*Author's photo*)

53. The pools of a modern garden situated within the Alhambra reflect the Partal, a building known as the Tower of the Ladies. (*Rapho-Guillumette*)

78

45

46

43

44

47

48

49 50

VI Monastery and Castle Gardens

Complex administrative problems and the combination of two such differing ideological segments as the Greek East and the Roman West had divided the Roman Empire, and, early in the fourth century A.D., Constantinople was established as the second capital. Rome was sacked in 410 A.D., the legions were recalled from Britain, leaving it defenseless, and Gaul and Spain were overrun. Invaders spread throughout the territories like a devastating plague, and under Attila the Huns ravaged both the Eastern and Western Empires. Rome was sacked a second time in 455 by Vandals, who approached it from the sea. The last Emperor of the West was deposed in 476, and finally the destruction of the once mighty Empire was complete.

During the chaotic centuries of the Dark Ages, the Christian Church steadily grew and offered men hope. Monasteries were founded in the fourth century and became important storehouses of learning, because the careful copying of old manuscripts and the preservation of others maintained the sum of man's knowledge practically intact. Since monasteries had to be self-sustaining, agriculture and horticulture were of great importance, and the monks preserved not only the faith but also the knowledge of plants and herbal lore. Garden plants were exchanged with pilgrims and travelers who sought a night's lodging and who brought news and fresh ideas with them.

The physic garden of medicinal herbs as well as vegetable plots, vineyards, and orchards were tended within and without the walls, and flowers were grown for the decoration of the church. It is a strange paradox that while Christian laymen considered

54. (OPPOSITE) Created for Francis I, this manuscript painting of "Love's Game of Chess" suggests a profusion of flowers within a walled garden. In the allegory a master leads his pupil to the orchard, or garden of Nature, for which Nature herself holds the key. Within, a choice must be made between three ways of living — according to Venus, goddess of love; according to Pallas, goddess of wisdom; or according to Juno, queen of the gods, who personified virtuous conduct. (*Paris, Bibliothèque Nationale*)

flowers in a church to be pagan, the monks decorated the altars with them and on feast days priests wore chaplets or wreaths. In England, especially, the sacristan's garden became a necessary adjunct to a church. This conflict of ideas concerning floral decoration arose because the laity recalled the wreathed Roman carouser and the monks were evolving a system of floral symbolism associated with the Virgin Mary and her Son. The lovely *Lilium candidum,* now known almost universally as the Madonna lily, symbolized her purity, and the rose was her attribute as the Queen of Heaven. Red roses frequently denoted Christ's blood.

Every monastery had a cloistered quadrangle, directly evolved from the classic Roman peristyle and usually attached to the south side of the church. Here the monks could walk in seclusion and enjoy the fresh air and sunshine. The cloister garth, usually square, was divided into four sections by intersecting paths. In the center would be a well, a fountain, or a *savina,* which was a tub of water, or a cistern, for watering plants and for drinking and washing. Also there might be a *piscina,* stocked with fish for Friday and Lenten meals. A few plants and small-sized fruit trees or palms usually adorned the cloister, a quiet secluded place of simple beauty. In other areas were the vegetable and herb gardens.

These are clearly indicated in an ideal plan which has been preserved in the library of the Benedictine Monastery of Saint Gall in Switzerland. The plan includes a main cloister, a vegetable garden divided into eighteen separate beds, and an orchard used as a burial ground. By the hospital and the physician's house a physic garden is shown, where plants with healing "virtues," were grown in sixteen rectangular beds. Clearly labeled, these include "*Lilium,*" "*Rosas,*" and "*Gladiola.*" The last-named flower has been identified as *Iris germanica,* for the South African gladiolus of our day was not known, and the various wild species of gladioli, or corn lilies, of the Mediterranean region apparently had no "virtues." *Iris florentina* is the iris most closely associated with the old-time herb garden. The monks mixed the petals of purple-blossomed varieties with alum to produce a beautiful green pigment used in the illumination of manuscripts.

The plants indicated on the Saint Gall plans are said to have been based on the list which the Emperor Charlemagne decreed should be cultivated in his gardens. The listing under *Capitulare de Villis Imperialibus* made in 812 reveals Charlemagne's intense interest in gardening. Over sixty useful and ornamental plants are included. The "white lily" mentioned was *Lilium candidum,* the rose can be identified as *Rosa gallica,* the poppy as *Papaver somniferum,* and other flowers incidental to the useful herbs were squills, feverfew, and marsh-mallows. European wildings are also mentioned. The fruit and nut trees listed were almond, apple, cherry, chestnut, fig, hazelnut, medlar, mulberry, peach, pear, plum, quince, and walnut. The list must have been copied and recopied and passed on to monastery and castle gardeners all over Europe.

There are no pictures, no written accounts, nothing to tell us what a castle garden looked like during the early Middle Ages. Troubadours and minstrels did not weave their romantic tales until the twelfth century, and not until the great period of the miniature painters of the fourteenth and fifteenth centuries are we given an inkling of their nature. From these paintings it appears that the mistress of the castle kept a garden well protected from trampling horses and romping dogs, where the plants which supplied what was later to be called the stillroom were grown. As chatelaine she had to see that there were means of doctoring the sick, caring for festering wounds, easing women's labor pains, and comforting babies with tooth- and earaches. Vermin had to be repelled, the dye pot replenished, and food, especially meat, had to be flavored and sallets concocted. Love potions

A garden party. Early-sixteenth-century Brussels tapestry depicting games which could be enjoyed in a garden. (*Metropolitan Museum of Art*)

and poisons were also brewed. The lore concerning such herbal uses and remedies accumulated slowly — at first based on ancient documents such as Dioscorides' *Materia Medica*, later collected into hand-copied herbals and finally printed in book form.

A garden patch growing useful plants was an oasis of quiet in the confusion of the crowded life of the castle compound. It was a place to enjoy the earthy, fragrant smell of growing things away from the more pungent odors of human beings and animals. After the twelfth century, when western Europe had seen the last of the barbaric invasions, the countryside became safer and life spread out from the walls of the castle or manor house. The small garden then developed into a larger enclosure where the pleasures of life could be enjoyed after the winter had passed. The miniaturists and the tapestry designers clearly reveal the joy which people found in escaping from their damp, poorly lit, noisy, and often bad-smelling indoor surroundings.

One of the miniature paintings in the superb-early fifteenth-century *Book of Hours* created for the Duc de Berry shows a castle garden, set in a corner of the walls, oriented to the best exposure. There is an arched trellis or *berceau* built along the inside walls to support vines, which formed a tunnel where one could stroll in seclusion. Flowering fruit trees and thick green grass are also seen. This, undoubtedly, was a true pleasure garden, though its component parts were utilitarian.

The period of the High Middle Ages, the twelfth, thirteenth, and fourteenth centuries, saw the development of knighthood, of orders of chivalry. Romantic love was celebrated in song and story and Courts of Love were established as a pastime; there noble ladies such as Eleanor of Aquitaine settled all questions submitted to them. What better setting could there be than a beautiful garden to discuss the problems of love? It was by now a special enclosed place, set apart from the main dwelling, where privacy could be found. At other times parties assembled there for outdoor meals, storytelling, music, dancing, or for a variety of games such as backgammon, cards, and chess. Frequently such gardens had a tank or small pool for bathing.

Garden culture in Europe made considerable gains during the Crusades. In the garden courts of the Middle East, the knights discovered colorful beauty and refreshment of spirit, and their eyes were opened to the wonders of new flowers and trees. Among the importations that followed were the fragrant damask rose, the carnation, jasmine, new bulbs, and trees such as the pomegranate, lemon, sour orange, and the magnificent cedar of Lebanon, none of which had been seen in northern Europe before.

In order to describe a typical medieval "pleasaunce" we should look over the walls and into the gardens of the fortified manors of France and Flanders through the eyes of their miniaturists. In glowing colors they have preserved the beauty and serenity of these relatively small enclosures. Prominently displayed are turfed seats constructed against crenellated stone walls. These were narrow, raised beds held in place by boards or stonework and topped with turf transplanted from the meadows. This was used as an easily replaceable ground cover — one which introduced many delightful wild flowers, creating a "flowery mede." Such familiar garden flowers as English daisies (*Bellis perennis*), columbine, bellflowers (*Campanulas*), purple crocus (*Crocus vernus*), calendula, lilies-of-the-valley, primroses, violets, pinks, snowdrops, and heartsease (*Viola tricolor*) were all European wild flowers. The old *Rosa canina*, lilies, peonies, and iris had already been cultivated within the herb garden, and carnations, often depicted growing in pots, became special favorites. Hollyhocks now made their appearance — brought from eastern Turkey and Persia, since they were native to those countries as well as to China.

In pleasure areas, the hardy little flowers sprang up persistently through the grass even though the mede was often "daunced upon," and tall flowers grew on top of the turfed bench, which was sometimes used merely as a back rest. The charming painting of a "Paradise" garden by an unknown fifteenth-century master shows a bench used in this fashion. Sometimes the lower portions of trees were protected by fashioning circular turf seats around them, held in place by wattle fencing woven of osiers.

It was not unusual for the pleasure area to be divided into a grassy section for games and dancing and a squared-off section for plant beds. These beds were usually raised several inches for good drainage and were always carefully edged with bricks, stones, or boards. This part of the garden was frequently protected by a low latticework fence, which kept out roaming dogs. Very often the wooden edging and the fences were painted in the heraldic colors of the owner.

Water, so important in any garden, is shown in a variety of wells and fountains on the pages of illustrated manuscripts. Some are Gothic fantasies, some are great marble basins, and some are simple stone troughs. The overflow of water was caught in channels and pools, often used for bathing, and men and women sometimes bathed together, for in the communal life of a castle, privacy appears seldom to have been the rule.

Another permanent garden fixture was the marble table with pedestal base. In religious paintings it displays the symbolic apple of redemption, or the bread and wine of the Eucharist. In secular scenes people gather around it playing chess. The players had to remain standing, as chairs were lacking; only occasionally do we glimpse small wooden stools.

There were small fruit trees in these medieval gardens — apples, pears, pomegranates, oranges, and lemons. Small clipped evergreens, yew or box trained into tiers, appear, and in more urban settings, larger versions became wonderful dining pavilions. Large trees trained in this manner were particularly favored by the Flemish. They appear in several engravings, most clearly in Peter Brueghel's famous spring scene. Otherwise, the art of topiary, which developed in imperial Rome, had not been revived, and complicated shapes such as animals and people were not attempted.

Within the garden area there were still other means of entertainment. Grass-covered mounts, often topped with small pavilions, offered vantage points for viewing the countryside or the whole garden vista and became particularly popular in fifteenth-century England after their introduction from France. Four of them had existed in the fourteenth-century gardens of the Louvre. An opportunity for private walks was provided by simple labyrinths of hedging, for the labyrinth had now moved outdoors from the churches; during the Crusades, the time of greatest religious fervor, patterns had occasionally been worked out in the flooring of some of the French cathedrals, such as Chartres. Over these, penitents moved slowly on their knees, while reciting their prayers at fixed stations. The terms labyrinth and maze are confusing, for they are often used synonymously. Some English writers have stated that the labyrinth lacks the blocked alleys of the maze, and one author claims that the labyrinth is always high and the maze low.

The delightful miniature paintings not only show us how gardens were planned and situated, but frequently acquaint us with the flowers that grew in them. The borders of illuminated manuscripts often seem to depict flowers simply for their beauty and familiarity, but sometimes scenes symbolically illustrate a religious story. The painting of a

"Paradise Garden" (sometimes called a "Mary Garden") by an unknown Rhenish artist of the fifteenth century shows a seemingly casual garden scene full of Christian symbolism. The enclosed garden, or *hortus conclusus*, symbolized the Virgin Birth; through an allusion to a passage from the Song of Solomon, "A garden enclosed is my sister, my spouse." Mary, the Queen of Heaven, is seated upon a cushion reading while her Child humbly plays on the ground. His royal lineage from the house of David is suggested by the iris, which had a regal connotation. Mary's purity is suggested by the white lilies, and red roses symbolizing divine love grow beneath the cherry tree at the left. Cherries signified the joys of heaven. Strawberries, the fruits of righteousness, whose trefoil leaves symbolized the Trinity, grow near the seated figures of Saint Michael and Saint George, and a sturdy vine stock, sprouting new growth, represents the "rod out of the stem of Jesse." On the table are apples, symbolic of the fall of man and his redemption by Christ. The water trough can be associated with Mary as the "well of living waters" and the lilies-of-the-valley in the foreground denote both her meekness and her purity. The goldfinches perched on the wall were associated with Christ's Passion, for they have crimson markings and eat the seeds of the thorny thistle.

Everything we observe about the garden in these paintings is corroborated by two famous writers of the late Middle Ages. Both the *Opus Ruralium Commodorum* (*Book of Rural Profits*) by Petrus Crescentius and Giovanni Boccaccio's Third Day in the *Decameron* were skillfully illustrated during the fifteenth century, the greatest period of the miniaturists. Crescentius wrote his book at the end of the thirteenth century, however. It remained in Latin manuscript for a hundred years before it was translated into Italian, French, and German and finally illustrated by engravers and the fifteenth-century illuminators. The sections on agriculture and farming were largely based on the ancient Roman treatises of Cato, Varro, and Columella, but Crescentius's descriptions of ideal medieval pleasure gardens are his own. He suggests three sorts of gardens: for people of humble origin, for the middle classes, and for noblemen and kings. All should be created on flat ground and should be square and have sections for fragrant herbs (rue, sage, sweet basil, marjoram, and mint), as well as for flowers (violets, lilies, roses and gladiolus, or corn-lilies). Although Crescentius did not mention them (possibly because they were so common in the Mediterranean countries) native oleander, snapdragon, and candytuft probably beautified the garden as well. It was suggested that rue should be grown for its beauty, greenness, and bitterness, which would "drive away poisonous animals from the garden," and that all should be enclosed by moats, rose hedges, hedges of fruit trees, or high walls. Crescentius also recommended that the location of the garden be "freed from noxious plants and large roots" and be soaked with scalding water to keep the remaining weed seeds from germinating. Turf, brought in from the fields, was to be laid between the beds and on top of raised benches. A few shade trees were to be planted "in the sun's path," not so thick as to kill the grass, and not manured, because that, too, could harm the turf. Trees were to be planted widely enough apart to prevent spiders from stretching their webs across from one tree to another and catching in the faces of those who walked underneath. Gardens were to be open to the north and east and sheltered against the south and west winds, which were "violent, impure and unsettled." Being an Italian he advised in favor of his own climate. A fountain was to be placed in the middle of the garden, and a pergola was used as a pavilion, for in the Italian summer shelter from the sun was all-important.

The lordly garden, as Crescentius described it, was a greatly enlarged area of twenty square acres containing natural springs. It had all of the above features, created on a grander scale — higher walls, larger pergolas stretching along the inside of the walls (as seen in the Duc du Berry miniature), and rows of orange, lemon, and pomegranate trees. He stated that ideally, in such gardens, there should also be a wildlife refuge, for hares, rabbits, roebucks, and stags. Near the castle a large tree covered with copper wire was suggested as an aviary for song and game birds. Nightingales, blackbirds, goldfinches, linnets, partridges, and pheasants are all mentioned.

Boccaccio's description of a garden in the Third Day of the *Decameron* (the first dated edition of which was published in 1471), might well have used Crescentius as a model. It has the same medieval walls and the same fountains, covered alleys and pergolas, flowered turf, and bird and animal denizens. The description is far more poetic, however, and it is entertaining to read further of how a group of young people spent their time in these lovely surroundings. The story concerns seven young ladies and three young men who fled plague-ridden Florence in 1348 to seek refuge in a villa on the hills of Fiesole probably the Villa Palmieri). In the garden they took turns being King and Queen of the Day and held daily storytelling sessions. The following passage is from the translation of the Bibliophilist Society edition of the *Decameron*.

> The garden, all walled about, coasted the palace. It had about it and athwart the middle, spacious alleys, straight as arrows and embowered with trellises of vines, yielding a rare savor about the garden. The sides of these alleys were walled about with roses, red and white and with jessamine. While the sun was highest one might go all about neath odoriferous and delightsome shade. Amiddleward the garden was a plat of very fine grass, enamelled with a thousand kinds of flowers, closed about with the greenest and lustiest of orange and citron trees, the which, bearing at once old fruits and new, and flowers, afforded the eyes a pleasant shade and were no less greatful to the smell. Midmost the grass plat was a fountain of whitest marble. From a figure that stood on a column in its midst, sprang a great jet of water, high towards the sky. With a delectable sound it fell back into the wonder-limpid fountain. The water which overflowed the full basin issued forth by a hidden way, encompassing the lawn by very goodly and curiously wrought channels.
>
> As the ladies and three young men went gladsomely about, weaving themselves the goodliest garlands of the various leafage of the trees, they hearkened to the carols of belike a score of different kinds of birds, and then wonder-stricken they noted that the garden was full of maybe an hundreds kinds of goodly creatures, rabbits, hares, grazing fawns and kids.

Boccaccio's garden was essentially medieval, but his writing marks him as a humanist of the early Renaissance, so let us use him as the connecting link between the Middle Ages and the Renaissance, that great period of history which wrought so many economic, political, and social changes in people's lives.

Plates

55. Re-created cloister garden of Cuxa. A simple fountain, borders of purple iris, apple trees, and soft green grass offer beauty and serenity. (*Metropolitan Museum of Art, Cloisters Collection*)

56. Cloister of the convent of the Quattro Santi Coronati, Rome. The fountain of this twelfth-century cloister is placed in the middle of a small square pool. (*E. Richter, Rome*)

57. A *Paradise Garden*, by an unknown Rhenish painter of the fifteenth century, shows elements of a typical medieval garden and is imbued with Christian symbolism. (*Städelsches Kunstinstitut, Frankfurt*)

58. A low stone wall, planted with turf from the fields, forms a seat for the Virgin and Saint Anne in the garden scene painted by a fifteenth-century Flemish artist. The flowery mede of the foreground includes certain plants favored by medieval Christian symbolists – daisies of innocence (also held by the Christ Child), dandelions (symbolic of the bitterness of grief and of the Passion), and the plantain, or "waybread." This latter, since it was so well known as a roadside weed, signified the well-worn path of those seeking the way to Christ. (*Bulloz, Paris*)

59. The usefulness of turfed seats beside garden walls is seen in this charming painting of the Virgin and Child, Mary Magdalene, and a donor. The garden is simply made of brick-edged beds. Painted in the late fifteenth century by the unknown Master of the View of Sainte-Gudule. (*Musée Diocésain, Liège*)

60. Within castle walls a checkerboard garden is further protected by a low-railed fence. Arches to support vines border it, and within the enclosure several fruit trees have been planted. A fountain spilling over into a convenient dipping pool lies just outside the enclosure. An illuminated manuscript depicting Susanna and the Elders, fifteenth century French. (*Philadelphia Museum of Art*)

61. Reproduction of a medieval herb garden at the Cloisters, New York City. Madonna lilies, peonies, roses, pinks, and a number of cooking and medicinal herbs are grown in raised, brick-edged beds. (*Metropolitan Museum of Art, the Cloisters Collection*)

62. Planting a garden. Page from a Flemish manuscript copy, circa 1460, of *The Book of Rural Profits*, by Petrus Crescentius. (*Pierpont Morgan Library, New York City*)

63. In a strangely quiet castle courtyard a medieval maiden (Saint Barbara) reads her book while she rests against a turfed seat. The flowers that might have grown within the garden or among the turf are beautifully depicted in the manuscript border instead. (*Pierpont Morgan Library*)

64. *The Concert*, an early-sixteenth-century French tapestry. Gathered around a large fountain set in the midst of flower-spangled grass, a group enjoys music in a garden. The lady playing the portable organ has a helper to pump the bellows. Seated on a wooden stool beside her, a man plays a lute, while another lady plays a viol. (*Musée des Gobelins, Paris*)

65. Between the inner and outer walls of this castle lies a little pleasure garden in which two lovers meet. A pot of carnations, a clipped evergreen, and a Gothic fountain are all important elements of the scene. French fifteenth-century manuscript painting by Renaud de Montauban. (*Bibliothèque Nationale, Paris*)

66. Within garden walls men and women bathe in a Fountain of Youth, while enjoying the pleasures of wine and music. Fifteenth-century Italian manuscript painting from *De Sphaera* in the collections of the Biblioteca Extense, Modena. (*Umberto Orlandini*)

67. This miniature painting from a fifteenth-century copy of *Le Roman de la Rose* shows a large garden area divided by a lattice fence into two separate areas of activity. The garden section at the right is divided into beds for herbs. That on the left, with a large fountain at the center, has a grassy space for dancing, strolling, or music-making. Large trees provide shade. (*British Museum*)

68. Surrounded by men and women attendants, a noble lady bathes in an outdoor tank – often a garden fixture in medieval times. Early-sixteenth-century French tapestry, one of a series depicting the life of the aristocracy. (*Musée de Cluny, Paris*)

69. A château garden of fifteenth-century France, created in a sunny corner formed by protecting walls. Illustration for the month of April from *Les Très Riches Heures*, the fifteenth-century illuminated prayer book painted for the Duc de Berry by Pol de Limburg. (*Giraudon*)

56

57
58

59

61

60

63

62

64

65

66 67

70. (OPPOSITE) View over Lake Maggiore from the gardens of Isola Bella. (*Author's photo*)

VII   *The Italian Renaissance*

Though the Renaissance would seem to be a precise period in history when a fully developed culture of great art, scientific achievement, and expansive trade burst upon a world long darkened by the turmoil of war, ignorance, and superstition, exact dates cannot, of course, indicate its beginning or its end. It can rather be likened to a flower, for it had a gradual burgeoning, a period of stunning bloom, and finally an overblown beauty. After the centuries of grinding, fear-ridden existence that followed the fall of Rome — fear of God, fear of a lordly master, fear of war, pestilence, hunger, and death — medieval man at last threw off the shackles of his burdensome existence and became fully aware of his many capabilities as an individual. This is the true meaning of the Renaissance — the rebirth of man.

During the Middle Ages, man had been primarily concerned about his relationship to God; now he became engrossed in his relationship to himself and his world; and a spirit of inquiry was abroad. Presaging the full flowering of the Renaissance were the great fourteenth- and early fifteenth-century writers Dante, Petrarch, and Boccaccio, the artists Giotto and Donatello, and the architect Brunelleschi. The artists achieved greater realism in depicting man; the writers helped develop a common Italian language and fostered an appreciation of the pre-Christian Roman culture. This was a culture which, like their own, had also stressed wealth, trade, city life, and the glorification of the arts. People became absorbed in all things pertaining to man's classical past. The "humanist" mind reveled in ancient manuscripts (preserved by the monks and translated by the Arabs) and marveled at the sight of newly excavated classical statues. Even Justinian I's laws were re-examined for use in the complexities of urban life.

Geographically, Italy had always been at the crossroads of the world. Trade was the very essence of her being, and urban life rather than the feudal system had long been the accepted way of living. With the Crusades, people's lives were profoundly changed by newly unleashed economic and intellectual forces felt throughout Europe. Mental horizons were broadened by new ideas and scientific knowledge, as well as by the rich rewards of travel. Economic conditions changed radically as the new wealth of consumer goods arrived from the East. As urbanization spread through Europe the merchant class became all-powerful. Trade and the continuing wars required financial support, and this was supplied by prosperous money-lenders. Those of Venice became famous throughout the world, and later on, in the city of Florence, the Medici family became pre-eminent, first as wool merchants, then as financiers.

By the fifteenth century, class consciousness in Italy had so completely broken down that social acceptance was apt to be based upon talent, the ideal *uomo universale* or universal man having versatile cultural gifts. Such a one was Lorenzo de' Medici, who was not only an astute financier and politician but a classical scholar, collector, musician, poet, and art patron as well. Such artists as Alberti and Vasari were also writers, painters, musicians, architects, garden designers, sculptors, and classicists. Architects often planned the gardens surrounding the palaces and villas they designed. Some created garden sculpture. Raphael was famous for his magnificent paintings, for his architectural work, and for the garden plan of Villa Madama, Rome, built for Pope Clement VII.

An early example of the *uomo universale* was Leon Battista Alberti (1404-1472),

Wood-engraved illustrations from the 1499 edition of the *Hypnerotomachia* of Poliphilus: (LEFT) Design for a patterned flower garden, or a parterre, meant to be outlined with low-growing herbs and filled with small flowering plants. (RIGHT) A marble-pillared pergola for vines such as Alberti suggested for every garden.

a contemporary of the first great Medici, Cosimo the Elder (1389–1464), who became known as "Pater Patriae." In *De Architettura* Alberti set forth the principles of villa and garden design befitting a cultured man of the Renaissance, for the most part merely reiterating what Pliny so explicitly set forth in the first century A.D. Classicism was truly to the fore. Nevertheless, it served to remind would-be creators and owners of gardens that,

Also from the *Hypnerotomachia*: a colonnade of marble and latticework in which stone vases hold topiary trees, each one clipped differently. (*New York Public Library*)

like the ancients, they, too, should select sites which "had a view of cities, land and sea, a spreading plain and the known peaks of the hills and mountains." There should be open galleries for enjoying sun or shade, and cool, shell-encrusted grottoes covered with porous stone and made "mossy" with the addition of green wax. Groves of fruit trees, ivy-entwined cypresses, and marble-pillared pergolas covered with vines should be included for their shade-giving qualities. Box-bordered paths and topiary work were indispensable, and concerning the latter Alberti reminded his readers that "the gardeners of former times flattered their patrons by writing their names in letters formed in box and other odorous herbs." Stone vases should be set about to ornament such an ideal garden, which would include fountains and flowing water and statuary, "if not indecent."

A carefully preserved diary of the fifteenth century written by Bernardo Rucellai, a wealthy Florentine who is thought to have commissioned Alberti to design his garden at Quaracchi, describes many of these elements. The plan was a simple, straightforward one, calling for a pergola connecting the house with an enclosed, private garden (*giardino segreto*), a small lawn, box-bordered and flower-filled beds, and clipped topiary work. Beyond the *giardino segreto* the main axis was continued as a tree-lined avenue leading to the Arno. All parts of the garden were well defined by the straight lines of its geometrical layout. The style demanded square beds and trees planted in orderly rows, and only plants and trees which could be clipped or trained were grown. The intense interest in gardening during this period was wholly in keeping with the humanist movement, for it was plainly characterized by respect for the cultural achievements of the past.

An allegorical romance written by Francesco Colonna, a Dominican monk who called himself Poliphilus, published at this time (perhaps in 1467), reveals a considerable degree of garden achievement during the quattrocento. In the story *Hypnerotomachia*,

111

concerning "Love's Struggle in a Dream," the author expressed his theories of gardening and architecture. Engravings added great importance to the later edition of 1499, which was translated into French and English, for they reveal medieval as well as Renaissance garden features, thus linking the two periods. This imaginary garden was planned as a series of concentric plantings through which the principal figures passed to reach the island at the center named "the place of heart's desire." There were meadows which one associates with the "flowery mede," centered marble basins or fish ponds, and latticework enclosures and trellises, all medieval in feeling. Contemporary elements included a classical colonnade displaying vases planted with clipped evergreens, antique statuary, a ruined amphitheater (its different levels planted with flowers), and several intricate parterres or "knot" gardens worked out with a variety of herbs. The Italians cherished a great variety of flowers, not only for their usefulness but also for sheer beauty. The old-fashioned roses, violets, iris, lavender, hyacinths, and primroses, the native gladiolus, and such plants as columbine, balsam, forget-me-nots, heartsease, and love-in-a-mist are all mentioned. These were planted with new introductions from faraway places — hollyhocks, carnations, narcissus, cyclamen, and jasmine, which had reached Europe during the Crusades. Traders and envoys such as the Flemish ambassador Busbecq, who served the emperor Ferdinand I at Constantinople, also sent back bulbs and plants from the Middle East. However, at the peak of the Renaissance garden style, most of this floral beauty was relegated to the small, private family garden.

The imaginary garden of Poliphilus is interesting as a forerunner of Italian Renaissance gardens, but those created by the Medici and their contemporaries excite our imagination more, for they can be brought to life with real people and history. The story of Renaissance garden art begins in Florence and culminates in Rome. It is, in particular, a story of the wealthy Medici family and of the affluent princes of the Church.

The softly rounded hills bordering the valley of the Arno became the favorite building sites for the country villas of Florentine families. Basking in the Tuscan sunshine, surrounded by vineyards and orchards, these villas provided relaxation from the confusion and violence of life in the bustling city of Florence. The patriarch of the Medici, Cosimo the Elder, owned a number of villas during his lifetime, as well as an impressive city palace. His favorite villa, which became the most famous, was at Careggi, outside the city limits. It was situated at the foot of the hills and had fine vistas over the plain and the most extensive grounds of any of his domains. The original fortified building was bought in 1417 and was remodeled by the architect Michelozzi, into what Giorgio Vasari, in his *Lives of the Artists* (first printed in 1550), called a "rich and magnificent building." The quotations from Vasari are from the 1897 edition (published by Charles Scribner's Sons). It incorporated within its walls a double loggia, which brought the house and garden into close relationship and was now considered to be necessary for providing shade in summer and protection on windy, cool days. Frequently it was enclosed on three sides by the permanent structure of a building, with its fourth side consisting of arches supported by columns. On occasion, it had two open walls, or even projected into the garden at ground level like a pavilion. When constructed as part of an upper story it became an ideal place from which to admire the garden or the distant view.

112

Cosimo gathered at Careggi a circle of brilliant people who considered the garden a proper setting for the discussion of philosophy and the reading of ancient Greek literature. Called the Platonic Academy, it was truly that in spirit and ideals and a deliberate imitation of the open-air academies of classical Athens. It became renowned as one of the most important intellectual centers in Europe. Cosimo developed the garden plan in a purely classical manner, to the extent that symmetrically designed, box-edged borders enclosed plantings of flowers and herbs. There were fruit trees, bay trees, myrtles, and cypresses, probably arbors, benches, and at least one fountain, at the center. Vasari mentioned that water had to be brought in specially, and when Cosimo's grandson, Lorenzo the Magnificent (1449–1492), inherited Careggi, he had this fountain adorned with Verrocchio's charming bronze sculpture, "Boy with a Dolphin," which is now placed in the courtyard of the Palazzo Vecchio. Cosimo's garden was famous as a place where rare and foreign plants were brought to be nurtured and studied. This interest in exotics was maintained by Lorenzo.

In the country, Cosimo the Elder also owned a villa and hunting lodge at Caffaggiolo, high in the hills overlooking Florence. The original garden no longer remains, though a sixteenth-century painting shows its simple design. Its hunting lodge, *Il Trebbio*, still stands, impressively overlooking first its garden, then the whole beautiful countryside. The garden is medieval, as it is a separate, walled unit, with regularly spaced beds for flowers and vegetables. One of the original pergolas is still in place. The villas and garden of Caffaggiolo are privately owned, and Careggi now belongs to a hospital.

The city palace on the Via Larga, now Via Cavour, which Cosimo commissioned in 1440, was destined to become as famous as Careggi as a center of learning. The massive and forbidding building which Michelozzo designed for his patron set the style for other fifteenth-century city houses of the great families. Inside, its arched and columned courtyard gave it an air of formal beauty and welcome. Beyond the courtyard lay a garden with great basin-like fountains and elaborate topiary work. Box was clipped into the shapes of elephants, dogs, stags, and ships in full sail. As pieces of ancient sculpture were acquired by the family, they were set in prominent places in the garden and, with the topiary shapes, gave the place an animated and populous air. Since city encroachments and additions to the palace by its subsequent owners, the Riccardi family, greatly cut down the size of the original garden, there is but a small portion still in existence today. What remains is well maintained but too small to have retained any of the atmosphere of a place which was once the setting for the colorful and splendid festivities accompanying Medici family weddings and royal visits.

It was the great Donatello, a favored protégé of Cosimo's, who aroused his initial interest in the acquisition of antiquities, an interest maintained by the grandson Lorenzo. Under Lorenzo's sponsorship the nearby gardens of San Marco became an academy for promising young painters and sculptors, where, under the tutelage of Bertoldo, a pupil of Donatello's, they could study and copy the ancient works brought there. Each one received a stipend according to his ability. Young Michelangelo, aged fifteen or sixteen, was sent to join the group in the garden and here his great talent was perceived almost immediately. Lorenzo soon persuaded the youth's father to let the boy live in the palace

with the Medici and be treated as a son. He was given a stipend of five ducats a month and a purple mantle.

An important step in garden development was taken at Fiesole when Giovanni de' Medici, the younger son of Cosimo the Elder, built a villa on a very steep hillside. We return to Vasari once more to learn that Michelozzo, starting in 1458, "constructed another magnificent and noble palace, the foundations for the lower part of which were sunk at a very great expense in the declivity of the hill, but this was not without its advantage, since the master contrived to place in that portion of the edifice, various cellars, store-rooms, and stables, useful appurtenances to the dwelling of a noble." The situation of the villa required a terraced development of its surroundings. However, decorative use of staircases and ramps had not yet been conceived of as the means of connecting the upper and lower terraces. The ancient Romans had not solved this problem satisfactorily either, and their gardens were laid out on level or slightly sloping ground. Entrance to the lower part of this Medici garden was through the underground rooms or by an indirect path. Only utilitarian stairways connected its parts. This villa was especially delightful during the hot summers; according to Politian, Lorenzo's friend and his children's tutor, "there is abundance of water here, and as we are on the edge of a valley, but little sun, and the wind is certain never lacking. The villa itself lies off the road, in a dense wood, but commands a view of the whole city." A charmingly simple and private small garden adjoined the house. Its entire plan was made up of two paths, with a large circular basin at their junction. Here, in sun or shade, was an outdoor room in which to linger with friends. When Lorenzo inherited the villa, upon his uncle's death, he spent much time with the members of the Platonic Academy, now part of his permanent household.

This type of secluded small garden close to the dwelling, was a precursor of the secret garden (*giardino segreto*) which ultimately became a necessary adjunct to every great Renaissance villa. It was a retreat where, when the garden became a complex of formal greenery and architectural detail, flowers could be grown, herbs could be properly cared for, intimate meetings could take place, and perhaps children could play. In fact, the *giardino segreto* retained the spirit of the medieval secular garden, although the details of its design became thoroughly Renaissance. In some such small garden where roses were cherished Lorenzo became inspired to write one of the charming poems of his young manhood:

> Into a little close of mine I went,
>> One morning when the sun with his fresh light
>> Was rising all refulgent and unshent.
> Rose-trees are planted there in order bright.
>> Whereto I turned charmed eyes, and long did stay,
>> Taking my fill of that new-found delight.
> Red and white roses bloomed upon the spray;
>> One opened, leaf by leaf, to greet the morn,
>> Shyly, at first, then in sweet disarray;

"Boy with a Dolphin" by Verrocchio. This sculpture originally graced a fountain in the garden of Cosimo de' Medici the Elder at Careggi. It is now in the Palazzo Vecchio in Florence. (*Alinari*)

> Another, yet a youngling, newly born,
>   Scarce struggled from the bud, and there were some
>   Whose petals closed them from the air forlorn;
> Another fell, and showered the grass with bloom;
>   Thus I behold the roses dawn and die,
>   And one short hour their loveliness consume . . . .[1]

Some say the garden was at Caffaggiolo, where Lorenzo lived during much of his youth, but wherever it was, the roses would have included damasks, *Gallicas* and *Rosa alba*.

The villa of Poggio a Caiano, ten miles from Florence, was the only one Lorenzo actually built for himself. It was naturally his favorite and became a place where he lived as lavishly as in the city. Its extensive area included woods for hunting, streams for fishing, and large gardens for merrymaking. We read of balls, masquerades, feasting, falconry, and May singing. Here too, experiments in agriculture were carried out and there was an extensive plantation of mulberry trees. For several centuries Poggio a Caiano received the world's eminent figures on their way to Florence, for even after Lorenzo's time the Grand Dukes of Tuscany (the younger branch of the Medici) enjoyed this princely pleasure house. We have no contemporary description of garden details, but a sixteenth-century painting shows many symmetrical tree plantings and garden areas on each side of the house. Its most distinctive feature in the painting is the delightful walled garden, very possibly made in Lorenzo's time, which suggests a *giardino segreto*. The villa is now a state museum and little garden area is left, for much of it was converted into an eighteenth-century "English park."

After Lorenzo de' Medici's death in 1492 the political fortunes of the Medici family fluctuated. They were twice exiled but returned in 1531 as the Dukes of Florence. Six years later a murder removed the last of the direct line of Cosimo the Elder, and a collateral descendant, Cosimo I, often called "the Great," governed as the Grand Duke of Tuscany. Another period of prosperity and splendor followed, under three generations of Medici rulers.

In 1540 a member of the Duke's artistic household, the sculptor Il Tribolo, was requested to draw plans for gardens surrounding the Villa of Castello. This garden is described by Vasari as "the most rich, magnificent and ornamental garden in Europe." There is also an enthusiastic description by the French essayist Michel de Montaigne, who visited it in 1580 while on a health-seeking tour through Switzerland, Germany, and Italy. Giusto Utens' lunette painting, dating from the end of the century, also reveals interesting details. Essentially the Villa Castello's garden is a symmetrical, large, walled enclosure, created behind the palace on a very gentle upward slope. It was of artistic importance because of the fine sculpture incorporated in its fountains and of scientific interest because of the engineering of its underground aqueducts. It had horticultural significance because of the variety and treatment of its trees and because of the introduction of such plants as jasmine from the East Indies. It was, as well, a stimulating place for entertainment. The painting shows two large rectangular pools in front of the villa, surrounded by a flat grassy area known as a *prato*, a space reserved for games or tilting matches. There was a secret

116

garden at each end of the palace, one of them perhaps reserved for the growing of medicinal herbs, for a statue of Aesculapius, the Greek god of medicine, is known to have been created for such a place.

The focal point of the garden is a large, tiered fountain of columns and basins topped by Bartolommeo Ammanati's dramatic bronze sculpture of Hercules and Antaeus. It was not always in its present position, for the center fountain at the time of Montaigne's visit supported a beautiful bronze figure of a woman wringing out her long wet hair. Sometimes referred to as Venus, but most frequently as "Florence Rising from the Waters," this statue by Giambologna is now at the neighboring Villa Petraia. Formerly there was a thick planting of cypresses, laurels, and myrtles around Castello's central fountain; this no longer exists, nor do the many thickly interwoven arbors of "odoriferous trees" seen by Montaigne, through which "the sun at its greatest strength could not enter."[2] The orange and lemon trees he saw, which were also mentioned by Vasari, are now represented by those planted in terracotta jars which traditionally take their places along the borders each spring. In May they are brought out from the *stanzone*, or lemon houses, of the upper level and are placed on their stone bases scattered throughout the garden area, still an almost universal practice in formal Italian gardens. Sunny walls still support espaliered fruit trees.

In the midst of the *bosco* at the top of the garden, in the center of a pool, one can still see the crouching figure personifying the Apennines. The large grotto underneath this hill received its water from the reservoir above, and at its entrance was a favorite conceit of the sixteenth-century garden designers, a water joke. Innocently approaching, one might suddenly be dampened by jets of water spurting from the pebbles in the pavement, turned on at will by a garden attendant. Within the grotto three large shell-encrusted niches held a remarkable collection of life-sized animals, some of stone, some of stucco, some incorporating real antlers and horns. The grotto was cool and served almost as a menagerie for nontravelers who had never seen a camel, an elephant, or a rhinoceros.

Another of Castello's marvels was the thickly screened room among the branches of an evergreen tree. That this tree was probably a holm oak is suggested by the saddening remains of another, with a rustic staircase encircling it, that still exists on the terrace of neighboring Petraia. Centered in a small marble table in the Castello oak was a marble vase from which a little fountain of water spurted. Montaigne added to his description of the tree that it was impossible to describe the many ways in which the water of the oak could be turned on, "in order to drench anyone at pleasure"! A system of copper tubing could also make the water "produce various sounds and whistlings." Yet another famous tree house was constructed at Pratolino, its great size and winding stair well depicted in a seventeenth-century engraving.

The only reference made to anything resembling topiary art at the Villa Castello was to the Duke's escutcheon which topped a gateway, "very well formed of some branches of trees maintained by fibers that one can scarcely discern." The fibers were probably willow, which Italian gardeners still use as twine after it has been soaked in water. A study of contemporary engravings from this time on reveals a marked lack of complicated topiary work. Hedges were clipped at varying heights, and occasionally one notices a pyramidal form, but height accents were usually provided by the many citrus trees in pots.

Nowadays, without the evergreens around the central fountain and other shade-giving elements, the garden of Castello has an impersonal look, lacking charm. Perhaps it is because a sense of enticement has been lost, for all is revealed at a glance.

Undoubtedly in the environs of Florence there have been gardens equally as beautiful as those of the Medici or even more so, but although many of the dwellings remain among the Tuscan hills, the gardens were less permanent and prone to neglect or fashionable change. The nineteenth-century influx of the English with their devotion to flower borders, green lawns, and large specimen trees in many instances destroyed the Italianate character of the villas they acquired, and while their gardens have colorful beauty they are not in keeping with the buildings they surround. Two small gems, however, which still preserve their Renaissance character, are the Villa Capponi at Arcetri and the Villa Gamberaia at Settignano. The Villa Capponi has three divisions — a grassy lawn for games, a parterre garden with citrus trees set among its beds, and a little secret, walled garden. Villa Gamberaia has been described as giving a "great effect on a small scale."[3] The four divisions of its main garden have been recently turned into a water parterre which charmingly reflects the clouds, the blue sky, and the green of the clipped shrubs. A tall hedge shaped into arches terminates the garden and provides windows from which to admire the superb view. The compact plan of the garden also includes a *giardino segreto*, grotto, bowling lawn, and *bosco*.

The grandest and most extensive gardens ever developed in Florence are the Boboli, which lie behind the huge Pitti Palace on the left bank of the Arno and are easily approached by the Ponte Vecchio. The original palace, which is now but a central section of the whole, was built in rivalry to Cosimo the Elder's on Via Larga. The rich Luca Pitti ordered each of its windows to be as large as the entrance door of the Medici palace. Financial difficulties suspended the building operation within eight years, although the family retained it until 1549, when it was sold to Eleanor of Toledo, the extremely wealthy Spanish wife of the Grand Duke Cosimo I. From then on several large additions were made to the palace and the development of the gardens began. Il Tribolo, who had designed those at Castello, was entrusted with the planning, but he died within a year and Ammanati took over. During approximately one hundred and fifty years, four different architects designed for the gardens and six generations of the Medici dynasty enlarged and embellished the palace, until it became one of the most impressive in the world. The garden is dominated by the horseshoe-shaped amphitheater behind the palace. It was created from the sloping fields of a hillside, once cultivated and called "Bogoli" or "Borgoli." At its far end steep ramps ascend to other levels, one of which holds the pool and fountain of Neptune. This statue, with a fabricated triumphal car, were originally used in a festival in 1565. At the top of another sharply inclined staircase is a statue of Abundance. From any level a wonderful view of Florence unfolds, and even while one is seated in the amphitheater some sections of the Duomo are clearly visible. For the pageants, masques, fetes, and wedding festivities which took place with the palace as the background, and for the processions that wound through the city streets, some of the most famous artists designed costumes, pasteboard arches, and stucco statues, invented clever automatons, and even superintended the productions. Giorgio Vasari was one such impresario and wrote of creating arches and

118

banners for the Emperor Charles V's reception, and of gigantic decorations made for the wedding of Cosimo the Great's eldest son and the Archduchess of Austria. Even the great Leonardo da Vinci designed a mechanical lion which spilled a shower of lilies from its breast to greet Francis I when he was entertained at the Milanese court.

One of the fetes which made Florence famous took place in the Boboli gardens on a summer night in 1651, in celebration of the marriage of Cosimo III de' Medici to Marguerite Louise d' Orléans. A booklet entitled *Il Mondo Festeggiante, Balletto a Cavallo*,[4] describing the pageant and including an engraving of the climactic entrance of a giant wood and canvas Atlas, was published in Florence in 1661. First there was a "ballet of troops of horsemen pacing in intricate figures to music from over a hundred voices and a hundred instruments." For this procession the cavalry was costumed to represent Europe, America, Asia, and Africa. Then, Atlas is said to have "lumbered in, cracked open and became a rocky mountain with pretty ladies on its top." He was accompanied by a gold float symbolizing the sun and a silver one for the moon. There was also "a vast machine of clouds in a niche, which rolled down with a sound like thunder, let out a four-horse chariot of

The great oak tree at Pratolino, which had a double staircase with rustic handrails and a platform among its spreading branches. Seventeenth-century engraving by Stefano della Bella.

Jove and then rolled back again." The splendor of this pageant was later rivaled by the French King Louis XIV, with his week-long *Festins du Roi*, for a copy of the booklet had been presented to him and the fame of such Florentine festivities had spread.

The early depictions of the Boboli gardens show the areas surrounding the amphitheater squared off into tree plantations or *boschi*, with a formal garden on the river side of the palace. Since this part of the garden encountered old city walls, further development had to take place on the opposite side of the palace in the wedge-shaped piece of land which sloped towards the Porta Romana. Throughout much of this section, as with many old and overgrown gardens, the geometric design of its circular complexities is not too apparent as one wanders under the dense shade of protecting branches. However, one is constantly aware of diagonal paths leading off from central meeting places like the spokes of

119

a wheel, and a labyrinth once existed in this section. Much of the original statuary and water is missing, for each subsequent owner made changes to conform with the spirit and fashion of his times. Topiary work admired by the English visitor John Evelyn in 1644 is no longer in evidence, nor are the aviaries, bowling green, or botanical garden. In accordance with the Medici tradition of interest in horticulture, experiments were made here in the growing of potatoes, pineapples, and mulberry trees, all marvels which had come to Europe during the great age of exploration.

Since the garden had to expand down the western slope, a long, straight cypress avenue, now grown dramatically tall and flanked by a pair of evergreen alleys, was developed to lead directly toward a lower level. Here was a large oval basin incorporating a delightfully formal little island called the Isolotto, whose design Vasari claimed. An iron railing encircles the pond, which is bridged at intervals. A colossal fountain of Oceanus occupies its center, patterned gardens surround it, and the whole small island is encircled by a wall displaying climbing roses and by lemon and orange trees in terracotta jars. It is said that this whole creation was inspired by the small water theater which had been uncovered at Hadrian's Villa at Tivoli. Its feeling, however, is far from classical; much of its statuary is grotesque and Baroque, for the last major changes in the garden scheme were made during the seventeenth century. Since that time it has remained virtually unchanged. Still maintaining its reputation of "a royal palace in the open air," the Boboli provides entertainment for thousands of visitors, and the custom of presenting plays and musicals in the amphitheater has been revived.

Each of these Tuscan gardens made contributions toward a well-defined Renaissance style of gardening. Since the hot, dry summers ruled out all but the spring-blooming flowers or those which could be tended in pots, year-round beauty was provided by the permanent greenery of clipped hedges, trees, and arbors. This green background was a perfect foil for a colorful array of fashion. Never in history had clothes been more strikingly designed or made of more elegant fabrics. The sparkle of jewels was added to the women's flowing gowns with their contrasting mantles. Men wore brocaded tunics or emblazoned them with heraldic insignia. Often the legs of their hose were of different colors, and many wore small red felt hats.

The greatest garden glory of the Renaissance flourished ultimately in Rome and her environs, but not until Florence had paved the way. Rome began developing her princely gardens more than a century after Cosimo de' Medici created his at Careggi. There had been many troubled years of rivalry between the papacy and the empire, of the Popes' "captivity" in Avignon, and of terrible schism within the Church. The city was a frightful morass of ancient ruins and squalid medieval dwellings. Life was violent, depressing, and unhealthy. Not until a forceful pope, Martin V (1417–1431), succeeded in returning the papal court to Rome and the States of the Church were brought in line through diplomacy and force did any semblance of order, hope, and security emerge. Then vainglorious popes lifted the face of the city by building monumental churches, palaces, and fountains, designed by the great artists of the sixteenth and seventeenth centuries. The Church soon accumulated the tremendous amounts of money needed to accomplish this through taxation and the sale of indulgences. But a tragic interruption took place in 1527, when Em-

"Entry of Atlas." An engraving of 1661 of festivities in the Boboli Gardens for the marriage of Cosimo III de' Medici to Marguerite Louise d'Orléans. (*Metropolitan Museum of Art, Dick Fund, 1940*)

peror Charles V's mutinous and unpaid troops sacked Rome. Nevertheless, since a pattern of living perhaps more worldly than spiritual had been established by the prelates of the Church, the rebuilding and beautifying of the city began again and its splendor grew.

Renaissance popes embraced humanism as did the temporal despots, and they extended their patronage to painters, sculptors, and architects, many of whom traveled back and forth between Rome and Florence. The princes of the Church lived as luxuriously as the princes of the city states. They developed beautiful gardens and often built magnificent pleasure palaces for entertaining, at the same time maintaining city dwellings closer by. Popes and cardinals enjoyed all the good things in life — good food, great libraries, gorgeous surroundings. They could collect marble statues or enjoy the pleasures of the flesh. Not for nothing was it said that churchmen could "easily be distinguished by their noble breadth of girdle"! Montaigne wrote, "The city is all court and all nobility, every man shares in the ecclesiastical idleness . . . it is nothing but palaces and gardens."

Nevertheless there were at times stern, far-seeing men such as Pope Julius II (1503–1513), who sincerely worked toward the glorification of Rome and the Church. Julius had grandiose visions, and his immediate interest lay in the rebuilding of Saint Peter's and the further enlargement of the Vatican, the palace of the popes. Before succeeding to the papacy he had acquired a sizable and fine collection of antique sculpture, which he now wanted to place within the walls of the Vatican. Also wishing to utilize further the pleasure house of the Belvedere which his predecessor had built on a hill close by, he commissioned Bramante (Donato d'Agnolo, 1444–1514) to design a connecting court which would provide a setting for the sculpture and create a protected passage from one place to the other. Thoroughly versed in the ideals of the Renaissance, Bramante studied and measured the ancient ruins of the city and had already built that classically perfect gem, the Tempietto. He was a logical choice for the designing of a great pleasure garden which was

121

to incorporate a private retreat and a large public area suitable for pageantry. His design for the Court of the Belvedere had far-reaching significance and was daringly unorthodox at the time. Perspective, proportion, and terracing solved his problem, for by the introduction of retaining walls, grand staircases, and ramps, various levels were connected. Never again would it be necessary to select only level or gently sloping garden sites.

The structural and artistic advantages of using whole architectural elements and not just details were considerable and the final result impressive. The Farnese Pope Paul III (1534–1549), a notable art patron who apparently agreed with Leo X's statement that one should enjoy the God-given Papacy, had an extensive and famous series of gardens on top of the Palatine Hill. In the last years of his life he entrusted the architect Giacomo da Vig-

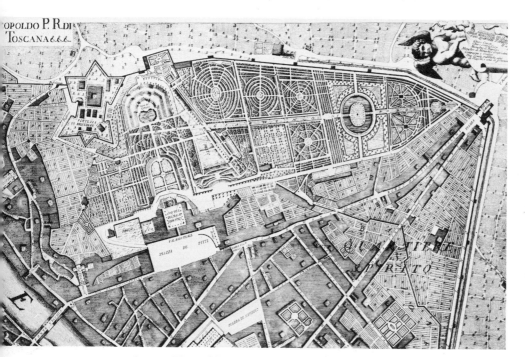

(LEFT) Plan of Boboli Gardens in Cosimo Zocchi's 1783 map of Florence.

(CENTER) View of the Vatican gardens below the Villa Pia, in the seventeenth century. A comparison can be made between this print and the sixteenth-century one (FAR RIGHT) in which N represents the villa. From Giovanni Battista Falda's *Giardini di Roma*, 1683.

nola (1507–1573) with the task of designing a grand entrance leading up to them from the Campo Vaccino, or what we now call the Roman Forum. For centuries the rubble of ancient buildings and soil from the hillside had been washed down and the level of the Forum had risen. Covered with grass, it was a grazing place for sheep and cows. At ground level Vignola created a wall and gateway leading to a semicircular *teatro* adorned with niches for statues. From there a ramp and staircases led up through several levels to the top, where two square aviaries, flanked with high retaining walls and connected with a balustrade, looked down over the scene and seemed to present the unified façade of a building which really did not exist.

The remains of fountains and a grotto still stand in the mysterious and overgrown gloom of this section of the Forum, topped by the original aviaries, though they no longer possess their original screened cupolas. Orchards, cypresses, and other trees added a softening green throughout this great approach to the top. The gardens of the Palatine were meant exclusively for the growing of flowers, trees, and shrubs, introduced as "exotics" from faraway places, for the Pope was greatly interested in acquiring all the new varieties possible. Later, the gardens were sold to the Duke of Parma, who had the parterres redesigned by Carlo Rainaldi. A small section of these gardens still remains, but the process of excavating the palaces of the Caesars has obliterated the greater part.

The Farnese gardens continued to grow in importance over a number of years, and a catalogue of their rare plants, published in 1625, indicates that morning glories, passion

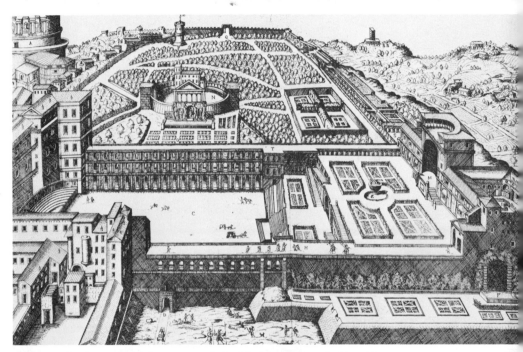

(RIGHT) Court of the Belvedere, designed by Bramante, which connected the Vatican Palace (left) with the Villa Belvedere (right). The court was the scene of jousts and pageants. This 1579 engraving by Ambrosius Brambilla was made just before the building of the Vatican Library across the lower terrace. From a collection of Antonius La Freri called *Speculum Romanae Magnificentiae*. (*New York Public Library*)

vine, and yucca had been introduced from Central America. All over Europe there was an intense interest in horticulture during this period, and in addition to plants from the New World, bulbs from Asia Minor such as tulips, new varieties of narcissus, and many kinds of lily were avidly collected. A handsomely illustrated garden book of 1633, *Flora — ouero Cultura di Fiori*, by Padre Giovanni Battista Ferrari of Siena, the keeper of the Barberini family's special garden, shows that a great variety of plant material suitable for growing in a *giardino segreto* or within a botanical collection was available. Besides the bulbs already noted, he listed fritillaria, muscari, and ornithogalum. A number of varieties of roses, Spanish and Persian iris, lilac, cyclamen, lychnis, and lobelia are mentioned, and sumac and trumpet vine from North America had also been received. This book is also a wonderful

Plates

71. Giambologna's figure of "Florence Rising from the Waters," which was formerly in the Castello garden of Grand Duke Cosimo I, and is now at the neighboring Villa Petraia. The beautiful marble fountain was the work of Il Tribolo. (*Alinari*)

72. The villa and gardens of Castello, designed by Il Tribolo for the Grand Duke Cosimo the Great. This lunette painting by Giusto Utens shows the two *giardini segreti* at each end of the dwelling, the thick planting of evergreen trees which surrounded the central fountain, and the fountain of "The Apennines" in the basin on the upper level. (*Soprintendenza alle Gallerie, Firenze*)

73. The garden of the Villa Castello. Its clear-cut design, great central fountain, and jars planted with citrus trees are all typical of the sixteenth century. The entrance to the grotto is through the columned opening in the center of the retaining wall at the back. Within the wall, staircases rise to the *bosco* above. (*Federico Mella, Milan*)

74. The Villa Medici, Fiesole. Its situation and its formal plantings followed Alberti's garden principles, but the terracing of the gardens was a daring and imaginative concept for the times. (*Alinari*)

75. "The Apennines," a colossal figure by Bartolommeo Ammanati, crouches in the pool in the *bosco* above the garden of Villa Castello. (*Alinari*)

76. A photograph taken in the early twentieth century showing the holm oak on the terrace of Villa Petraia. Its rustic staircase led to a dining platform. (*Alinari*)

77. Griffins guard the entrance to the lemon garden of the Villa Capponi at Arcetri, just outside Florence. Still retaining its original sixteenth-century character, it is a small outdoor room sheltered from cold winter winds, fragrant in summer and green throughout the year. (*Courtesy of Mr. Henry Clifford. Bertoni photo*)

78. The Isolotto at the Boboli Gardens today is essentially as it was three hundred years ago. The little garden in the center still has its formal beds, terracotta jars holding lemon and orange trees still form part of the balustrade, and dark walls of ilex still enclose the whole area. (*Alinari*)

79. The amphitheater which lies behind the Pitti Palace in Florence. The fountain terrace and the walls of the courtyard, seen in the foreground, provided the base on which a stage could be built for outdoor spectacles. (*Alinari*)

80. The elaborate grotto which today's visitor sees as he enters the Boboli Gardens is a remarkable combination of stuccowork, sculpture, and fresco. Michelangelo's "Prisoners" (copies are now in place) were surrounded by fantastic shellwork creatures. (*Touring Club Italiano, Milan*)

81. The garden of the Villa Gamberaia at Settignano has a panoramic view of the Tuscan hills. It is not an extensive garden, but its magnificent site gives it great scope. The clear-cut design, the meticulous shaping of its topiary work with clipped cypress formed into an arched colonnade, and the planning of all its parts make of this garden a small gem in keeping with all of Alberti's ideas. (*Tet Borsig*)

82. The Villa Medici garden, Rome, now the Académie de France. Its design has hardly changed since the sixteenth century. The view is seen from the upper terrace. (*Touring Club Italiano, Milan*)

83. From the loggia of the Villa Medici one looks past Giambologna's Mercury into the main garden area. The *bosco* is on the left, sculpture gallery on the right, and above it a path through the woods leads to the mount. (*Anderson*)

72

74

73

75 76

79

80

82

83

source of information concerning the drying of flowers, their distillation, their use as sweetmeats, their packing for shipment, and their artistic arrangement either in vases or in set pieces created over wicker forms.

The importance of the sixteenth-century architect to the garden can also be appreciated in a study of the exquisitely designed Villa Pia of Pope Pius IV (1559–1565) in the Vatican grounds and in his successor's, Villa di Papa Giulio III. The first is a truly secluded retreat consisting of a very small palace facing a loggia on an oval, paved courtyard.

Planned less as a retreat than as a place for entertainment, Pope Julius III's classic pleasure house, just off the Via Flaminia and below the Borghese Gardens, was perfectly designed for enjoyment during a hot Italian summer. Its shallow rooms, curving colonnade, sunken *nymphaeum*, and cool underground passages, interspersed with lawn and garden, made it an ideal place for seclusion or for sociability. Small formal garden areas, the descendants of former *giardini segreti*, are still retained, and there is a charming colonnade with a beautifully frescoed ceiling representing a trellis of roses and grapes. This garden side of the villa is supposedly the re-creation of an ancient Roman one; Vignola, as superintendent of the works, and Vasari, Michelangelo, and Ammanati had a part in its completed design. Vasari said he "always committed to drawing the caprices of the Pope, which were then given to Michelangelo to revise and correct." In the Pope's time the gardens, lavish with fountains, statues, and trees, stretched all the way to the Tiber.

In Rome there still remains an almost perfect example of a Renaissance pleasure garden, where flower beds and ilex woods can weave a spell that evokes the sixteenth century. The Villa Medici, which became Académie de France after Napoleon bought it from the Grand Dukes of Tuscany, has retained its original character with few changes, and it is a delight to walk its paths and explore its wooded depths. The villa, close by Trinità dei Monti, occupies a part of the Pincian Hill, the ancient *Collis Hortulorum* associated with Lucullus, Domitian, and Sallust. Just as there is contrast between the light and shady sections of the garden, there is contrast between the formidable façade of the palace and the delicate, open feeling of its garden elevation. Garden and villa were completed soon after 1580, when Cardinal Ferdinando de' Medici acquired the property. The occupants of the villa and their guests entered the garden area through an open loggia, and went down a few steps to the open area reserved for active games and entertainments, thence into the main garden with its six symmetrically divided beds. Like other members of the Medici family, Cardinal Ferdinando took an intense interest in old and new sculpture. Important pieces had dominant positions in the garden, and long sculpture galleries extended its width. An entire collection of bas-reliefs was purchased to ornament the façade of the villa, and classical busts and statues were placed in the niches incorporated in its design. These *stucchi* added delicacy to its appearance, and the idea was copied soon at the Villa Borghese. Giambologna's *Mercury* stood in the loggia with two stone lions, but ultimately these were sent to Florence with other priceless treasures. Copies are now in place and a few casts are set about the grounds. The sculpture gallery also functioned as a retaining wall for the hill behind it, and its balustraded roof still serves as a terrace from which a bird's-eye view of the garden can be enjoyed.

Immediately behind it is a *bosco*, now wildly overgrown, but a moss-covered path still leads to the ancient mount, so well seen in early engravings. From the little stone summer-house on its top there is a most wonderful view of the city. Giovanni Battista Falda's late-seventeenth-century engraving shows a flower garden down below the other side of the mount, and an earlier print reveals that covered walks, or *berceaux*, existed in the garden divisions close by the palace and near the loggia. These are now a part of the extensive but formally planned wooded area through which one strolls upon entering the villa's grounds. As one walks up the cobblestones of a sloping drive, it is easy to recapture the mood of the past and imagine the clattering of horses' hoofs and the jingling of harness. However, the *bosco* must be imagined as it was originally planted, orderly and controlled, without the romanticizing effect the old stone pines bring to it today.

With Florence re-establishing the classic principles of formal gardening, and with Rome contributing the elegance of architectural elements, there remained but one final addition to complete an Italianate style. This was the dramatic flourish of water, spilling in quantity down the terraced hillsides now selected for garden sites, providing both motion and sound in a variety of moods. The hills north of Rome where Tivoli is situated, and the Alban hills beyond the eastern campagna became the favored locations for summer palaces. Rome was expanding rapidly, the elevation of the hills was invigorating, and a water supply was plentiful. Aqueducts had brought water to Rome in ancient times and popes rebuilt them during the Renaissance, but this water was channeled directly to the city's public fountains and further distributed to the private gardens of the rich. Now, where water was tapped at its source, the restraint of a single jet could be cast aside and the garden architect could be lavish with fountains and cascades.

The supreme example of a "water garden" is at the Villa d'Este at Tivoli, little more than twenty miles from Rome. It was begun sometime after 1550 for Cardinal Ippolito d'Este, a son of Lucrezia Borgia, and was then developed by successive cardinals. Pirro Ligorio, who had been studying the ruins of Hadrian's Villa nearby, designed both villa and garden, and Orazio Olivieri was the hydraulic engineer. A branch of the local river Anio, diverted and channeled, provided unlimited amounts of water, and the high rise of ground a logical course for its descent. But since, in the Renaissance garden, all was controlled by man, the water never flowed naturally, but was led into fountains which became white thrusting curtains, cascading falls, and plumelike jets. Banisters are used as chutes, and water spurts from stonework and even gushes from the breast of the Sphinx. In contrast to all this movement, great rectangular pools reflect in their soft green depths the slow motion of clouds and the breeze-swept branches of trees.

The design of the garden is so logical and its terraces are connected with such ease that it is possible to explore all its reaches without tiring, in spite of the forbidding drop of its hillside. The several cross-axes serve to rest and divert the visitor, for each has something to be admired: a fountain, statuary, or an impressive view. Along one crosswalk which runs parallel to the façade of the villa are placed the Hundred Fountains. Eagles and fleurs de lys, representing the crest of the Este family and the recognition of the cardinal's ambassadorship to France, are lined up along a wall with small obelisks and stone boats. Their jets and arcs spurt brightly and gently into long troughs, and their wall is now green and soft with maidenhair ferns.

There were many written descriptions of the wonders of this garden, and a number of engravings were made by artists, all of which reveal its development. The earliest print shows that the flat area at the foot of the hill had transverse latticework arbors, or *berceaux*, with herb gardens (*giardini de semplici*) on either side. Here was the main entrance for the cardinal's visitors, who next looked up at the great villa on the summit of the hill and approached it by way of staircases, sloping walks, and diagonal ramps. From the top there was a fine view over all the gardens, now obscured by their greenery, and an extended vista over the countryside. Later, the *berceaux* disappeared, and Piranesi's eighteenth-century engraving shows that they had been replaced by the *rondello*, where fountains and eight statues representing the Liberal Arts were eventually enclosed by a circle of cypresses, now grown majestically impressive.

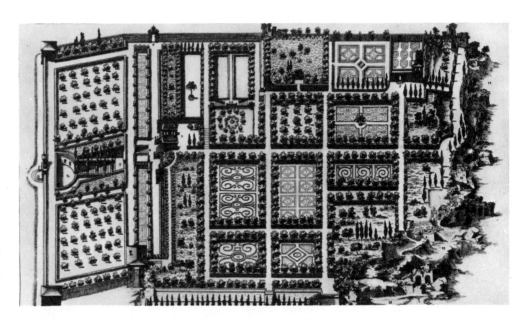

The Farnese gardens, designed by Giacomo da Vignola and developed by Pope Paul III, originally covered most of the Palatine Hill, but the parterres were later redesigned by Rainaldi.

(OVERLEAF) The entrance to the Farnese gardens from the Roman Forum. From Falda's *Giardini di Roma*, 1683. (*New York Public Library*)

The Villa d'Este was one of the places greatly admired by Montaigne during his travels, although it was as yet incomplete. The "water inventions" captured his fancy, and his description of the famous water organ is particularly interesting.

> The music of the organ, which is real music and a natural organ, though always playing the same thing, is effected by means of the water, which falls with great violence into a round arched cave and agitates the air that is there and forces it, in order to get out, to go through the pipes of the organ and supply it with wind. Another stream of water, driving a wheel with certain teeth on it, causes the organ keyboard to be struck in a certain order, so you hear an imitation of the sound of trumpets.

He also spoke of water which fell in another section of the garden with such force and such suddenness that it made "a noise of cannon shots"; and of the wonderful Fountain of the Owl, a place where "you can hear the song of birds, which are little bronze flutes . . . and then, by other springs set in motion, an owl appearing at the top of the rock, makes

135

this harmony cease instantly, for the birds are frightened by his presence." The effectiveness of the great reflecting pools was not lost on Montaigne either, for he spoke of "the rainbows seen in their interlacing shafts of water so natural and vivid, that they lacked nothing of one we see in the sky."

Montaigne was also greatly impressed with the Tuscan villa at Pratolino which the Grand Duke Francesco de' Medici built in 1568 in seeming rivalry to the Villa d'Este: "he purposely chose an inconvenient, sterile and mountainous site, . . . without springs, so as to have the honor of sending to get water five miles from there, and his sand and lime another five miles. It is a place that has nothing level about it." Pratolino's water devices were varied and justly renowned. Benches and stairs squirted water on the unsuspecting; doors opened and statues came to life through its power. There was a figure of Pan which stood up and played his pipes as people came near, and also a marble statue of a woman doing her washing. Water dripped from the white tablecloth she was wringing out and a basin

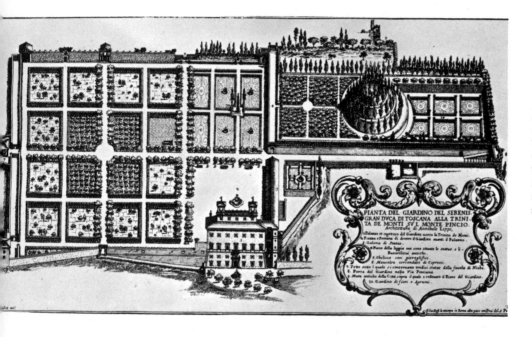

Falda's engraving of the Villa Medici in 1683. Previous to this the two square divisions of the *bosco* immediately to the left of the palazzo, as seen in the engraving, had trellised arbors crossing them at right angles.

nearby appeared to be boiling the water for the wash. Another marvel of the garden was the gigantic fountain figure of the Apennines with a little room inside its head. This alone remains today of all the original garden ornaments. In 1819, when it was much overgrown and the hydraulic water devices no longer in working order, the garden was changed to the prevailing English park fashion, and three years later the villa was torn down. Montaigne thought the spring water of Pratolino excellent and that of the Villa d'Este "muddy and ugly," and he wrote that although the Villa d'Este excelled "in ancient statues and in situation and beauty of prospect," the Pratolino palace was more beautiful.

By the end of the sixteenth century, in places such as the Villa d'Este and at Pratolino, we see a reaction against the classically restricted garden rules that had prevailed so long. Contemporary statuary rather than antique was included, and artists created complicated

138

Piranesi's 1765 engraving of the Villa d'Este. In the foreground are the statues and fountains of the *rondello*, but the artist seems to have placed its cypresses farther up in his composition. From *Veduta di Roma* by Giambattista Piranese.

figure fountains planned for specific locations. The tiered-basin fountains of the Tuscan gardens became outmoded. There was less conformity in architecture as "C" curves, scrolls, and volutes were introduced. More and more the Baroque intention of impressing was achieved by dynamic line movement, by a combination of the beautiful and the grotesque, and by the exaggeration of effects. Uninhibited emotion appeared in painting and in sculpture, and lavish display often·found its way into the very structure of the garden. This is seen in the prodigal use of water at the Villa d'Este and in the grotesque detailing of the water organ, with women's legs twisted into pilasters! Some of the statues surrounding the Isolotto at the Boboli combined the traditional with the grotesque. Both the Farnese Villa at Caprarola and the Villa Lante at Bagnaia show tendencies toward the Baroque style in their statuary and other embellishments.

In the spring of 1550, Vignola was commissioned by Cardinal Alessandro Farnese to build a palace with gardens about thirty-five miles north of Rome in the hills of the Monti Cimini. He had already completed his commission for the cardinal's grandfather, Pope Paul III, at the Farnese Gardens on the Palatine. Here at Caprarola, on a hillside overlooking the vast panorama of open country, stood the remains of an old fortress which became the foundation of the new building. Its pentagonal shape was retained on the exterior and a huge several-storied circular courtyard was created inside, surrounded by elegantly frescoed staterooms. The problem of designing a garden for such a huge and forbidding building was difficult, and Vignola accomplished it in the most direct way, probably realizing that anything in close proximity, if too elaborate, would only appear trivial. After grand

An early view of the Villa d'Este at Tivoli. In the lower part of the garden, where visitors entered, labyrinths no longer exist, nor do the herb gardens. An engraving by Giacomo Lauro, *Antiquae Urbis Splendor*, 1612. (*New York Public Library*)

A plan, engraved in 1815 by Jacques Barozzi, of the Villa Farnese at Caprarola, its adjoining gardens, and its casino. The scale of the immense pentagonal palace can be sensed by comparing it with its garden casino on the hill (far right). (*Columbia University, Avery Library*)

staircases and a piazza were designed for the front, the two sides of the pentagon facing the hill behind became garden façades for two separate square gardens, completely walled in, except where small drawbridges connected them with the *piano nobile*, or first floor of the villa. A moat still surrounded the old fortress. In keeping with the severity of the architecture, these gardens were completely simple, with symmetrical garden beds squared off and paths intersecting at the center. One had a grotto that dripped "like the sound of rain" and was at one time planted with roses. It also had a long arbor. The other was planted with small fruit trees and had a fish pond in its center. The gardens have been replanted in this century, and include camellias and a magnificent collection of red-berried hollies. They do not evoke the sixteenth century, but the shiny foliage is always an attraction.

The greatest glory of Caprarola, however, is the casino and its surrounding garden. Quite separate from the villa and its two adjacent gardens, it lies further up the hill beyond the intervening woods. After Cardinal Alessandro's death in 1592 his grandson, Cardinal Odoardo Farnese, began this project, and although Vignola died in 1573, long before its completion, it is generally agreed that the design was his. The casino was built as a hideaway for the cardinal and perhaps a few intimate friends, as a place free from formality and protocol. It is reached by an easy walk up through the woods by way of an opening in the wall of the orchard garden, and is startlingly lovely to come upon. The approach leads one to a round pool with a single tall jet, past a long water chain, past a fountain overlooked by two stone river gods, and up some stairs to the garden in front of the casino. The clipped box parterre of the terrace is bordered by stone *canephorae* (basket bearers of ancient Athens) standing on stone benches built into the wall. On its other side the casino faces gateways leading to woods beyond. There are open loggias on each side of the building. A special government permit is needed today for a visit to this section of Caprarola, as it is reserved for the summertime use of the President of Italy.

Connoisseurs consider the garden of the Villa Lante at Bagnaia to be the most exquisite of all these noble garden creations. Smaller than the other great gardens of the sixteenth century, it was nevertheless acclaimed from the very beginning when Cardinal Gambera supposedly commissioned Vignola to design it, soon after 1566. There is no documentary proof that Vignola was the actual architect, but since he had been the designer of the Farnese Villa at Caprarola, not far away, it is quite possible that his superior talents were called upon here also. Certainly the manipulation of both sites was masterly. At least there can be no doubt that the same artisans worked at both villas, for there are striking similarities in stonework. Montaigne claimed that the hydraulic engineer who was in charge of the water inventions at Tivoli also directed the work at Villa Lante although he seems to have been in error about his name. Water is the main theme at this villa, as it is at the Villa d'Este, but at Lante, instead of a central villa, there are two small identical ones, and the water of the garden, starting high on the hillside, flows in between them on its way to the large square basin below. The water is not flung dramatically about by fountains but pursues its downhill course through a variety of runways both above and below ground, bursting into jets and falling intermittently. Always it is like a lively stream, never a rushing river. It first issues from a grotto between twin loggias at the top of the hill, appears in a fountain basin, races down a rippling water chain, spills over basins guarded by moss-covered river gods, disappears, and emerges anew, but more placidly, in a long table trough in which wine could be cooled, and after jetting from a circular fountain finally appears in the grand finale of four reflecting pools in the *quadrato* at the bottom of the garden. Here it has emerged completely from the wooded hillside where giant plane trees, ilexes, and oaks have shaded it, and is at last displayed in the open, surrounded by the serenity of formal garden beds. The most important fountain is on a balustraded island in the center of the *quadrato*.

This garden was another place Montaigne visited and found enchanting, saying, "It easily takes the prize for the use and service of water." The four little stone boats in the divisions of the great pool interested him, for in those days each one still held its two musketeers and a trumpeter who shot water at the central fountain. At that time this was the double-tiered basin shown in the 1612 engraving by Lauro. This same print shows both villas finished, but only one was completed in Cardinal Gambera's time. One of his successors, Cardinal Montalto, built the second and had the large fountain of the pool replaced by the figures of four youths, sometimes referred to as Moors, holding high his family emblem, the hills of the Monti Cimini, with a star on top. Cardinal Gambera's crest, a crawfish (*gambero* in Italian), is seen several times in the garden. It appears in stone relief and in an elongated form becomes the water chain or *catena d'acqua*, its head and claws spilling the water into the shell-like basin above the Arno and Tiber river gods.

This is a garden for *al fresco* living, with enough water tricks to enliven any gathering. There were gentle sprays from the pavement to soak one's legs, jets from the circular fountain to wet a visitor suddenly, and arcs of water from the roofs of the loggias to surround one.

An unusual addition to the formal garden section is the enclosed park at one side. The Italians always included *boschi* for shady walking, usually planted with regularity, but here the woods were quite separate and wild, only the diagonal paths giving a semblance of order. Scattered here and there were fountains, trellises, and a labyrinth, all seeming to presage the English parks of a hundred and fifty years later. The outstanding feature in this area outside the main garden is the great circular reservoir, glacially blue, in which Giambologna's statue of Pegasus is surrounded by little winged children.

Perhaps the most extraordinary garden ever conceived is that created by Pierfrancesco Orsini, in 1572, below his family villa in the small town of Bomarzo near Viterbo. Scorning the steep hill behind his palace he selected some wooded valley land below, which had a little stream and natural outcroppings of limestone. What was called a garden was really an outdoor sculpture gallery of nightmarish monsters and ogres, fashioned from the natural stone. A giant, holding his enemy by the legs, tears him apart. A dragon snarls at two fighting lions, while an elephant crushes a gladiator in his trunk. A giant turtle with a mossy back stumbles through the undergrowth while balancing a robed figure. Two gigantic heads loom from beneath a bank, one with staring, empty eye sockets, and a wide-open mouth in which a person can stand. There is a stone dining table inside, and along the lips Dante's words are engraved: "Ogni Pensiero Vola" — "Every thought flies." Is this the entrance to Hades? Near the entrance to this "garden" there was a three-headed dog, Cerberus surely? It is claimed that Turkish prisoners of war, taken at the Battle of Lepanto in 1571, were brought here to carve these fantastic creatures. At one time there must have been some semblance of order in one section of the "garden" at least, for there are traces of low retaining walls, and many large stone urns are scattered about. These have an affinity with the beautiful small temple, said to have been planned as a memorial to the duke's dead wife. Here again the architect Vignola is claimed as the designer. Small specimen trees have recently been planted where the underbrush has been cleared, and when they reach maturity a mood of mystery which the visitor senses here will once more prevail.

Since medieval times wealthy noble families had built residences on the slopes of the Alban Hills, whose villages became known as the Castelli Romani. One of the villages, Frascati, experienced great building activity at the close of the sixteenth century and the beginning of the seventeenth. Here the aristocracy, mostly of the Church, created spectacular pleasure houses a thousand feet above sea level, with views which encompassed volcanic lakes, the campagna, and, in the far distance, the sea.

Popes not infrequently presented villas to nephews who were cardinals, or financed their building. Clement VIII bought a small villa in 1598 for his kinsman, Cardinal Pietro Aldobrandini, which, within five years, developed into one of the most imposing of all Baroque Italian villas. Its architect was Giacomo della Porta, a pupil of Michelangelo. Its two waterworks specialists were Giovanni Fontana and the same Orazio Olivieri who had been employed at the Villa Lante and the Villa d'Este. Halfway up a hill, the austere façade of the palace with its broken pediment, still looks down upon Frascati. Its unusual enclosure of stone and wrought-iron fencing has oval openings, like eyes, as if for scrutinizing visitors, but the protective tunnels of greenery bordering the straight entrance approach have always extended a gesture of hospitality. Today there is one magnificently old central *allée* with grazing pastures sweeping down on either side, but an old print by Falda reveals that in the seventeenth century there were regularly planted trees of several varieties. The villa's impression of grandeur is furthered by the broad, horizontal terraces and diagonal staircases which firmly link it with its surroundings. Under these terraces are the storage and service quarters; the roofs of the kitchens have

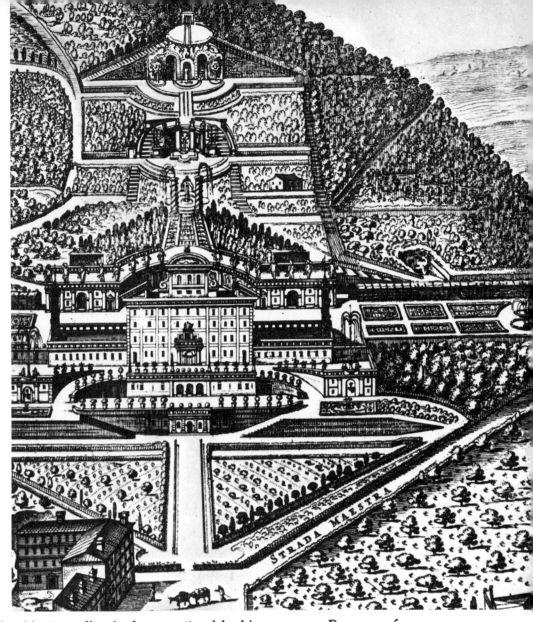

Detail from an early engraving of the Villa Aldobrandini on its steep hillside at Frascati. The Hague: A. Alberts.

become side terraces, their chimneys disguised as medieval-looking turrets. Because of the slant of the hillside there are only two stories at the back of the building, which looks over a rather shallow courtyard, the other side of which has a great semicircular retaining wall holding back the wooded hill above. This is known as the water theater or *nymphaeum*, for it has grottoes and rooms with ornamental water, cool refuges for hot summer days. Visitors always were impressed with the continually dancing copper ball in one room, where a hole in the pavement let in wind which kept the ball moving.

In the central niche of the *nymphaeum* stands Atlas, bearing a watery world on his back, for he is the terminus of a spectacular water cascade which rushes down the length of a precipitous slope, passing through rustic fountains and little gorges. The watercourse is narrow, for woods are allowed to come close and are clipped only where they grow directly above the water theater. It takes daring and care to clip these ilex hedges, for they are at least thirty feet high, with little room to maneuver tall ladders between their base and the balustrade which runs along the top of the theater. The walls of trees are always kept green, for as ilex loses its bottom branches, laurel is planted to

143

inferius situm est Castellum Bagnaia.

Plan of the Villa Lante at Bagnaia which gives some idea of its descending levels. The original fountain seen by Montaigne is clearly shown. Engraving by Giacomo Lauro, 1612. (*New York Public Library*)

maintain the green down to the ground. The close combination of the wild and the formal in this hillside garden is indicative of the Baroque relaxation of previous conventions.

The Frascati villas were visited, admired, and painted by a number of European travelers including John Evelyn, the English diarist and garden author, and Hubert Robert, the romantic French painter. Many of the villas passed from the Church to the family descendants of the cardinals who built them; others were exchanged or sold by the families. But for three hundred years such places as the huge Villa Mondragone, the Villa Torlonia (originally the Ludovisi Villa), the Villa Falconieri, the Villa Muti (famous for its box parterres), and the Villa Lancellotti have been meccas for countless garden-lovers. With the passage of time, some lost their initial splendor, and their gardens fell into decay. The Villa Mondragone, for instance, became a Jesuit college with little pretense of keeping up its beauty. But the destruction and subsequent economic difficulties of World War II wrought the most devastating changes. The Villa Aldobrandini became the headquarters of a German communications center and a target for Allied bombings. The Villa Falconieri was seriously damaged and the Villa Torlonia was demolished. Prince Aldobrandini has restored his villa and gardens, and the grounds of the Villa Torlonia are now a public park where the desolately dry water staircase and the vacant niches of the water theater below it are but empty shells of their former beauty.

On either side of Rome, there still exist two great parks, one public, the other private, which were acquired and developed during the first half of the seventeenth century by the cardinals of the Borghese and Pamphili families. Each family owned city houses, but the lavish casinos built within the parks a short distance away made versatile and showy places for entertainment and magnificent backgrounds for fine art collections. Cardinal Scipio Borghese, a favorite nephew of Pope Paul V, was an assiduous acquirer of properties. He bought and enlarged the Villa Mondragone for himself and another property for his sister, at Frascati. In 1605 he also bought a large tract of land, three miles in circumference, just

144

beyond the Pincian Gate, where he built a beautiful casino. It had formal, patterned flower gardens immediately adjacent to it and was especially noteworthy because the rest of the land was developed into a lovely but regulated woodland area, scattered with Baroque foundations, sculpture, a small dining pavilion, a large rectangular fish pond on which swans and waterfowl swam, enclosures for gazelles, deer, other wild animals, rabbits, and birds. Hundreds of pines, cypresses, planes, oaks, and other trees were planted, but in an orderly fashion, and the whole area was divided by straight avenues and walks. When the influence of the English park of the eighteenth century was felt formality was forgotten, and the other, now familiar, features of the Borghese Gardens — the large amphitheater, the lake in front of the small temple, and fake ruins — were added. A greater variety of trees and shrubs was also planted. Cardinal Borghese opened the section nearest the city gate to the Roman populace, following the tradition of ancient emperors, and setting the pattern for the present. All this property and additions made to it remained in the hands of the Borghese family until 1901. Subsequently bought by the Italian government, it is now Rome's finest public park, and the art collection housed in the casino ranks as one of the world's great treasures. This was the second great art collection made by the family, for Camillo Borghese, who married Napoleon's sister Pauline Bonaparte, was persuaded to sell his brother-in-law two hundred works of art to enrich the Louvre.

A seeming rival to the Borghese domain was that owned by the Pamphili family on the Janiculum hill, on the opposite side of the city. The acquisition of a small villa by the man who was to become Pope Innocent X was followed by the building, in about 1645, of the delicately decorated casino for his nephew the Cardinal Camillo Pamphili. The addition of an undeveloped hunting preserve molded this into a holding far greater than that of the Borghese Villa. It was the parklike surroundings, rather than elaborate parterres, which made both these domains unusual for their time. The Pamphili garden also succumbed to the English park style in the early nineteenth century, so only parts remain of the original authentic Italian Baroque garden. It is still owned by the descendants of the Doria Pamphili family.

The Italian style culminated in the overblown last period of the Baroque era, from which it was impossible to advance further. The late Baroque style in painting and architecture often overwhelmed with the intricacy and extravagance of its unrestrained design. We have already seen curves and arabesques appearing in the shaping of flower beds and hedges. Some say this was the influence of the French, who loved linear pattern, and certainly there must have been an exchange of ideas through the many travelers of the period. But it seems rather to have been a natural reaction to what had been a set style for so long. In the late seventeenth century there was less harmony in the combination of plant materials. In gardens such as that of the Villa Garzoni at Collodi, we see palm trees combined with cypress, while agaves mingle with box. Tall hedges are scalloped in contrast to the straight lines of terraces, while some clipped shrubs have a softness hardly compatible with stone retaining walls.

The Villa Garzoni and its hillside garden are two separate entities because of the nature of the site. The proximity of a little village and of a busy stream made it difficult to interrelate palace and garden; therefore, the garden, which was meant for display, was created at one side, seemingly flung across the hill for all to see. Placed with the native Italian flair for developing sites, a central watercourse presided over by a statue of Fame, five descending terraces, and a pair of sloping flower gardens brought the plan down to ground level. Here there are two large round pools with forty-foot water jets, and a box-edged parterre. In the spring the garden is filled with brightly colored cinerarias, and wisteria is introduced in a stylized form, clinging to tall pillars. Since their introduction, probably during the nineteenth century, both flowers have remained popular throughout Italy. Terracotta-colored statues add another note of color, and there are lemon trees in jars. From the top of the garden one looks down across a valley where the road lies, toward a terraced vineyard, not a "grand view" but one of domesticity. On the upper levels of the garden were entertainment facilities, which were reached from the villa by stairways and walks through the woods. A little theater with wings of clipped evergreen was created at one end of the upper terrace, and among cypresses on the brow of the hill were once baths and an eighteenth-century bath house. Some tastes find complete beauty at the Villa Garzoni, but others criticize it for the diversity of its different design elements.

Isola Bella, of the same period, charmingly unreal, magical in its spell, is a delight to all. It floats like a great flower-strewn barge in the waters of Lake Maggiore, surrounded by the snow-capped mountains of northern Italy. According to a possibly fictitious story, which is nevertheless in keeping with fairy-tale enchantment, the ladies of the Borromeo family disliked their castle on the mainland because they were disturbed by the cries of the prisoners in the dungeons. Therefore Count Carlo Borromeo conceived the idea of building a palace on the rocky island offshore. Work was started about 1630. Sharp rocks were leveled, boatloads of soil were brought over from the mainland, and hundreds of workmen shaped the terraces, laid out the gardens, and started the architectural work under the celebrated Roman architect Carlo Fontana. The Count's son, Vitaliano, carried the burden of most of the work, for his father died soon after the imaginative project was begun. By 1670 the terraced gardens were completed, but the palace was finished only recently, fortunately in accordance with the original plans. The formal garden, which one enters from the rear of the palace, leads directly to the great eminence of ten rectangular terraces overlooking the lake, their walls softened by the green of hedges, vines, and espaliered trees. Flanking each terrace, a statue or an obelisk is silhouetted against the sky. Seen from the water they appear to be pennants fluttering over a great castle, the more so because of the two hexagonal pavilions which give the impression of turrets at each side. As in the Hanging Gardens of Babylon, here, also, are cool arcaded retreats beneath the terraces, their different levels constantly attractive with flowers and verdure. Facing the palace is a great Baroque wall of pebble work which encloses within its shallow curve a number of grottoes or niches filled with statues and the repeated forms of scallop shells. It is bizarre, but time and the elements have mellowed its effect.

Many beautiful shrubs and trees have been added as time has passed. Today, the classic cypresses, pines, and laurels are joined by cedars of Lebanon and Japanese maples. There are the magnificent colors of azaleas, camellias, mimosa, rhododendrons, and oleanders, and the pansies, tulips, and cinerarias of the spring are followed by the potted flowers of summer. The gardens are laid out in formal parterres or shaded walks, and there is a fine green lawn, which can flourish in the equable climate and over which dazzling white peacocks strut. There are no fountains, for there was no need to compete with the shimmering expanse of the lake, but there are round pools and the dripping grottoes repeat the sound of water lapping against the bulwarks. The thought has often been expressed that Isola Bella gilded the lily of the Renaissance.

During the eighteenth and nineteenth centuries gardening felt two great influences. The French *parterre de broderie* with its intricate designs and its use of many new and colorful small flowering plants changed the aspect of many an old, and created many a new garden. Change was also wrought by the complete turning away from formality and the vogue for the English park. But neither of these modifications could ever destroy what was the basic contribution of the Italian style of gardening, a form of garden artistry in which a beautiful effect was retained throughout the four seasons. Its permanent elements

Water joke table in the early-seventeenth-century Italianate gardens of Hellbrun Castle, Salzburg. Engraved by F. R. Danreiter. (*New York Public Library*)

were evergreen trees and shrubs, stone staircases, balustrades and statues, and water in the form of flowing fountains, stately jets, pools, and gushing cascades. Designers were both daring and ingenious in their site planning and developed their gardens to include shady walks for hot summer days and sheltered ones for the winter. The garden had its large expanses for show and entertainment and its smaller, more intimate portions for seclusion. It was a place of beauty and pleasure the year round.

147

Plates

84. Cypresses in the gardens of the Villa d'Este. A drawing by the French artist Jean Honoré Fragonard made in the summer of 1760, when he was a guest there. (*Albertina Collection, Vienna*)

85. The oval fountain presided over by water deities at the Villa d'Este, Tivoli. This is at one end of the terrace of the Hundred Fountains. It is possible to walk under the circular falls of the fountain without getting wet. (*Alinari*)

86. Walk of the Hundred Fountains, which drips with both water and greenery. The stone fleurs de lys and the eagles belong to the d'Este family coat of arms. (*Alinari*)

87. View of the water organ and the Fountain of Neptune above one of the large reflecting pools at the Villa d'Este. (*Alinari*)

88. The Villa d'Este seen through the *rondello* of giant cypresses. Only the bases of the statues seen in Piranesi's engraving are left. (*Alinari*)

89. The garden of Villa Lante, Bagnaia. In the foreground is the Fountain of the Lamps, one level above the water garden, which is called the *quadrato*. Parterre gardens lie on either side of it. (*Anderson*)

90. The terrace in front of the casino at Caprarola is bordered with these stone canephoroe, ceremonial basket-bearers of ancient Athens. (*Anderson*)

91. A view of the approach to the casino garden of Caprarola. Two river gods flank a huge urn-shaped fountain whose waters descend down a water chain and thence into the pool in the foreground. The upper loggia of the casino looks out over far reaches of country. (*Anderson*)

92–94. In the garden of the Villa Orsini at Bomarzo, weird stone creatures are carved from rocky outcroppings. (*Touring Club Italiano, Milan*)

95. One of a pair of fountains on the terraces above the ascending staircases of the Villa Aldobrandini. This was a fine vantage point from which to admire the superb view over the Roman campagna. (*Anderson*)

96. The Atlas fountain and water staircase of the Villa Aldobrandini at Frascati. Little runnels of water spiral around the two pillars of mosaic and feed into the descending balustrade. The small plume of water ejects from a star, the crest of the Aldobrandini family. (*Anderson*)

97. Part of the garden of the Villa Garzoni at Collodi. (*Touring Club Italiano, Milan*)

98. Isola Bella, a seventeenth-century island garden in Lake Maggiore. (*Alinari*)

99. The water theater at Isola Bella is topped by a unicorn, which is the heraldic device of the Borromeo family. (*Alinari*)

100. The gardens of Villa Pietra, at Florence, epitomize the enduring quality of Italian garden art. Year-round beauty comes from the various greens of its plantings, the architectural richness of the stonework, and the simplicity of its fountains. In early spring the grass plots are spangled with tiny wild flowers. (*Azienda Autonoma di Turismo, Italy*)

101. The green theater at Villa Marlia, near Lucca. Its stone players represent the principal characters in Italian pantomime — Columbine, Pantaloon, and Pulcinella. This has been a favored spot for musicales. (*Alinari*)

102. Within the gardens of the Villa Marlia tall hedges wall separate enclosures, each one an outdoor room with its own character. Begun in the mid-seventeenth century and once the property of Napoleon's sister Elisa when she was the Grand Duchess of Tuscany, the gardens are now owned by Count and Countess Pecci-Blunt. (*Alinari*)

84

148

85

86

87 88

90

92

91

93

94

98

99

100

101

VIII   *French Grandeur*

The term "the French garden" immediately evokes a picture of Versailles and the splendors of the court of Louis XIV. The nobility and the princes of the church before and after Louis XIV's long reign from 1643 to 1715 built great châteaux with large and beautiful gardens, but during his reign, as during that of Francis I, it was often more expedient for the nobles to spend much of their life at court, to obtain the King's favor. While they were away at court, their country estates fell into sad disrepair. The gardens of Versailles, although conceived and created by the great André Le Nôtre, were not brought into being simply through the magic of a blinding vision. Behind their creation lay a hundred and fifty years of changing traditions in France, the gradual break from medieval Gothic traditions leading to the absorption of Italian Renaissance ideals and the adaptation of the Italian garden to a relatively flat terrain.

During the last half of the fifteenth century, France emerged from medieval feudalism to become an absolute monarchy. After the Hundred Years' War and when the last remaining fiefs of Burgundy and Brittany had been acquired, the ruling power in France was centralized. Instead of strengthening his country through peaceful pursuits, Charles VIII, reigning from 1483 until his death in 1498, decided to march into Italy and claim his inheritance of the Kingdom of Naples. Although his success was short-lived and the French army had to withdraw, the campaign showed that Italy could be exploited in the future. In time, armies were led there by both Louis XII and Francis I.

During the various French occupations, Frenchmen saw Italy's accomplishments in the fine arts and admired the beauty of her pleasure gardens. French kings sensed that the

103. (OPPOSITE) Sixteenth-century Flemish tapestry showing Henry III of France, one of Catherine de Médicis's three sons, and his queen, Louise de Lorraine, witnessing a water fete. Mock naval battles such as this were fought on the River Cher before the château of Chenonceaux. (*Alinari*)

use of permanent greenery in basic designs, combined with the drama of fountains and elegant sculpture, could be adapted and developed for the royal gardens at home.

The first seeds of the Italian Renaissance were planted in France when Charles VIII returned from Naples with paintings, sculptures, and other treasures. In addition, he imported twenty-two Italian artists to beautify his castle and grounds at Amboise. Neapolitan gardens, he exclaimed, "only lacked Adam and Eve to make of them an earthly paradise." Charles did not live to see his garden at Amboise completed, and his successor, Louis XII, moved his court to Blois, where the Italian gardener Father Pacello di Mercogliano created a most impressive group of gardens. These gardens consisted of three large terraces, as shown in Jacques Androuet Du Cerceau's engraving.[1] Since the château retained its moat (as did many French castles until the end of the seventeenth century), the terraced gardens had to be reached by a bridge. Each separate garden consisted of geometrically patterned beds; of these the "Queen's garden," on the middle terrace, was the most elaborate. Inside its walls were trellised arbors called *galeries*, and an octagonal chapel, named after Anne of Bretagne, joined the two-storied building or *orangerie* at the rear of the lowest garden. Above it lay a very large *potager*, or vegetable garden. Another important feature was the central wooden pavilion, which contained a marble fountain. The details in Androuet Du Cerceau's engraving are strikingly similar to those in a miniature painting of the same period — of the King of Navarre plucking a marguerite — which clearly shows garden beds protected by lattice fences, *galeries* covered with vines, and an imposing marble fountain and pavilion of Italian inspiration. The changeover from the medieval to the Renaissance garden was a gradual one, and we see aspects of each type, both in the engraving and in the painting.

The Château of Blois, engraved by Jacques Androuet Du Cerceau.

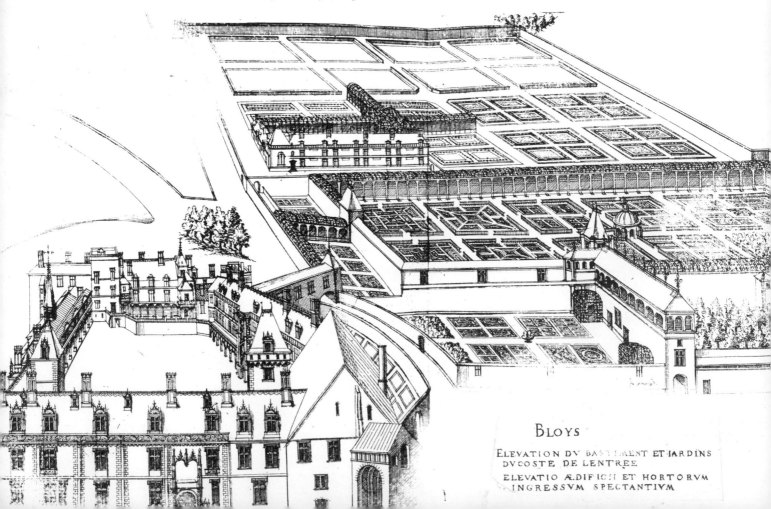

BLOYS

ELEVATION DV BASTIMENT ET IARDINS
DV COSTE DE LENTREE

ELEVATIO ÆDIFICII ET HORTORVM
INGRESSVM SPECTANTIVM

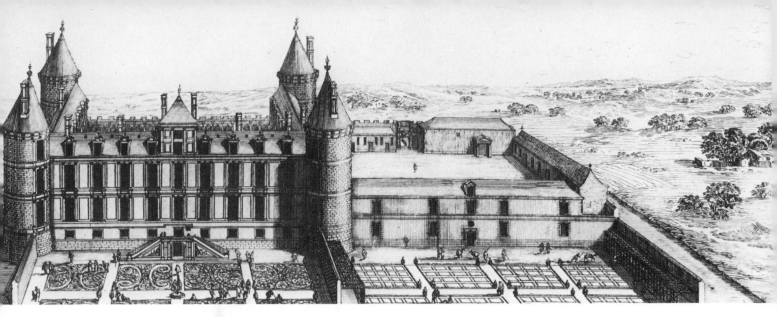

At the Château of Bury the pleasure and kitchen gardens were separate. (*New York Public Library*)

It is also interesting to note in many other sixteenth- and early-seventeenth-century engravings the number of châteaux that included moats, even though these were no longer necessary for defense. The reflections in castle moats of clouds, turrets, and walls were appreciated for their beauty, and artificial lakes and canals were built to perpetuate this beauty.

Francis I, who succeeded to the throne in 1515 and died in 1547, was more interested in literature, painting, and architecture than in the art of gardening. Like Charles VIII, he returned from Italy with a group of artists and artisans, the foremost in his retinue being Leonardo da Vinci. An inveterate builder, Francis I enlarged Blois by adding a wing with Italianate arcades and then built the immense dream castle of Chambord and constructed Fontaine-bel-eau on the site of an ancient hunting lodge in the forest. Of the three vast estates only Fontainebleau, as it became known, which became the king's favorite home, had any significant gardens. There the great pond, where carp are still kept, was formed out of a marsh. The excavated earth was thrown up into banks on the two long sides, one planted with a promenade of pine trees, the other less formal. Below the famous Jardin des Pins was a garden laid out in square beds in which herbs and flowers in knotted designs were grown. Another intricately patterned garden, with a fountain and statue of Diana at the center, was constructed below the north walls of the château. This was surrounded on three sides by a moat or canal. Garden planners had not produced the ideal effects obtained when the lines of both garden and architecture are directly related, so the irregularity of the castle wings made the placement of the Diana garden look somewhat haphazard.

One unusual feature at Fontainebleau, inspired by the Italian garden designers, was an arcaded grotto whose rusticated stone columns incorporated human figures in their design. This was at one end of the Jardin des Pins within the lower walls of the château. A grotto's relationship to the ancient *nymphaeum* seems to have had special significance in Renaissance Italy, and after it was adopted in France, it became a usual part of the garden, lasting through the period of Versailles's greatest glory and throughout the romantic phases of the nineteenth century. Some were made of boulders and trees with openings to the sky, and later examples were usually elaborately encrusted with shell-work designs.

Today the most complete picture of a sixteenth-century château and its gardens is to be seen at Villandry, in the Loire Valley. Here a magnificent restoration by its previous

167

Plates

104. View of the gardens of Villandry. This superbly re-created garden, built in three terraces, is in the valley of the Loire. The box gardens in the foreground form one half of the symbolic Garden of Love, which is Gothic in inspiration. (*Edwin Smith*)

105. Versailles. The Basin of Latona and the *tapis vert*. (*Rapho-Guillumette*)

106. The Bagatelle rose garden, Paris. The Empress Eugénie's favorite garden house overlooks this section of the garden. (*Edwin Smith*)

104

owner, Dr. J. Carvallo, shows the horticultural and agricultural divisions of a large castle domain. A great medieval *donjon*, linked to a Renaissance building by Francis I's secretary of state, Jean de Breton, forms the château, which lies beside a hill. The gardens are built on three terraces, their walls delineated by a canal and by long vine-covered arbors. The uppermost level has rows of square clipped trees, vineyards, an orchard, and a large beautiful sheet of water called "the mirror," which is used as a reservoir for irrigating the gardens below. The middle tier is a right-angled area containing the formal pleasure garden, entirely formed of flower-filled designs of box. It contains a unique symbolical Garden of Love, Gothic in inspiration, which consists of the four large, square compartments nearest the château. One compartment has box motifs of hearts and flames which represent *l'amour tendre*. A second compartment symbolizes *l'amour tragique*, its beds shaped like dagger blades and usually filled with red roses. The third, *l'amour volage*, or fickle love, has simplified shapes of butterflies, chrysalids, and folded love letters. The fourth, *l'amour folie*, has twelve hearts filled with varicolored flowers spinning like a pin wheel. The long right-angle of this pleasure garden is geometrically designed in box, crossed by gravel walks, and accented with spirals of topiary. At the far end of the garden was once a labyrinth the counterpart of which can be seen in many of the engravings by Androuet Du Cerceau. In fact all of the garden restoration at Villandry is based on this series of engravings. The earlier garden was replaced in the eighteenth century by an English park, and there are no other exact records of the original design which could have been copied.

Below the box gardens at Villandry lies a great *potager*. The plots of this vegetable and herb garden differ in design, and charming rose-covered bowers of latticework mark the crossings of the main paths. Except for field-grown crops, which sometimes included peas and beans, all the vegetables for the table were grown in a *potager*. According to an old French book, translated by John Evelyn in 1675, the following produce was common at the time: melons, cucumbers, and gourds; artichokes, chard, asparagus, cabbage, lettuce, and cauliflower; the root vegetables — beets, parsnips, carrots, salsify, radishes, turnips, skirret, rampion, and Jerusalem artichokes; many kinds of pot and salad herbs, and, of course, onions, leeks, and garlic. At Villandry, the subtle variations of green in the leafy vegetables and herbs of the potager, the dark-hued borders, and the incidental color from flowering and fruit-bearing plants present an unforgettable picture. Here, too, espaliered fruit trees have been trained against sun-warmed walls and along the low latticework fences which enclose each vegetable square. In the sixteenth century, France already had many varieties of apples, cherries, figs, peaches, pears, and plums; and under the supervision of a chatelaine, these fruits were conserved in honey, pickled in salt and vinegar, or dried.

Engravings of the sixteenth and early seventeenth century show how completely the pleasure garden was separated from the utilitarian area. At the château of Bury the flower garden was placed immediately before the main dwelling, while the vegetable garden was screened off from it by a trellised arbor and placed alongside the *basse-cour*, or stable. Symmetrical gardens, canals, and groves of trees were now planned to complement the Renaissance châteaux, as was the custom in Italy.

The medieval château of Verneuil was brought "up to date" in the late sixteenth cen-

One of the great attractions at Saint-Germain-en-Laye was the fantastic shellwork grotto, designed by the Francini brothers, in which the figure of a woman played a water organ. Engraving by Abraham Bosse, 1624. (*New York Public Library*)

PORTRAIT. DES. CHASTEAVX. ROYAVX. DE. SAINCT. GERMAIN. EN. LAYE.

Plan of the terraced gardens of Saint-Germain-en-Laye, fifteen miles west of Paris. The gardens overlooked the Seine, which flowed near the tree-line shown at the bottom of the picture. (*Larousse*)

tury, when its pleasure garden of flower beds (called "*parquets*" by Androuet Du Cerceau), its groves of trees, and ornamental waters all were laid out in perfect symmetry which repeated the lines of the château's architecture. Canals of water, developed from the old idea of the moat, ornamented the lowest level of the garden. There were also two large gardens for vegetables, and a vineyard. Often used within the design of such parquets were labyrinths of the low-growing plants — lavender, marjoram, mint, and thyme — which edged the beds. The usual flowers grown were violets, wallflowers, pinks, heartsease, lilies-of-the-valley, primrose, columbine, bellflowers, peonies, iris, calendula, crocuses, snowdrops, and *Lilium candidum,* all of which had been typical of the medieval garden.

Another early garden planned as an integral part of a château design was that of Anet, built by the famous architect Philibert de l'Orme (sometimes spelled Delorme) for Diane de Poitiers. A huge rectangular garden, enclosed with galleries, lay symmetrically behind the building. The fountains — statues of the mythological Diana (one by Benvenuto Cellini) — the garden pavilion beyond the parquet garden — directly on axis — and the extensive park beyond were described by Androuet Du Cerceau, who said that there was at Anet "everything that could make a place perfect." Unfortunately practically all was demolished during the Revolution. Today one wing, the chapel, and the grand portal remain, but in a setting that is more pastoral than formal, a mere echo of bygone glories.

Even more than Anet, we associate Chenonceaux with the lovely Diane de Poitiers. Though twenty years older than Henry II, she had been chosen as his mistress by his father, Francis I. Francis acquired Chenonceaux when, angered by an alleged slur upon his mother's integrity (she had been accused of using money intended for the army), he had the accuser, his own treasurer, put to death and revenged himself further on the impoverished family by acquiring the Treasurer's newly built château. It remained unoccupied until inherited by Francis's son. Only a king could accomplish this type of retaliation. Henry VIII of England had already taken over Hampton Court after ridding himself of Cardinal Wolsey, and, later, Louis XIV was to imprison Fouquet for life while commandeering the artists who created Vaux-le-Vicomte to work for him at Versailles.

The château of Chenonceaux was built on the foundations of a mill on the river Cher. As one of the first improvements, Diane de Poitiers added a bridge connecting it to the opposite bank, where a large garden, no longer in existence, was made in the most romantic setting. Another garden, still referred to as "the Diane garden," was made at the river's edge, to the left of the main entrance to the château. Basically it is a great platform of earth dug from surrounding canals and supported with turf and stone levees for flood protection. The terraces above command a view of the intricate pattern of paths, *broderie,* and clipped trees. Perhaps there once existed a shady *berceau,* or tunnel of greenery, for the garden seems to cry out for shade. Early descriptions tell of the many fine gifts of plants, trees, and shrubs which were originally made to this garden, as well as of the confiscations that were made from other places.

After Henry's death, his queen, Catherine de Médicis, who had coveted Chenonceaux, forced Diane to exchange it for Chaumont. Catherine then set about making elaborate improvements, adding another large formal garden at the right of the entrance court and creating a park. With true inspiration she had a two-storied gallery built above the bridge,

Plates

107. Sixteenth-century miniature painting of Henry, King of Navarre, plucking a marguerite for Margaret of Valois. (*Bibliothèque Nationale*)

108. The four parts of the Garden of Love at Villandry symbolize "tender love" (hearts and flames), "tragic love" (daggers and swords), "fickle love" (butterflies and love letters), and "foolish love" (spinning hearts). (*Metropolitan Museum of Art. Photo: Roche*)

109. The château, box gardens, and *potager* of Villandry. The four-part Garden of Love can be seen at the rear of the château. (*French Government Tourist Office*)

110. Vaux-le-Vicomte's *parterre de broderie* was re-created with great skill in box, brick dust, earth, and sand by Henri Duchêne at the end of the last century. The surrounding parterres of fine grass emphasize its complexity of design. (*Art Pictural*)

111. The gardens of the two rival châtelaines of Chenonceaux, Diane de Poitiers and Catherine de Médicis, flank its entrance court. (*Conservateur du Château de Chenonceaux*)

112. The scrolling lines of a seventeenth-century *parterre de broderie* embellish the restored garden of Diane de Poitiers at Chenonceaux. (*French Government Tourist Office.*)

176

Inueni vnam preciosam margaritam quam inti mo coide collegi :-

Jardin d'Amour
Villandry

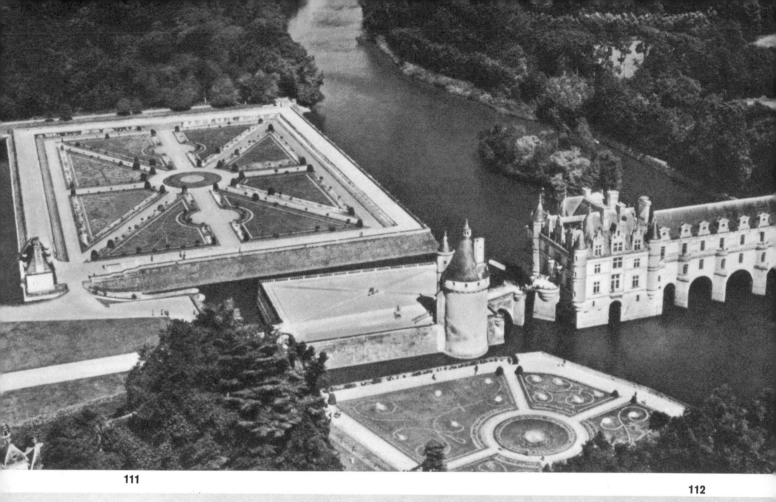

111

112

and today, as we see it reflected in the quiet river waters, we cannot help but think of the many gay and the many tragic persons who lived here, and of the many festivities and dramas which took place. On the merrier side, there were constant banquets and balls; we read of mock naval battles on the river Cher, of fireworks, and of an occasion when court ladies, disguised as mermaids and nymphs, greeted a kingly entourage with song before being pursued by satyrs and rescued by handsome cavaliers. During Henry III's time there was one banquet at which "the most beautiful and virtuous ladies of the court appeared half-naked, with their hair loose, like brides," who, "with the Queen's daughters, waited on guests."

In 1564 Philibert de l'Orme built the palace of the Tuileries for Catherine near the royal palace of the Louvre in the area now occupied by the gardens behind the Arc du Carousel. The site, along the right or north bank of the Seine, had long been occupied by tile workers and potters; although the gardens the queen planted were not truly outstanding, the grottoes they contained, fabricated by the great potter and modeler Bernard Palissy, have historical significance. After long years of experimentation with glazing techniques and materials Palissy had become famous for his enameled pottery. The queen became his patron and gave him a site for his kiln within the palace grounds. We do not have descriptions of the several grottoes he made there but he wrote of another one which was probably very similar — a subterranean pool filled with realistically modeled fish and reptiles, coral, seaweed, pebbles, and moss. In his ceramic work Palissy used rich purple and blues, strong green, pale yellow, and a mottled brown which resembled tortoise shell. Below the splashing waters spewed out by animals along the rim, the creatures at the bottom of the pool seemed positively animated. A further liveliness was added by the translucence of the glazed walls and ceilings, an effect Palissy obtained by firing right inside the grottoes. Had any such fantastic creation survived, it would indeed have been a rare work of art, for even the smallest piece of Palissy ware is greatly treasured by museums and collectors. Unfortunately the grottoes at the Tuileries lasted a very short time; they disappeared when Henry IV (crowned in 1589, died 1610) changed the gardens to suit his taste, and that of his queen, Marie de Médicis.

Changes were not confined to the Tuileries. Henry and Marie altered the gardens of all the royal palaces. Italian ideas were introduced in the new gardens of Saint-Germain-en-Laye and in the relandscaping of Fontainebleau. Newer, decidedly French elaborations of the old-fashioned, compartmented parquet embroidered the Tuileries gardens and those at the new palace of the Luxembourg, which the queen built for herself after she was widowed.

The palace of Saint-Germain-en-Laye consisted of two buildings. Francis I had reconstructed a feudal château high above the Seine, and later this was paired with a new one which Henry II built close to the edge of the bank. The new gardens created under Henry IV and Marie descended by terraces and stairs right down to the river. In his diary, John Evelyn wrote that the gardens had "an incomparable prospect towards the River and the goodly Country about it." The plan bears a striking resemblance to that of the Villa d'Este at Tivoli, where diagonal lines of descending walks and stairways also lead down a hill from one terrace to another. Two Italian waterworks engineers, the Francini brothers;

the French architect Du Perac, who was influenced by Italian design; and a French gardener, Claude Mollet, were called upon to collaborate in the execution of this great work, which included beautiful fountains and large reflecting basins, a shady *bosquet* of trees, and box designs that traced out the royal cyphers. The fantastic shell-encrusted grottoes were famous for the water-animated figures of a woman playing an organ, Mercury playing a trumpet, a dragon that flapped its wings, and nightingales and cuckoos that sang.

In the gardens at Fontainebleau, new additions and alterations were undertaken. The Diana garden was made an integral part of the building complex, and the fine classical statue, thought to have been the original from the Temple at Ephesus, was taken to the Tuileries by the king and replaced by a bronze replica cast by Barthelemy Prieur. A second copy replaced this eighty years later and is the one we see there today. The figure rests upon a pedestal in a sunken circular basin into which water spurts out of pipes concealed in four stag's-heads cast of bronze. A platform garden was built out into the carp pond. Here stood Michelangelo's statue of Hercules, now lost. It had been moved from its earlier position in the court overlooking the pond. Other changes included a large parterre garden formed out of the meadowlands and vegetable gardens; at the center of the long canal which once bisected it was placed an elaborate fountain representing the Tiber river god. For the sake of shade and coolness the walks beneath Francis I's pine trees were left untouched and there were green covered galleries.

Fontainebleau was already fit for any king, but Louis XIV and Napoleon Bonaparte were also to leave their marks upon it. During Louis's reign the designs within the grand parterre were embellished further with the king's and queen's initials, L and M, cut in box.

Alexandre Le Blond's four main types of parterres. The dark borders and areas within the designs were meant to be filled with black earth. Some areas contain brick dust, powdered tile, iron filings, or Smith's dust; others are planted with grass. The dotted areas represent light-colored sand. (*The Pierpont Morgan Library*)

Fascinating topiary men and animals in the garden of Marimont. Israel Silvestre engraving, 1673.

The canal in the garden was filled in and another created at a lower level. The garden of Diana became the garden of the Orangerie, and the aviary made by Henry IV was remodeled into a conservatory. Under Le Nôtre's guiding hand the new canal, dominated by a cascade in the supporting walls of the parterre, stretched dramatically into the park.

An important step in the course of French garden design had been taken at the Tuileries when its old squared parquet gardens were replaced with a *parterre de broderie*. Theorists and writers agreed that the patterned regularity of the old geometrical style had become tiresome, and that graceful curvilinear lines were more natural and suitable. Since the layout of a garden could best be appreciated from above, ornamental gardens became *parterres* ("on the ground"), and terraces were usually constructed above or around them for better viewing. Intricate arabesque and foliate designs were developed in dwarf box (which France acquired at the end of the sixteenth century) and color was no longer provided by flowers alone, but also by brick dusts, clay, and sands, which were used to fill intervening spaces. The sculptural quality of low relief with which the garden was now endowed was akin to the arts of the embroiderer or lace maker or of the goldsmith and wrought-iron artist, and the designs had a close affinity to the popular floral silk brocades, wallpapers, and ceramics of the day. Only the lowest-growing flowers were used in working out the main decorative pattern of a garden, the taller flowers being used elsewhere and largely for cutting. The asymmetrical nature of the curvilinear patterns required the planning of several compartments to complete a whole scheme, "such that a garden makes one single parterre, divided by wide paths," as Claude Mollet wrote. Mollet, the king's chief

A Parterre of Cutwork for Flowers.

gardener, had executed the elaborate plans which Jacques Boyceau designed for the Tuileries. From this time on, the main attraction and the most decorative element in a pleasure garden was the *parterre de broderie*.

By the time Henry IV, the first French Bourbon king, had begun his reign, another dynasty, that of the Mollet family, had been established in the gardening world. Jacques Mollet was master gardener at Anet. Claude, his son, after working for the king at both Saint-Germain-en-Laye and Fontainebleau, was made head gardener of the Tuileries in 1599. Later he worked at Versailles for Louis XIII. In turn, his son André became master gardener to the Queen of Sweden, and worked for a few years in England, where Charles II employed his services at Hampton Court. To the credit of the Mollet family are two

(LEFT) Ornamental trelliswork was often used in seventeenth-century French gardens. As many designs for them were published as for *broderies*, such as this one by Perelle. (*Metropolitan Museum of Art, Rogers Fund, 1920*).

(RIGHT) The flower garden or *bouquetier* at Liencourt. This was but one of many gardens which adorned this aristocratic residence. (*New York Public Library*)

important books on garden theory — Claude Mollet's *Théâtre des Plans et Jardinages*, published posthumously in 1652, and André Mollet's *Jardin de Plaisir*, 1651 — which, together with those of Boyceau and Olivier de Serres, make the seventeenth century a period rich in source material. Jacques Boyceau wrote *Le Traité du Jardinage*, which was published posthumously in 1638, and Olivier de Serres, *Le Théâtre d'Agriculture*, published in 1600.

The *parterres de broderie* were frequently set off by tall clipped hedges, trellised walls, arcades, and pavilions referred to as "carpenter's work." These were not necessarily meant to support vines or roses but were used more or less as purely architectural decorations. They were too elaborate and impractical to survive long, but as a characteristic of the seventeenth-century pleasure garden they were important. According to Claude Mollet, every garden should have a parterre, lawns, and *bosquets* in which walks crisscrossed. Equally important, he said, were long radiating *allées* of trees, frequently forming a three-part pattern called a *patte d'oie*, or goose foot, which led out into a park or hunting forest.

We can easily visualize these large gardens, with members of the court and their attendants strolling about with little else to do except talk, gossip, flirt, and intrigue, but contemporary engravings also show such gardens busy with gardeners who had the box parterres and hedges to clip, graveled paths to rake, weeding to keep up with, flowers to transplant, orange trees to set out, galleries of "carpenter's work" to paint, and of course, constant watering to do.

Extravaganzas in topiary work were minimized as gardens grew larger, and by the eighteenth century topiary was decidedly "out." Whimsies, such as animals, men, birds, and ships hewn out of living plant material, apparently lacked the grandeur and formality of the new age. Both Palissy and de Serres had previously described elaborate topiary

work they admired, but in 1728 Alexandre Le Blond wrote, "at present nobody gives in to these trifles in France, how well soever they may be kept . . . we chuse rather a plain regularity less clutter'd and confus'd, which indeed looks much more noble and great."

Flowers, once so loved in castle gardens, began to play a minor part in the ornamental *broderie*. They defined the outside borders, and a few low-growing ones filled in parts of the designs, but it became more usual for flowers to have a separate parterre garden known as a *bouquetier*, or a *parterre fleuriste*. These were filled with the old-fashioned native flowers as well as with the new bulb introductions from Asia Minor and the plants developed from seeds brought home by Crusaders. The collection of flower engravings made in the previous century by Pierre Vallet called *Le Jardin du Roy Très Chrestien Henry IV*, reveals exactly what grew in a royal flower garden in 1608 and what must have continued to be planted in later years. The bulbs included iris, crown imperial (*Fritillaria imperialis*), the checkered lily (*Fritillaria meleagris*), tulips, hyacinths, grape

185

Four illustrations by Israel Silvestre of Louis XIV's fete at Versailles, "The Pleasures of the Enchanted Isle." (ABOVE LEFT) The opening event was a *course de bague*. The king is shown exhibiting his skill on horseback. (ABOVE RIGHT) An elaborate banquet was served at the end of the first day's activities. (BELOW LEFT) An enormous framework between the trees of an *allée* formed the proscenium arch of an outdoor theater. A Molière comedy was played and a ballet danced. (BELOW RIGHT) The large pond at the head of the canal became a setting for a ballet on the third day of the festival.

hyacinths, crocus, *colchicum, ornithogalum*, jonquils, narcissi (double, single, and *poetaz*), and Martagon lilies. There were also German iris, cyclamen, anemones, ranunculus, foxglove, canterbury bells, primroses, auriculas, peonies, fraxinella, pinks, cornflowers or field poppies, monkshood, pelargonium, snapdragons, and Christmas roses (*Helleborus niger*). There were roses of course: the French loved and cultivated the damasks, the Gallicas, and centifolias.

As this complete separation of the flower garden took place, the elaboration of the parterre took four different forms. These were carefully described in Alexandre Le Blond's *Theory and Practice of Gardening* and were differentiated as: Parterres of Embroidery, Parterres of Cut-work, Parterres of Compartiment, and Parterres after the English Manner.

Le Blond named the "Parterre of Embroidery" the finest, and recommended that it should "possess the principle Place, and lie next the Building." Box imitated embroidery upon the ground and sometimes was accompanied with "knots and scrolls of Grass-work." In a flowerless garden such as this the spaces between the design elements were sanded, "the better to distinguish the Foliage and Flourish'd-work of the Embroidery." Other areas were usually completed with black earth, brick dust, and the reddish-brown iron filings or dross from the anvil known as Smith's dust. All of these designs were asymmetrical and delicate in feeling.

The "Parterre of Compartiment" was a self-contained symmetrical design, each half repeating the design of the other. It, too, was made up of box scrolls and grass-work and colored earths, but flowers were allowed in the borders.

(OPPOSITE) Plan of Versailles engraved by Lepautre in 1714. The magnitude of the gardens and park can best be imagined by observing the relative size of the palace area. (*New York Public Library*)

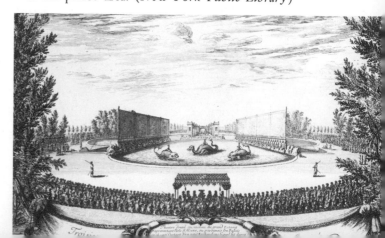

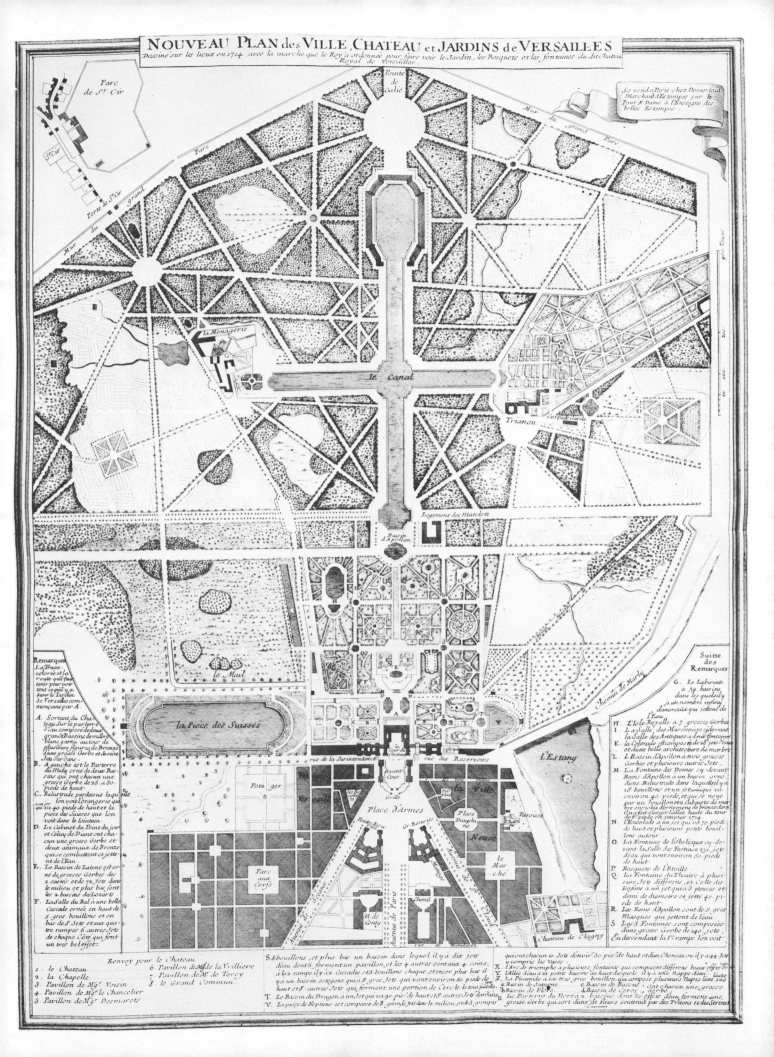

NOUVEAU PLAN des VILLE, CHATEAU et JARDINS de VERSAILLES

Dessiné sur les lieux en 1714, avec la marche que le Roy a ordonnée pour faire voir le Jardin, les Bosquets et les fontaines du dit chateau Royal de Versailles

Se vend à Paris chez Demortain Marchand d'Estampes sur le Pont N. Dame à l'Enseigne des belles Estampes.

Parc de St. Cir

le Canal

la Menagerie

Trianon

Bassin d'Apollon

le Mail

la Piece des Suisses

L'Estang

Place d'Armes

Parc aux Cerfs

Remarques

La Trasse colorée et la route qu'il faut tenir pour voir tout ce qu'il y a dans le Jardin de Versailles commençau par A.

A. Sortant du Chateau sur le parterre d'eau composée de deux grands Bassins de marbre blanc garnie autour de plusieurs figures de Bronze d'une grosse Gerbe et de seize Jets d'ar dans.

B. A gauche est le Parterre du Midy orné de deux Bassins qui ont chacun une grosse Gerbe de 28 à 30 pieds de haut.

C. Balustrade pardessus laquelle l'on voit l'orangerie qui va à un jet qui va 40 pieds de haut et la piece des Suisses que l'on voit dans le lointain.

D. Le Cabinet du Point du jour et celuy de Diane ont chacun une grosse Gerbe et deux animaux de Bronze qui se combattent et jettent de l'eau.

E. Le Bassin de Latone est orné de grosses Gerbes des 2 corsets et de 72 Jets dans le milieu et plus bas sont les 2 bassins de Lezarts.

F. La Salle du Bal à une belle Cascade ornée en haut de 5 gros bouillons et en bas de 8 Jets et aux quatre rampes 6 autres Jets de chaque côté qui font un très bel effet.

Suitte des Remarques

G. Le Labirinte a 39 bassins dans les quelsily a un nombre infini d'animaux qui jettent de l'Eau.

H. L'Isle Royalle a 7 grosses Gerbes.

I. La Salle des Maronniers cy devant la Salle des Antiques a deux fontaines.

K. La Colonade d'architecture et de 28 jets d'eau et d'une belle architecture de marbre.

L. Le Bassin d'Apollon a trois grosses Gerbes et plusieurs autres Jets.

M. La Fontaine des Domes cy devant Bains d'Apollon a un bassin orné d'une Balustrade dans laquelle il y a 18 bouillons et un jet qui va environ 40 pieds, et qui se noye par un bouillon et 2 Cabinets de marbre enrichy dornemens de bronze dorés On a fait elargir la Salle haute du tour On a fait elargir la Salle en janvier 1714.

N. L'Enselade a un jet qui va 70 pieds de haut et plusieurs petits bouillons autour.

O. La Fontaine de l'obelisque cy devant la Salle des Festins a 231 jets d'eau qui vont environ 80 pieds de haut.

P. Bosquet de l'Etoile.

Q. La Fontaine du Theatre à plusieurs Jets differens, et Celle des Enfans a un jet qui a 2 pouces et demi de diametre et jette 40 pieds de haut.

R. Les Bains d'Apollon sont de 5 gros Masques qui jettent de l'eau.

S. Les 3 Fontaines sont composées d'une grosse Gerbe de 140 jets, En descendant la 1re rampe l'on voit

Renvoy pour le Chateau

1. le Chateau
2. la Chapelle
3. Pavillon de Mgr. Voisin
4. Pavillon de Mgr. le Chancelier
5. Pavillon de Mgr. Desmarets
6. Pavillon de Me. la Villiere
7. Pavillon de Mr. de Torcy
8. le Grand Commun

8 bouillons, et plus bas un bassin dans lequel il y a dix jets d'eau dont 6 forment un pavillon, et les 4 autres sont aux 4 coins, à la 2 rampe il y a 2 Cascades et 8 bouillons chaque, et encor plus bas il y a un bassin octogone qui a 8 gros Jets qui vont environ 80 pieds de haut et 8 autres Jets qui forment une portion de Cercle le tout puisse.

T. Le Bassin du Dragon a un jet qui va 90 pieds de haut et 8 autres Jets d'ardans.

V. La piece de Neptune est composée de 8 grands jets dans le milieu, et 3 groupes

qui ont chacun 10 Jets d'envir 30 pieds de haut et d'un Cheneau ou il y a 44 Jets y compris les Vases.

X. L'Arc de triomphe a plusieurs fontaines qui composent different beaux effets de l'eau.

Y. La Piramide a un très gros bouillon qui compose plusieurs Napes l'une sur l'autre.

Z. Bassin de Flore.

a. Bassin de Bacus.

b. Bassin de Ceres.

c. Le Parterre du Nord a 2 bassins dont les 2 gros d'eau forment une grosse Gerbe qui sort d'une fleur de fleurs soutenue par des Tritons et de Serenes.

Plates

113. The Château of Fontainebleau engraved by Jacques Androuet Du Cerceau. It shows the gardens as they had been developed for Francis I and his immediate successors. (*Larousse*)

114. An air view of Fontainebleau reveals the simplification of the old parterre and the disappearance of any formal setting for the statue of Diana. (*Conservateur de Fontainebleau*)

115. Night illumination of the fountains of the Apollo Basin, Versailles. (*French Government Tourist Office*)

116. Versailles, painted in 1668 by Pierre Patel the elder, before Louis XIV made it his official residence. The central section between flanking wings was his father's hunting lodge. The main vista and the parterres are virtually unchanged. (*Giraudon*)

117. The *Parterre du Midi*, above the orangerie, is the only garden at Versailles with *broderie* designs. It overlooks the water known as *La Place des Suisses*. (*French Government Tourist Office. Photo: Jean Roubier*)

118. The classic colonnade was built by Jules Hardouin-Mansart in one of the *bosquets* at Versailles. It was often the setting for musicales. (*French Government Tourist Office*)

119. Versailles. The Apollo Basin at the foot of the *tapis vert*. (*French Government Tourist Office*)

120. Crowned with flowers, this sphinx charmingly guards the Belvedere of the Petit Trianon. (*French Government Tourist Office*)

121. The marble figures of the Baths of Apollo have been moved three times at Versailles and now occupy an artificially made rocky cavern in the *jardin anglais* of the Petit Trianon. (*French Cultural Services*)

122. Once the property of Madame de Pompadour and later changed into a *jardin anglais*, the gardens of Champs have been redesigned in the old manner by Henri Duchêne. Its palisades of clipped trees and the precision of its *parterre de broderie* make it a masterpiece. (*French Embassy, New York City*)

123. The ingenious way in which André Le Nôtre designed the grand parterre of Chantilly and related it to the water-encircled château is seen to advantage in an air view. The little parquet garden on the island dates from the sixteenth century. (*Aero-Photo*)

124. Marie Antoinette's little mill in the *hameau* at the Petit Trianon. (*Musées Nationaux*)

188

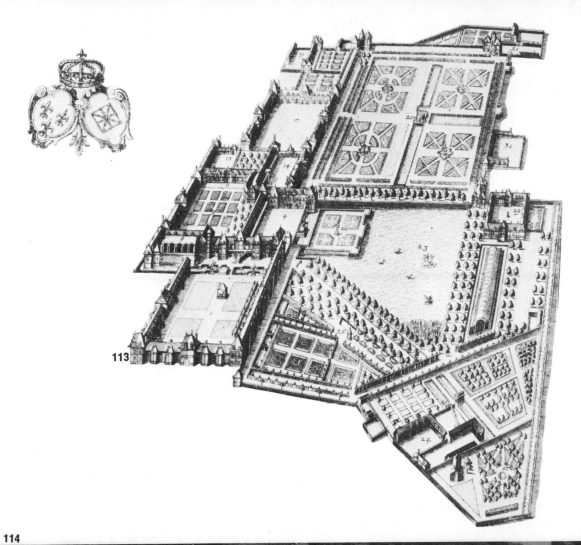

113

114

116

115

117

119

118

122

123

32

34

138

149

The "Parterre after ye English Manner," declared to be "the plainest and meanest of all," had a large grassy area, and little elaboration of design. There were borders of flowers separated from the grass-work by sanded paths two or three feet wide, and frequently orange trees from the *orangerie* were placed along the parterre.

The symmetrical "Parterre of Cut-work" was designed especially for flowers, and the beds were edged with box. Paths within the design, which included neither grass nor embroidery, were sanded and permitted walking in the parterre "without hurting anything."

Le Blond considered the following design motifs appropriate: "branches, flowers, foliage, palms, tendrils, roots, volutes, knots, clasps, chaplets, cartouches, trefoils, plumes, frets, wreaths, and real flower forms — roses, pinks, and tulips." Animal forms he dismissed as being "heavy and clouterly." He emphasized that the embroidery be "light, regular, and not confused."

Besides the parterre, this theoretician was particularly interested in the use of water, which he called "the soul of a Garden" and its "principle Ornament." Without it the scene was "dull and melancholy." The difficulty of introducing water to gardens was much greater in France than in Italy, where hillsides allowed it to fall by natural gravity. In France it had to be raised to reservoirs by pumps and then conveyed through miles of lead pipes to the fountains. Some pumps were worked by hand or by horses, but wind and water mills were more frequently used because they could work continuously. The water problem was so complex that in the greatest gardens of France and perhaps of all history — the gardens of Versailles — it was never satisfactorily solved.

And so we come to the time of Louis XIV and the creation of Versailles, the work of its master gardener André Le Nôtre and the preliminary episode in the unfolding of their story, Nicolas Fouquet's fiasco at Vaux-le-Vicomte. It was a humiliating disaster for Fouquet personally, but the garden heritage of France was greatly enriched by the accomplishments there.

On the death of Cardinal Mazarin, Nicolas Fouquet, *Surintendant des Finances*, had expected to become Chief Minister of France. Ambitious and extraordinarily wealthy, he embarked on the building of a château and gardens of the greatest magnitude and splendor, which were completed in a little over five years. His first disappointment came when the twenty-two-year-old Louis XIV decided to be his own first minister; but the second disappointment was so utterly devastating that Fouquet died a broken man. Pride dictated that he show his magnificent estate to King Louis, so in the summer of 1661 he planned an elaborate reception for the whole court. The king did not attend, but his brother and sister-in-law were present. After hearing about it, Louis was consumed by curiosity; and on August 17, having received a second invitation to Vaux, he came, accompanied by several thousand people who arrived both by coach and on horseback. By the time the festivities finished, the King, envious and angry, had already begun to plot Fouquet's downfall and was planning a far grander palace of his own at Versailles.

The finance minister, who had lined his pockets well from the King's treasury, was socially charming and had impeccable taste in the realm of art and architecture. He was also a born organizer, and the talents he employed for the creation of Vaux included those of the architect Louis Le Vau; Charles Le Brun, the decorator and painter; and André Le Nôtre, the garden designer.

André Le Nôtre (1613–1700) had worked with his father in the royal gardens of the Tuileries, and his formal education had included geometry, drawing, and architecture. Before he worked at Vaux he had already completed several important commissions, but it was under Fouquet's auspices that his precepts regarding garden design first blossomed into a style that could be called his own. In the construction of Vaux, three whole villages were displaced and the course of a river was diverted to prepare the land for the formal grounds and parks. Parterres were placed on either side of the château, which was surrounded by a moat. A truly elegant *parterre de broderie* (now present in a magnificent restoration), lay before the garden façade as the *pièce de résistance;* and a broad walk, forming the main axis, led toward the water cascades and the colossal statue of Hercules on its distant green hillside, the culminating feature of the design. This long promenade was accented by a round basin with a high *jet d'eau*, and along the way slight changes of level were effected by broad steps. Because of the difference in levels, the two transverse water areas, the canal and water theater, came as unexpected and delightful surprises to the visitor. Equally clever was the initial leveling of the whole rectangular area behind the château and the raising of a terrace on one long side to correct a slope. All along the walks, jets cast their water into the air. There were shady *bosquets* and statuary, and thickly planted trees at the far sides of the parterre area. The wide terraces around the château allowed it to be seen from all angles and to welcome the sun into most of the rooms.

Fouquet's guests that August afternoon strolled around the gardens and then went indoors for a banquet served on gold plates, while Jean Baptiste Lully and his musicians performed. A play by Molière was presented, in which that famous dramatist played the leading part, and then a midnight supper was crowned by an immense display of fireworks. The King had seen enough. He refused Fouquet's invitation to spend the night in the royal suite prepared for him, and without giving indication of his real anger that one of his ministers should dare to live in greater splendor than he, drove back to Fontainebleau, where he arrived at dawn. Louis soon appointed the trusted Jean Baptiste Colbert as his Minister of Finance and found enough evidence to convict Fouquet.

The King soon commandeered all the talent that Fouquet had used at Vaux and started the plans for his palace at Versailles, which he intended to make the largest and grandest in all Europe, worthy of the absolute monarch he intended to be. He considered Fontainebleau too old-fashioned, he hated Paris and the Tuileries, and Saint-Germain was much too small for his growing court. He had enjoyed staying at his father's hunting lodge at Versailles, and this was the place he wished to dedicate in the form of a glittering palace to the power and glory of France.

Louis XIII's hunting lodge, situated on a knoll overlooking woods, fields, and ponds, was of modest size with a small garden and park, until his son, Louis XIV, enlarged the domain to approximately fifteen thousand acres and enclosed it with a wall. Le Nôtre's grandiose plans for the vast new garden development took him six years (1662–1668) to complete, during which time the château gardens, which occupied the previous King's entire park, the grand canal, and the *Petit Parc* were created. Displaying his talent for organizing space, Le Nôtre laid out the gardens along a grand east-west axis running through the center of the palace façade, but he did not terminate them in a grand gesture of dramatic architectural design. Instead, he achieved a terminal drama through distance, for the axis became a vista stretching to the horizon. While this great perspective was established early in Le Nôtre's planning and was thereafter maintained, the garden divisions and their detailing were constantly changed. Louis and his garden designer had great rapport, and an idea of one always seemed to spark the imagination of the other, so work and change and growth went on unceasingly. Even a lady's whim could dictate the addition of something new.

In May 1664, barely two years after the garden work had begun, it was sufficiently advanced to allow the King to arrange a three-day fete — a worthy sequel to Fouquet's and as grand as the Medici celebrations, of which he had heard, in the Boboli Gardens at Florence. Though it was announced to be in honor of his wife and his mother, it secretly rewarded the Duchesse de la Vallière for bearing him a child. During the fete his mistress played the part of the heroine in a pageant called "The Pleasures of the Enchanted Island," based on an episode in Ariosto's *Orlando Furioso*. On the first day of the fete there was a test of horsemanship called a *course de bague*, followed by an elaborate outdoor banquet in the evening. On the second day a comedy and a ballet were performed in a green theater formed between trees in the gardens. As at Vaux, Molière and Lully were the entrepreneurs. For the third day of festivities the pond at the foot of the garden, now known as the Apollo Basin, had been turned into a water theater with tapestries from the château hung as scenery. In front of a fabricated palace of Alcina with fearsome beasts guarding it, another ballet was performed. The finale was a fireworks display which supposedly consumed the enchanted palace and its island, thereby breaking the spell.

The King had invited hundreds of guests, and they stayed on for seven days. It was perhaps then that Louis began to think of enlarging the château further; certainly by now the gardens were more grandiose than the building itself. In 1668, the architect Le Vau began work on the great edifice we see at Versailles today. It evolved gradually, with further additions made by Jules Hardouin-Mansart ten years later, and reached completion when the Royal Chapel was added during the last years of Louis's reign. Long before this the King had decided to make Versailles not only his official residence but also the seat of government, which it became in May 1682. He constantly watched the progress of the work in the gardens and wrote the first guide to them.

Le Nôtre, with mathematical precision, fashioned parterres, *bosquets*, and outdoor rooms on either side of the grand axis. It was a huge concept, unified geometrically with the main lines related to the palace. Thousands of large trees arrived by ox-cart from all parts of France, and many failed to survive. Their shade provided coolness and contrast to the huge sun-drenched terraces which stretched along the garden façade of the palace. A variety of entertainment could be planned within the *bosquets*. The circular marble colonnade was an enchanting setting in which to listen to music, and dancers enjoyed the ballroom with its marble pavement and grassy tiers for spectators. In the labyrinth couples could find privacy and escape the stiffness of court etiquette, while on the long canal courtiers and their ladies could be rowed in gondolas.

It is difficult to agree with the cynical personal opinion of Saint-Simon[2] that it was "disagreeable to make the smallest use" of the gardens. He sharply criticized the lack of shade and the scorching expanse in proximity to the palace. The stones of the paths hurt his feet, and he considered the *bosquets* damp, unhealthy, and evil smelling.

Throughout the gardens an incomparable richness is still evident. Thousands of statues, marble vases, and bronze and gilded lead figures occupied nearly a hundred sculptors and used the best talents France could provide. Running as a main theme throughout is the symbolism of the sun and the universe. The sun god Apollo and his mythical companions recurred throughout the sculptured groups in deference to King Louis, *Le Roi Soleil*. In the planning of the garden, "*Toutes les figures et les ornements qu'on y voit ne sont point placés au hasard, mais dans leur ordre de relation avec le soleil ou sa personnification.*" ("All the figures and ornaments which one sees are placed not at random, but in their order of relationship with the sun or its personification.")[3] On the south front, for example, the flower garden and orangerie emphasize in symbolic decorations Flora and her lover Zephyr, and Hyacinth and Clytie (heliotrope), turned into flowers by Apollo. The legend of the Sun King and his universe is echoed in the statues of the seasons, of dawn, midday, evening, and night, of the four continents and the four elements of earth, air, fire, and water. The Fountain of Apollo, at the head of the canal,

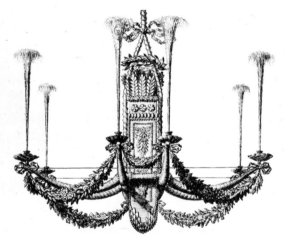

The Grotto of Thetis was decorated with candelabra made of shells. Engraving by F. Chauneau, 1676.

shows the sun god in his horse-drawn chariot, emerging from the sea. His return from his daily journey to the ministrations of the nymphs of the sea goddess Thetis is depicted in the Grotto of Apollo's Bath. Latona, the mother of Apollo, and his twin sister Diana surmount the huge basin overlooking the *tapis vert*.

The three sculptured groups which comprise "Apollo's Bath" have had three different settings, necessitated by enlargement of the palace and a change in garden fashion. Originally they were in shell-encrusted niches of *rocaille* within a marble pavilion at the north side of the palace. This was called the Grotto of Thetis and was one of the king's favorite settings for musicales. Later the figures were transported to one of the *bosquets*

200

The engraver Hyacinthe Rigaud (1659–1743) wrote that the beautiful parterre of the Grand Trianon was bedecked with all kinds of the rarest flowers. (*Metropolitan Museum of Art. Photo: Roche*)

to replace Madame de Montespan's whimsy, the Bronze Tree Fountain, and in 1778, in acknowledgment of the fashionable *jardin anglais*, they were moved once again, this time to a huge artificial cavern in the English Park of the Petit Trianon.

For fifty years the work continued at Versailles. Fourteen hundred jets were installed for the fountains, but though the king's hydraulic engineers worked continuously, the problem of supplying enough water for them to function as planned was never properly resolved. After horse-driven mills and windmills failed to bring enough from the river and pond for the reservoirs (there is a large one beneath the Royal Terrace), a system of draining the water table for miles around into a series of pools and conduits was adopted. Seven years were spent building the great pumping *Machine de Marly*, which raised water from the Seine, but even this failed to provide enough, and its waters were soon reserved for the fountains of the king's newly built "hermitage" at Marly. The most grandiose scheme was the bringing of water from the Eure River by aqueduct. Soldiers were ordered to dig a twenty-three-mile-long canal, but the project was never finished. The arches of the aqueduct may still be seen behind the Château de Maintenon. This was not the only time troops labored at Versailles. A regiment of Swiss Guards turned a swamp into an ornamental lake south of the palace, and to this day it is called *La Pièce des Suisses*. In the end the King had to be content to have just the main fountains playing during the daytime. Only on special occasions were they all functioning at once, and there were times when those the King enjoyed during a promenade were turned off as soon as he had passed.

Except for the *jardin fleuriste* or cutting garden tended by Jean de la Quintinye as part of the huge *potager* in the area now known as *La Pièce des Suisses*, floral color appeared only within the borders and embroideries of the Versailles parterres. Le Nôtre himself was a bit contemptuous of flowers, saying that they served only to please the eyes of the nursemaids and wetnurses who could look down upon them from the upper story of the palace.

After the first exhilaration of planning the gardens and enlarging the palace, the crowds of people who surrounded King Louis made him yearn for more privacy. In 1687, he pulled down the little pleasure house known as the Trianon de Porcelaine, at the end of the northern arm of the canal, to make way for a larger colonnaded palace of pink marble now called the Grand Trianon. (The name Trianon came from the hamlet which had been acquired in the enlargement of the park.) The Porcelain Trianon, famous for its plaques, vases, and pool linings of blue and white faïence, was equally appreciated for its gardens and flowers: the newer and larger Trianon was even more lavishly planted, and the flower beds constantly replenished from the hothouses and large nursery. Le Nôtre wrote, "This garden is always filled with flowers which are changed every season in pots and one never sees a dead leaf, or a shrub not in bloom. It is necessary to change continuously more than two million pots . . . carrying out, removing and bringing back." The fragrance of jasmine, narcissi, hyacinths, lilies, heliotropes, carnations, and tuberoses filled the air, but Saint-Simon claimed that on one occasion the King and his court departed because the scent in the garden was overwhelming. The Trianon had no grand vista, though it did have *bosquets* and basins with water jets. Its royal suite overlooked a flower garden and the guest wing was shaded by trees. Compared to Versailles, the Trianon, which the King gave as a wedding gift to Madame de Maintenon, whom he had secretly married, was comfortably informal. It always remained among the more favored royal residences, and in the reign of Louis XV an important botanical garden was established there.

Louis XIV's "hermitage" of Marly-le-Roi overlooked a large water parterre and twelve detached guest houses. (*Bibliothèque Nationale, Paris*)

The King's other favorite retreat was at Marly, in a narrow, enclosed valley which Louis deliberately chose as a site because it was secluded and offered no vista or "means of making one." The retreat was planned for three-day visits, and the King's friends were assigned to individual guest houses which lined the central water parterre. Louis changed his mind about a view and had a hill leveled to achieve one; then cascades were fashioned behind the small "hermitage" (a beautiful classic building designed by Mansart) to make an impressive water staircase with jets and marble statues. As the gardens grew, clipped trees were trained into elaborate canopies, avenues were cut into the woods, and statues were added. Once more the expense had been tremendous, and Saint-Simon bitingly commented, "Such was the development of a haunt of snakes and vermin, toads and frogs, that was selected solely on the ground that it would entail no expense. Marly was typical of the King's bad taste in everything, and of the proud pleasure which he found in subduing Nature, from which diversion neither the most pressing need of war, nor religious zeal could ever turn him." Marly was destroyed during the Revolution and all we now see are the remains of the great pumping machine and the surrounding park.

The royal residence at Marly was one of the few in which André Le Nôtre played no major part, but he was kept busy remaking or adding to existing gardens of the French crown and nobility. He simplified the design of the Tuileries by introducing more turf, reterraced it, and planted more trees to make it essentially what it is today. At Fontainebleau the parterre was refashioned and the canal lengthened. New gardens were made for the King at Saint-Germain; for the King's minister, Louvois, at Meudon, and for its next owner, the Grand Dauphin; for the Duc d'Orléans, at Saint Cloud; for Colbert, at Sceaux, and for the Duc de Condé, at Chantilly.

Chantilly offered Le Nôtre the greatest problem. Because of the shape of the water surrounding the château his formula of a central axis in line with the dwelling and enclosed with trees could not be followed. Instead he designed a huge terrace with an impressive vista at one side of the château and gave it a monumental staircase that led down to the parterre. Because of the close proximity of a river and many natural springs there was no difficulty in obtaining water, which Le Nôtre made the central theme. With the rhythmic repetition of round basins and a channeled river crossing the gardens, the château is mirrored from all angles and seems to float on its surroundings. Woods were planned on either side of the parterre, and cascades, a pavilion, a menagerie, a hunting lodge, and a chapel were built in the park. Chantilly, one of Le Nôtre's earlier achievements, was also one of his finest; he himself always considered it one of his best.

This great landscape artist was loved and respected by his patrons and associates even though he did not belittle his own accomplishments. He felt that he had a God-given genius and wrote his own epitaph, which reads in part, "The force and scope of his genius made him so outstanding in the art of gardening that he can be regarded as having invented their principal beauties and carried all others to their utmost perfection. The excellence of his work accorded with the grandeur and magnificence of the monarch he served and by whom he was showered with benefactions. Not only did France profit from his industry but all the princes of Europe sought his pupils. He had no comparable rival."[4] The gardens of Versailles were in themselves Le Nôtre's best epitaph: all the ruling heads of Europe felt compelled to imitate them.

After King Louis's death in 1715, the nobility, surfeited with court etiquette and imposed leisure, returned to their family estates. During the reigns of Louis XV (1723 to

(LEFT) Jean Jacques Rousseau's tomb at Ermenonville. (*New York Public Library*) (RIGHT) The principal pavilion and the *jeu de bague* in the Parc Monceau. Etching after Louis Carmontelle, 1779. (*Metropolitan Museum of Art. Photo: Roche*)

1774) and Louis XVI (1774 to 1793) the whole social tenor was gayer than it had been during the latter part of the *ancien régime*. The arts reflected the change and heavy baroque decoration gave way to the greater delicacy of the rococo. Garden design at first followed the Le Nôtre formulas set forth by Le Blond in his *Theory and Practice of Gardening*, but gradually a change came about through a simplification of *broderies*, through a freer type of landscaping with winding paths cut through the *parcs*, and finally, through a full adoption of the naturalistic or "landscape style," which was the new fashion in England. The garden of the average aristocrat was designed not for ostentatious pageantry but for agreeable outdoor enjoyment.

Jean Honoré Fragonard and Hubert Robert painted many joyful garden scenes which, in a romanticized way, reflect the light-hearted gaiety of the period and depict a variety of garden activities. People went boating, they picnicked, played games, pushed each other on swings, masqueraded, and made love in the garden. From these pictures, as well as from eighteenth-century literature, we see a frivolous society, dominated by the feminine sex.

In France, as in England, reaction against stiff garden formality was first voiced by philosophers and writers. Addison's criticism of formality and Pope's ridicule of topiary were both quickly translated into French, and Voltaire wrote:

> *Jardins, il faut que je vous fuie,*
> *Trop d'art me révolte et m'ennuie.*
>> (Gardens, I must shun you,
>> Too much art revolts and bores me.)

Jean Jacques Rousseau, condemning the artificialities of society in general, advocated a "return to Nature" and the "simple life." In his *Julie, ou la Nouvelle Héloïse* he described an ideal garden of meadows, brooks, glades, and flowers. Elsewhere he railed against gardens in which one found only flowers of porcelain, figures of apes, trellises, sand of all colors, and beautiful vases filled with nothing. His nature cult admirably fitted the English idea of a naturalized garden, which many French aristocrats saw put into practice across the Channel.

During the eighteenth century, France also responded to the Chinese influence in the

In the same park, the Dutch windmill pumped water over a rocky cascade. The faked ruins of the Temple of Mars within the Parc Monceau were made even more realistic by the addition of a dead tree. Etchings after Carmontelle, 1779. (*Metropolitan Museum of Art. Photos: Roche*)

field of decorative arts as well as gardening. The French Jesuit Father Attiret's description of the gardens of the Emperor of China at Peking was read with wonder and interest, and soon the picturesque garden became known as the *jardin anglo-chinois*. Jesuit painters, for their part, were employed at the imperial court to paint landscapes, portraits, animals, and flowers. They used Chinese materials and a pseudo-Chinese technique but added Western perspective.

One of the earliest French expressions of the naturalistic style was worked out at Ermenonville. The Marquis de Girardin was well acquainted with a number of English gardens, and in 1766 he began work on what became a ten-year enterprise. The Marquis was a great admirer and patron of Rousseau, and he patterned his romantic garden largely after the philosopher's ideals and descriptions. Shortly before Rousseau died, he provided him with a refuge in one of the entrance pavilions of his estate, later arranging for a tomb to be placed on a little poplar-covered island in the lake. At Ermenonville, little brooks wound naturally through the woods and a waterfall tumbled from the lake. Flowers and shrubs never appeared in beds, since a natural landscape was intended. Within the grounds were a desert area of stones and small pines, a hermitage, a Temple of the Philosophers, a thatched cottage, a grotto, the tomb of a young man who had committed suicide in the park, and a rustic farm or *hameau*. Carved on walls, small obelisks and tree trunks throughout the landscape garden were sayings of Horace, Virgil, Petrarch, Rousseau, and Voltaire. These were intended to invoke the proper moods for each successive scene. On special occasions hidden musicians provided woodland music and sometimes played from boats on the lake.

In a quite different and frivolous mood, the famous Parc Monceau was created, just south of Paris. Apparently the Duc de Chartres wished to provide something that would appeal to every taste. Louis Carmontelle, who had much to do with planning the special effects, wrote that the design of a "natural garden should be an itinerary," to be explored gradually, never revealing all its tableaux at one time. He wrote admiringly of English lawns but claimed that French gardens were not made in exact imitation of the English. Rather, he said "we love that happy liberty which produces new and piquant effects" belonging to "our ideas, taste and uses." The *parc* included pavilions, belvederes, tombs,

205

and ruins, and such "piquant" items as a merry-go-round *à la chinoise*, a minaret, a Tartar tent, an Italian vineyard, and a Dutch windmill — "a small confusion of many things" as a rival gardener wrote. The principal pavilion was built of different-colored marbles and trimmed with bronze garlands. The merry-go-round could take only four riders, the men seated on dragons and the women on cushions held by the reclining figures of Chinese attendants. To steady themselves they hung on to metal parasols which were ornamented with tiny bells. People could ride on camels and be served by attendants appropriately costumed for each theme. Walking nowadays through this Parisian park, not far from the Place de l'Etoile, one still finds a tomb, a pyramid, columns of the fake ruins of the Temple of Mars (which were made even more realistic by the planting of a decaying tree), and what is left of the Roman *naumachia*, a colonnaded pool for mock sea battles.

Monceau also had a *hameau*, which was a picture-book type of country farm supposedly representing the ultimate in rustic simplicity. The idea was much copied in the gardens of the aristocracy, who liked to take part in the simple life and milk cows, feed

(LEFT) The park of Bagatelle included this Chinese-inspired bridge. (*Metropolitan Museum of Art*)

(RIGHT) The grounds of Malmaison were planted in the manner of an English landscape park, with the exception of Empress Josephine's famous rose garden. White swans, her favorite emblem, are, to this day, kept in the small artificial lake. (*The Pierpont Morgan Library*)

poultry, or churn butter. One of the first farms was seen at Chantilly, when in 1780 much of the property was made into a *jardin anglais*. The spirit of make-believe and a pseudo-simplicity pervaded the *hameau*, which, in actual fact, provided its aristocratic visitors with much of the comfort and luxury to which they were accustomed. The interior of one building, an imitation of a hunting *rendezvous*, was described as being one "superb dining room." Tree trunks and turf formed the seats, flowers grew from the floor, and whole trees lined the walls. Window openings here and there among the branches let in daylight and at night suspended lanterns shone with sparkling light.

Marie Antoinette's *hameau* at the Petit Trianon, the most famous one of all, was the last general improvement made to the little palace before the holocaust of the Revolution. Here the Queen, so out of touch with her people and so out of touch with reality, enjoyed the happiest moments of her married life.

Louis XVI had given Marie the Petit Trianon as a wedding present, and she found

206

there the same kind of respite that Louis XV and Madame de Pompadour had sought. She and her children often stayed there for months. Some of the formal gardens at the Petit Trianon were retained when the "landscape style" was first introduced in 1781. The new alterations provided informal winding walks, and imported specimen trees. An octagonal belvedere was placed upon a setting of rocks, and the famous white marble Temple of Love was built on a small island in an artificial stream. The latter became a part of the view that Marie Antoinette enjoyed from her bedroom window.

Another well-known "English style" garden was created at Bagatelle, in the Bois de Boulogne, where Louis XVI's youngest brother, the Comte d'Artois, had bought a piece of property that included a small and very dilapidated house. Marie Antoinette teased him about this and he wagered her that he could transform the place during the short time in which the court left Versailles for its annual autumn sojourn at Fontainebleau. A pavilion and gardens were made in sixty-four days. Having won his bet by working his men and the horses night and day, the count and his gardeners, François Joseph Belanger, Lerouge,

and a Scotsman, Thomas Blaikie, continued to make improvements. Following accepted custom, formality prevailed close by the pavilion, but a more natural aspect was provided by a river, lake, and grottoes. A little island, with poplars and a tomb in imitation of Rousseau's tomb at Ermenonville, was made here and soon copied all over Europe. Bagatelle was not admired by the French. One commentator compared its rural atmosphere to the disorder of a "*coquette en négligé*." It has undergone many changes in character and ownership since the Revolution. In the last year of the Terror the National Assembly took it over as an amusement area and promenade for the Parisians, and in the Empire period it served Napoleon as a hunting preserve. In the years of the Restoration it was reacquired by the Comte d'Artois after an absence of twenty-four years. During the Second Empire it changed hands among several English owners, including Sir Richard Wallace, who hurried his priceless art collection to London when radicals endangered the place during the first year of the Republic. Finally, in 1905, the city of Paris bought it for a park of horticultural interest and this is how we know it today. With the exception of the pavilion and the lake few traces of the old garden remain. Bagatelle is now most famous for the exceptional beauty of its rose garden, though the garden of annuals and the modern iris garden are equally lovely.

Interest in the English "picturesque" style lasted well into the nineteenth century. Changes made in English gardens were copied in France and many fine gardens were destroyed in the making of artificial landscapes. Fontainebleau saw changes. Rambouillet, Champs, and many of the châteaux of the Loire, including Villandry, all succumbed. It was during the Reign of Terror and the aftermath of Revolution that gardening reached its lowest ebb in France. The gardens of the aristocrats lay neglected and overgrown with weeds, and broken ornaments littered the paths. At Versailles furious mobs swept through the palace, but in the gardens much of the sculpture was left, even though everything else was left to fall into sad disarray. Napoleon did not favor the former glory associated with Versailles and therefore neglected it, but the Grand Trianon and Fontainebleau pleased him, and these he restored.

The dwelling most closely associated with Napoleon and his first wife, Josephine de Beauharnais, is, of course, La Malmaison. The future empress bought this property in 1799, three years after their marriage, and it always remained her home. Here, she not only made continual improvements on the picturesque landscape, in the style of an English park, that surrounded the strikingly severe dwelling, but created a world-famous rose garden of all known varieties, some two hundred and fifty in all. Her horticultural interests were varied, and many newly discovered plants and shrubs were sent her. Camellias, hydrangeas, mimosa, rhododendrons, and catalpas all found a place in the landscaping, and dahlias, geraniums, and phlox were introduced to the flower gardens. There was a large greenhouse for exotics.

The aftermath of revolution lasted many years and a long time elapsed before people again had enough money to spend on pleasure gardens. Impoverished aristocrats returning from exile and new owners of properties once belonging to the victims of the guillotine found so many overgrown gardens and estates that discouragement must have been general. Without large staffs for maintenance, the classic old parterres were forgotten, and those we now see at such places as Champs and Vaux le Vicomte are restorations.

In nineteenth-century France there was little possibility of any original contributions to gardening. Economics and political events disrupted the life of the country so continuously that the easiest way of caring for grounds was to let them fall into the landscape pattern. In keeping with the Romantic movement in literature and painting, new gardens were apt to be planned in Gothic or rustic styles. One theorist, Gabriel Thouin, classified naturalistic gardens into five different types: *jardins champêtres* were made up of meadows, orchards, brooks, and flowers; *jardins sylvestres* were forested with trees, had rocks and waterfalls and woodcutters' cottages; and *jardins pastoraux* contained meadows in which cattle and sheep were allowed to graze. These gardens included stream-fed lakes, and among their adornments were windmills, bridges, and shepherds' huts. The fourth style was *jardins romantiques*, which called for an irregular plan with sharply varying contours. Trees with a variety of seasonal effects were planted, and water was introduced

In 1819 Gabriel Thouin published a work containing suggestions and sketches for "all kinds" of gardens. This plate depicts such embellishments as ruined Roman monuments and temples, ancient tombs, fountains, rocks and caverns, swings, a swan house, a boathouse, a Chinese aviary, various boats (including a gondola), and a lighthouse. (*Metropolitan Museum of Art. Photo: Roche*)

in cascades, falls, and fountains. To such scenes were added vases, statues, grottoes, ruins, tombs, and temples. The last style, *jardins paysages*, represented a combination of the first four worked out on a vast scale with "grand waters." Because these gardens were too large for promenading, one was expected to ride through them in a carriage. How strictly French garden enthusiasts adhered to these types is problematical; certainly they were not universally copied. With an innate love for formalism in all the arts, Frenchmen could never desert the formal garden completely.

Gradually, as in all the countries of Europe, the exciting new plants received from China, South Africa, and Central and South America made French gardeners less concerned with style. Instead, their interest became centered upon flowers and their hybridization and on colorful shrubberies and specimen trees with unusual foliage. Beds of flowers dotted lawns, and mosaic culture, a system of forming patterns of solid colors from low-growing flowers, was adopted for show areas. The resplendent colors of scarlet geraniums, dwarf orange marigolds, blue lobelias, pink begonias, and gray echeverrias emblazoned them.

In summary, it can be said that the era of grand gardens in France was the seventeenth century. After the seventeenth century there was a wave of enthusiasm for the parterre and vista, then a swing to the fashionable *jardin anglais*, and finally, during the nineteenth century, a drift back to the patterned garden of flowers, along with most other gardens of Europe and America.

IX

*Versailles and
Italian Fashions Copied*

The splendor of Louis XIV's Versailles was the envy of every reigning monarch and prince in Europe. During his reign and the Regency after his death, royal visitors came to be entertained or to follow in the fashionable footsteps of others. "A young man," said Frederick II, "passed for an imbecile if he had not stayed for some time at Versailles." All spent vast sums of money building or enlarging palaces, planning gardens, and hiring architects and designers, in the hope of emulating Louis's achievement. Their accomplishments were impressive, but Versailles could not be surpassed, for the wealth and genius were not to hand. Throughout the Continent, however, we can still see the magnificent results of their efforts at displaying their wealth, power, and culture. The gardens not only were imitated by royalty but have inspired efforts by both English aristocrats and American industrial magnates.

Italy's High Renaissance garden characteristics of carved stone-work and watery displays have frequently inspired other creations on a grand scale. This happened to a lesser degree during the century following Louis XIV's death, when Versailles's fame was at its zenith, although countries such as Austria, bordering on Italy, had always felt Italian influence. The architectural beauty of the style and the drama of its water effects are still impressive and beautiful.

The photographs which follow are a small selection of gardens created in the "grand style" in Europe and America, and even China.

Plates

125. The Nymphenburg was a summer palace of the Bavarian kings, built several miles from Munich, famous for its gilt vases and statues, its fountains and canals. It no longer has parterres, though it still retains an over-all formal pattern of paths, drives, and canals. A large part of it was made into a landscaped park in the late eighteenth century. Several original and charming pavilions remain. (*German Information Center*)

126. The castle of Herrenchiemsee, Bavaria, built by Ludwig II between the years 1878 and 1885, was designed in direct imitation of Versailles. (*German Tourist Office*)

127. The parterres of the Mirabell Gardens in Salzburg have been greatly simplified over the years, but the four statues with their rocky pedestals are still in place near the central fountain. The palace was built in 1606 by Bishop Wolf Dietrich, and the gardens were laid out about that time. (*Austrian Information Service*)

128. View of the colonnade called the Gloriette on the hill above Schönbrunn Palace, Vienna. A beautiful parterre garden was laid before it, terminated by a basin and the Fountain of Neptune. The Empress Maria Theresa, who reigned from 1740 to 1780, guided the development of the gardens, which were laid out according to a plan by Le Nôtre. (*A. Defner*)

129. The pink summer palace of Queluz, Portugal, five miles outside of Lisbon, was built in the mid-eighteenth century. Its gardens had a French architect, Jean Baptiste Robillon. The severity of their topiary and neat box hedges is relieved by the contrast of blue and white terracotta urns filled with pink geraniums and by statuary. (*Portuguese Government Tourist Office. Photo: "Sni-Yan"*)

130. Sixty miles north of Madrid, not far from Segovia, on the slopes of the Sierra de Guadarrama, Philip V built a summer retreat called La Granja (The Farm). This Bourbon king, a grandson of Louis XIV, was thoroughly familiar with Versailles and made a conscious effort to achieve something equally grand. La Granja's site is in wooded hills, with mountains for a background. Water was conveniently abundant and there are many fountains throughout the gardens. This photograph shows the marble cascade of the main parterre. (*Spanish National Tourist Department*)

131. Petrodvorets is the summer palace outside Leningrad (formerly Saint Petersburg), built for Peter the Great by Alexandre Le Blond, who came to Russia as the architect-general of the new capital. The long canal stretches down toward the Gulf of Finland. *Bosquets* on either side of the canal shelter several summerhouses. Peter the Great brought in forty thousand trees to landscape the grounds, which the Soviet Government maintains as a public park. (*V. Malyshev*)

132. A serenely beautiful Italian water parterre, overlooking the lake, has been designed in this century for the east front of Blenheim Palace, Oxfordshire. Its green and watery surfaces recall two other famous water gardens, those of the Villa Lante and the Villa Gamberaia in Italy. (*British Travel and Holidays Association*)

133. The sumptuous royal palace and gardens of Caserta, Italy, belonged to the Bourbon kings of Naples and were begun in 1752. Caserta's parks and gardens had all the traditional parts of French gardens of *le grand siècle*, parterres (now lawns), *bosquets*, avenues, pools, and fountains. Below the cascade, statues tell the story of Diana and her nymphs who were interrupted, while bathing, by the huntsman Actaeon. Diana turned him into a stag, and he was torn to pieces by his own dogs. (*Anderson*)

125

128   129

134

135

136

Plates

134. In 1906 Pierre S. du Pont began developing Longwood Gardens at Kennett Square, Pennsylvania. There are water gardens, a rose garden, herbaceous borders, naturalized woodlands, and extensive conservatories. At the foot of the main Fountain Garden is a canal in which fountains glitter and sway. Imported Italian stonework ornaments many sections. (*Longwood Gardens*)

135. America's industrial magnates of the late nineteenth and early twentieth centuries wholeheartedly embraced European art and architecture. Selecting a site in the mountains of North Carolina, just outside Asheville, George W. Vanderbilt commissioned Richard Hunt to design a French château, and Frederick Law Olmsted planned its grounds. The estate is called Biltmore. Extensive formal gardens surround the mansion, and there are miles of winding drives, a famous azalea collection, and a rose garden containing about five thousand bushes. (*Samuel A. Bingham, Jr.*)

136. Vizcaya was the name given to the Italian palazzo and formal gardens created by James Deering on Biscayne Bay, Miami. Many hundreds of European artisans worked to carve the gardens out of a tropical mangrove jungle, their work being completed in 1921. Jasmine instead of European box was used to trace out the parterre embroidery, and clipped live oaks flank the center panel of green turf. Much of the stonework throughout the gardens was carved by Italian sculptors from Florida coral. The stone barge acts as a breakwater. (*Miami-Metro News Bureau*)

(ABOVE) The fame of Europe's gardens was such that even the Emperor of China wanted to copy them, although only as a small part of the very extensive gardens of the summer palace of Peking. Two Jesuit missionaries, Father Michel Benoit and Father Giuseppe Castiglione, were asked to make a series of gardens featuring "foreign waterworks." These were called *Hsieh Ch'i Ch'u*, "Harmonious, Strange, and Pleasant." The Labyrinth of *Hsieh Ch'i Ch'u* was surrounded on three sides by rushing water. The Chinese were more used to having quiet pond waters in their gardens, with the possible exception of a dripping waterfall.

(OVERLEAF) This was called the Hall of Peaceful Seas. The grand staircase had a water balustrade spurting jets. Below was a fabulous water clock in which the twelve animals of the Chinese twelve-year cycle of time took turns in spewing out water for exactly one hour. (*New York Public Library*)

(LEFT) A game of ninepins played in the gardens of the Nymphenburg. A very early eighteenth-century engraving by Mathias Diesel. (*Metropolitan Museum of Art.* Photo: *Roche*)

(OPPOSITE) 137. *Allées* of tall, clipped hornbeams radiate from the garden façade of Schönbrunn Palace, Vienna. (*Photo Researchers*)

(BELOW) This eighteenth-century view of the Mirabell gardens in Salzburg shows the impressive and formal gardens, some of which were laid right over the city fortifications. (*New York Public Library*)

138. (Opposite) At Hampton Court: the restored Pond Garden and the Banqueting House.

X *English Traditions*

Garden glory passed successively from Renaissance Italy to seventeenth-century France, and thence to England in the eighteenth century. Since then Britain has virtually ruled the garden world; she has been a style-setter, a pioneer in the collecting of plants, a disseminator of plant knowledge, and above all, a magnificent contributor to floral beauty.

England's garden tradition is long established, for undoubtedly gardens were created during the Roman occupation of nearly four hundred years. Early dwellings were huts but as wealth accumulated, farms and villas were built with luxurious baths, running water, and central heating. In the Roman town of Calleva Atrebatum (now known as Silchester), for example, there were detached houses, each with its own garden. We can suppose the gardens grew lilies, peonies, roses, and violets, names little changed from the original Latin *Lilium*, *Paeonia*, *Rosa*, and *Viola*. Certainly there were orchards and vegetable and herb gardens, and cherry, pear, mulberry, and walnut trees were introduced.

After the Romans left, the warring Anglo-Saxons and Danes could have had little opportunity for the peaceful growing of garden flowers. On the other hand, we are reminded that the invaders had utilitarian gardens of some sort, for the word "orchard," which is retained in the English language, comes from the Anglo-Saxon *ortgeard* or *wortgeard*, sometimes spelled *wyrtgeard*. *Wort* was a plant (Saint Johnswort, lungwort, sneezewort, and others), and *geard* was a fence, or dwelling. What we call "orchard" formerly meant a plant yard, not necessarily a whole area given over to the growing of fruit trees. Another ancient word was the Danish "garth" or enclosure.

When Christianity gained a firm hold on the island, gardens were grown within or close to the walls of the newly built monasteries, mostly for medicinal herbs. From the sacristan's garden flowers were fashioned into crowns and garlands for the priests, and decorations were made for the church. After the Norman conquest baronial castles were constructed with small garden enclosures within their walls, and they were illustrated in illuminated manuscripts and described by the poets. A fourteenth-century poem, *The Flower and the Leaf*, formerly attributed to Chaucer, describes an arbor "That benched was and eke with turfës newe"; and also "The hegge as thick as a castle wall." In another poem Chaucer speaks of a flowery mede "With many a freshe and sondrye floure,/That casten up ful good savoure." And in the early fifteenth century, James I of Scotland, imprisoned as a very young man in Windsor Castle, looked down from a window and saw "a garden fair, fast by the Touris wall; and in the corner set an arbour green." Arbors, alleys, flowery medes, and seats turfed with "camomile, penny-royall, daisies and violets, seemely and comfortable," all occupying only a small space within the walls of a castle: this was the courtly garden of the Middle Ages — in England as in Flanders and France. It was a simple, unpretentious kind of gardening, carried on during the long periods of strife and unrest when England waged the Hundred Years' War with France, when the Black Death, a catastrophic epidemic of plague, decimated the population, and when quarreling English nobles embarked on the Wars of the Roses in which Yorkists with emblematic white roses and Lancastrians with red battled for the throne. Not until 1483, when Henry Tudor defeated Richard III at Bosworth and became Henry VII, was there any degree of stability in which peaceful occupations could prosper.

The introduction of gunpowder during the age of the Tudors made castles indefensible and therefore obsolete. This fact, together with a more stabilized economy, gave birth to the first great age of domestic architecture in England. Fine country houses were built, the sizes varying according to the degree of nobility and wealth of their owner. (The so-called "stately homes" of the Elizabethan Age and later were built on huge land holdings acquired, for the most part, at the time of the dissolution of the monasteries during the reign of Henry VIII.) The Englishman's inherent love of the country and outdoor life soon led to the inclusion of a garden in almost every building scheme. However, the gardens of Tudor and Elizabethan times were intricate, artificial, and confined; they served as outdoor rooms to be lived in and enjoyed in the same way as the indoor ones. In a country which does not experience great summer heat, it seems strange that shady "alyes" of arched trees or shrubs, such as "Privit, Sweet bryer, White Thorne or Pyracantha" (as John Parkinson wrote), and rose- and jasmine-covered wooden arbors were so widely considered necessary. Yet in bad weather they provided shelter. (Experienced gardeners wrote advising others that paths underneath the arbors should be laid with sand, paving stones, or "sawings of marble" instead of earth, which became muddy in the rain.) Probably the reason for the popularity of the arbor was that it often offered more privacy than the indoors, where the family, relations, and retainers were ever present. When we read one of Henry VIII's love letters to Anne Boleyn, "No more to you at this present, mine awne darling, for lake of time; but that I would you were in myne arms or I in yours; for I think it long since I kyst you," it is easy to imagine the couple meeting under such a dense, clipped, green arbor.

Knot gardens made their appearance in England at the beginning of the sixteenth century. A contemporary researcher has uncovered an early mention of payments made to gardeners by the Duke of Buckingham and the Earl of Northumberland for "diligence in making knots" and for "clypping of knottes."[1] This was in 1502, thirty-five years after the first edition of the Italian *Hypnerotomachia* of Poliphilus (and three years after the first illustrated edition of the same work). Whether Buckingham and Northumberland were the first gentlemen in England to copy an Italian idea is unknown, but there must be a connection between the simultaneous appearance in both countries of such similarly intricate garden patterns. It is possible that the Dutch were the intermediaries. In any event, English gardeners loved knot gardens and played with them for a hundred years or more. Francis Bacon (1561–1626) scoffed at them as "toys" and said one might "see as good sights many times in tarts."[2] But this was written a hundred years after their introduction, when gar-

Closed "knottes" from Lawson's *The Country House-wifes Garden*, 1638.

dening had grown extremely artificial, with colored earths, coal, and brick dusts used for color instead of flowers. Gervase Markham, in *The English Husbandman*, 1613, listed the following materials and the colors they produced:

Yellow — yellow clay or sand
White — chalke beaten to dust or well-burnt plaster
Black — coale dust
Red — brick dust
Blue — white chalk and black coal dust mixed
Green — natural property belonging to a garden

All to be sifted and beaten with a Beetell. [A "Beetell" was a large, heavy wooden mallet.]

Plates

139. The yew hedge at Sudeley Castle, Gloucester-shire, has been clipped and trained into a gallery with openings called *clairvoyées*. Its density provides a sheltered walk in inclement weather. The castle was once the residence of Henry VIII's widow, Catherine Parr. In the early nineteenth century it passed into private ownership and the garden was replanted. (*British Travel Association*)

140. The Elizabethan knot garden at New Place, Stratford-upon-Avon. Traditionally, English knots filled a square space; if the knots were quartered, the four parts often differed in pattern. Typically, this garden has a trellised arbor of "carpenter's work" surrounding it. (*Trustees and Guardians of Shakespeare's Birthplace*)

141. A low-growing maze described by Thomas Hyll in 1563, which would remain green throughout the year. (*New York Public Library*)

142. Hatfield House, Hertfordshire, seat of the Marquess of Salisbury, has patterned gardens and a very fine maze. This is of yew and has grown to well over a man's height. (*Aerofilms Ltd.*)

143. Details in Holbein's paintings of Henry VIII and his family show his heraldic beasts, set on green and white painted poles, in the gardens at Whitehall. These Tudor colors also appear on the rails of the garden beds. The people in the garden are Henry's jester and the jester's wife, Jane the Fool. (*British Ministry of Works*)

144. Topiary is featured in the open knot garden of Elizabeth I's hunting lodge, Great Fosters, Eg-ham. Hedges of this height were often used in the old days for the spreading out of laundry. (*J. Arthur Dixon*)

145. Haddon Hall has terraced gardens with a stone balustrade and staircase reminiscent of Italy. (*British Travel Association*)

146. One of the two banqueting- or pleasure-houses which terminate the balustraded terraces above the forecourt at Montacute House in Somer-set. Such features were common additions to the gardens of the late sixteenth and early seventeenth centuries, a period when many "stately homes" were built in England. (*The National Trust*)

230

141

143

142

144

145

146

A later author pointed out that both coal and chalk were dirty underfoot and should be used only to fill a pattern. Brick dust was gritty and made a hard path to walk on, as did ground shell.

The designs of knots were intricate and usually confined within a square. Low, dense-growing plants such as thyme, hyssop, rosemary, germander, thrift, and, at a later date, dwarf box, were planted in interlacing ribbon-like designs, in heraldic designs, or in fanciful shapes. If flowers filled the intervening spaces solidly, a "closed knot" was formed, but if paths of grass, sand, or brick led through the garden beds it was called an "open knot." The green plants had to be kept shorn, and the fragrant clippings were taken indoors and added to the rushes which were customarily strewn on floors.

John Parkinson, author of *Paradisi in Sole Paradisus Terrestris*, published in 1629 ("*Paradisi in Sole*" is a play on his name "Park-in-Sun"), described the advantages and disadvantages of using herbs for garden knots of Jacobean times. Thrift provided "ever living green" but grew so thick and bushy that it provided shelter for snails. Germander spread underground and sent up shoots in unwanted places, while hyssop's stalks grew too thick. He found marjoram, savory, and thyme too short-lived because of drought in summer and freezing weather in winter. Lavender cotton was the most fashionable plant but would rot if left beneath the snow. Juniper and yew were useful, but the ideal plant material, in his opinion, was the Dutch dwarf box, which grew slowly and had "long lasting continuance." There were certain "dead materials" which customarily bordered the open knots. Parkinson mentioned lead, "four fingers wide," which was easily bent to form desired lines, but which became "over-hot for Summer and over-cold for Winter." Oak boards were popular for lining long straight edges, but were subject to rot, and "tyles" had to be continually repaired. "Whitish or blewish pebble stones," uniform in size and merely laid upon the ground, were the "latest invention," and, with no pretense of elegance, he said the shank bones of sheep, "well cleansed and boyled, stuck in the ground small end downwards and the knuckle head upwards," were the best choice to "prettily grace out the ground." Since he admired this custom, it seems surprising that he dismissed as "too gross and base" the fashion of using jaw bones enjoyed in "the Low Countries and other places beyond the Sea."

The flowers which grew within the Tudor knots were of little variety, and their period of bloom ended with summer; but the green knot designs were pleasant to look upon at all times, and clipping them on warm days brought out their fragrance. Since fragrance was considered important for combating pestilential air, much thought was given to achieving it. The English had brought their native wild flowers into cultivation — columbine, foxgloves, violets, cowslips, primroses, and daisies (*Bellis perennis*), to name a few. In addition, plants brought from the Continent at various times became garden favorites — the peony, pot marigold (*Calendula officinalis*), larkspur, hollyhock, pansies, pinks, wallflowers, Martagon lilies, the Madonna lily (*Lilium candidum*), damask and musk roses. Many other plants were introduced during Queen Elizabeth's reign.

Of great significance during Tudor times were the gardens of Hampton Court which Cardinal Wolsey created twenty miles up the Thames River from London. Medieval in

(LEFT) Henry VIII's mount and summer-house in his New Garden at Hampton Court were probably similar to those seen here. (*Metropolitan Museum of Art. Photo: Roche*)

(ABOVE AND BELOW) Among the fountain designs by William Worlidge, 1688, can be seen a statue of a woman "that at the turning of a private cock, shall cast water out of her nipples," and "the Royal Oak." (*Pierpont Morgan Library*)

aspect, with walls, turf benches, arbors, and alleys, they had the newer addition of "knottes." About them, one of Wolsey's retainers, George Cavendish, wrote a little poem:

> My gardens sweet, enclosed with walles strong,
>> Embanked with benches to sitt and take my rest
>> The knotts so enknotted it cannot be exprest
> With arbours and alyes so pleasant and dulce
> The pestilent ayers with flavors to repulse.

The palace itself was one of the most beautiful examples of Tudor architecture, and Wolsey furnished it magnificently. He enjoyed the luxuries of drinking water and bathrooms.

After Henry VIII deposed Wolsey for failure to obtain an annulment of his marriage to Catherine of Aragon and for opposing his wishes regarding Anne Boleyn, to say nothing about Wolsey's faltering foreign policy, he took over Hampton Court, which he had long coveted. Henry set about making many changes in the gardens and also in the park, where he enjoyed hunting and archery. Provisions were made for bowling and a tiltyard, and several indoor tennis courts were added to the palace. The King's New Garden was created where the Privy Garden is at present, and the colorful Pond Garden, sometimes called Anne Boleyn's Garden, was planted and still remains enclosed by its original walls. Set about the gardens on poles were heraldic animals called the "kynges and queenys Beestes." Privy purse expenses reveal payment to a stone carver for "foure dragones, scyx lyones, five greyhounds, five harttes, foure unicornes serving to stand about the ponddes in the pondyard." Other items were for painting the "beestes" and for painting the poles with green and white "oyle." The rails which protected the flower beds were also painted in green and white, the colors of the house of Tudor. Perhaps the most spectacular addition was the huge mount raised at the river end of the New Garden. This was planted with "quicksets" (living greenery), probably hawthorn, and, a few years later, with yew, cypress, and bays. Around the mount was spiraled, "like the turnings of cockle shells," a rosemary-bordered path. This led to an elegant three-story summerhouse, generously glassed and topped by a lead cupola which displayed another "beeste" with a vane. Around the mount were other gaily painted wooden animals, sixteen bronze sundials, and beds planted with spring and summer flowers, including two hundred roses.

No garden was complete without topiary or "antike worke," an art brought to England (and the Netherlands) in the sixteenth century from Italy, via France. The favorite shrub for topiary was yew, which grew slowly, lived long, and could be cut and coaxed into quaint and playful shapes. William Lawson, the author of *The Country Housewife's Garden*, suggested the shapes of "men armed in the field, ready to give battle," and of "swift-running grey-hounds." Francis Bacon's frequently quoted opinion concerning topiary, that "images cut out in juniper or other garden stuff, be for children," did not rule out for him "little low hedges with some pretty pyramides." His ideal garden was square, "encompassed on all the four sides with a stately arched hedge" grown "upon pillars of carpenter's work, of some ten foot high and six foot broad." Over the arches he wanted "an entire hedge of some four foot high, framed also upon carpenter's work, and upon the upper hedge, over every arch, a little turret with a belly, enough to receive a cage of birds, and over every space between the arches some other little figure with broad plates of round coloured glass gilt for the sun to play upon." It is hard to reconcile this with his request that the garden "be not too busy."

Mazes were also "proper adornments upon pleasure to a garden." Some mazes were low-growing as described by Thomas Hyll in 1563: "Isope and time, or winter savery and time, wyl endure grene al the yeare throw," and "some set their mazes with lavender cottons." Other mazes were allowed to grow tall, "framed to a man's height" as Lawson put it, and so high that people could get lost in them, as one can today at Hatfield House, Hever Castle, and Hampton Court. Usually there was a central feature — a mount, an arbor, a summerhouse, or even a single tree-rose, which Hyll suggested for his low-growing maze.

Clipping the arbors and mazes, shaping the topiary specimens, and shearing the knots were not the only controlling measures that had to be taken; there were hedges to be trimmed as well. In the common people's gardens these were kept low, for they could be "profitable to the huswife for the drying of linen, cloathes and yarne."

In Queen Elizabeth's time (she was crowned in 1558 and died in 1603) gardens had become sophisticated enough to incorporate ornamental fountains. Frequently these were referred to simply as conduits and appeared in a variety of forms including basins with or without statuary. A few, copied from the Italians, were used for practical jokes, and even Queen Elizabeth had one placed at Hampton Court to "play upon the ladies and others standing by, and give them a thorough wetting." There was another at Nonsuch, the palace on which Henry VIII spent a large sum in imitation of Chambord. Bacon thought fountains and moving water "a great beauty and refreshment" but felt that pools made "the garden unwholesome and full of flies and frogs." Lawson commended both a conduit and an orchard "hard by a pleasant river" where one could sit on a mount and "angle a peckled trout."

The Continental custom of fashioning banqueting platforms among the branches of trees was occasionally copied in England. Lime trees were usually chosen, and several levels of platforms connected by a staircase were sometimes constructed. Parkinson described one at Cobham, "a great bodied Lime tree, bare without boughs for eight foote high, and then the branches were spread round orderly ... and from those boughs the body was bare again for eight to nine foote (wherein might be placed halfe a hundred men) ... and then another rowe of branches to encompasse a third arbour with stayres made for the purpose to this and that underneath it: ... upon the boughes were laid boards to tread upon, which is the goodliest spectacle mine eyes ever beheld for one tree to carry." Tree houses are frequently seen in Dutch and Flemish engravings, and there is a large one in Brueghel's spring scene.

Another addition to the Elizabethan garden was the garden house, summerhouse, or banqueting house, for outdoor entertaining and relaxation. In style and material the summer house was usually architecturally allied to the main dwelling. It might contain a table, chairs, even a fireplace, with painted "landskips" such as those in the banqueting house at Hampton Court. A contemporary author, John Worlidge, recommended the garden house as a place remote from "the frequent disturbances of your Family and Acquaintance," and John Rea suggested it for the more utilitarian purposes of sorting out and drying bulbs before they were "wrapped and put into boxes."

Perfect examples of such pleasure-houses stand at the far corners of the grassy forecourt of Montacute, in Somerset. This superb "stately home" was built between 1588 and 1601. Local Ham stone, used throughout the gardens for flights of steps, was also used for balustrades surrounding the fountain pools and those which connect the paired small houses to the mansion. These are pinnacled with obelisks and centered with airy, columned pavilions of unique design. At Montacute, the large-scale planting of lawns and yew hedges on several levels suggests the Italian in style. At one side of the forecourt is a lawn, formerly a bowling green, and on the other side, at a lower level, a square formal area, centered with a fountain and basin, which at one time probably had flower beds. Over the entrance door at Montacute a carved welcome reads, "Through this wide opening gate,/none come too early, none return too late," and one can easily imagine the warmth and gaiety and all the bustling activities connected with this great house in earlier days. At one time, it is said, young ladies of the household led their horses up the gentle risers of the wide inside staircase and exercised them on rainy days in the long gallery on the top floor!

At Haddon Hall in Derbyshire there is the same kind of emphasis on architectural detail reminiscent of the Italian manner as at Montacute, although the style of the two buildings differs greatly. Haddon Hall itself is medieval, but the gardens belong to the sixteenth and seventeenth centuries; their steep terraces are connected by an impressive staircase and

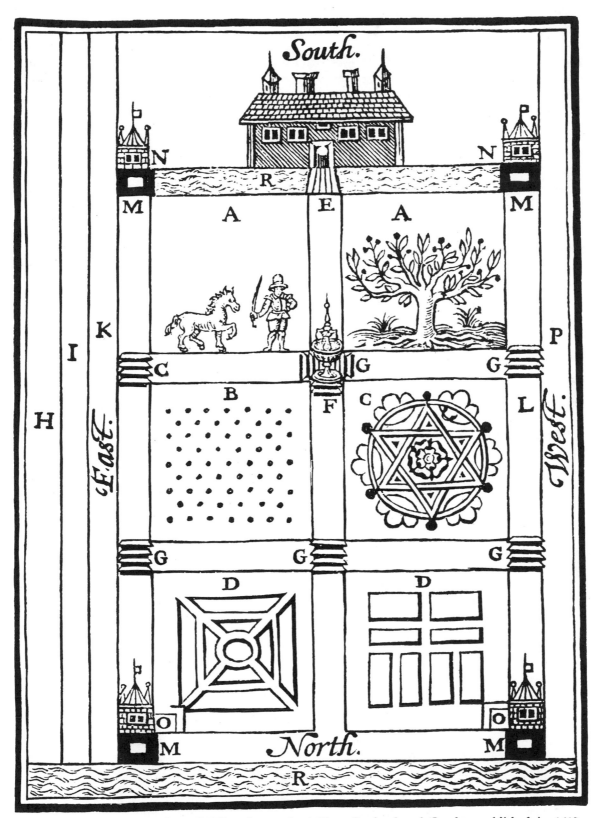

Ideal plan for a garden, from William Lawson's *A New Orchard and Garden*, published in 1618, displaying topiary, knots, a fountain, mounts topped with garden houses, and "fruit trees standing in comely order." The knot design (C) combines the six-pointed Masonic star with the Yorkist rose.

protected by fine stone balustrades. It was during these centuries that gentlemen of wealth and intellectual curiosity began to travel to the Continent in search of culture, for the Renaissance had captured their interest. Thus, they established the precedent for the "grand tour," which became a part of the education of many young noblemen.

The greatest change that occurred in the gardens of the Elizabethan and Jacobean periods was wrought by the introduction of new flowers from faraway places. English mariners were exploring the New World and bringing back new plants, to the delight of gardeners. At the same time, refugee Flemings, who emigrated from the Low Countries under threat of Spanish persecution, brought with them flowers that had recently reached Europe from Asia Minor. Now gardens became so enriched with bloom that they truly became flower gardens. At last flowers had won a place of their own quite apart from the useful plants. Lawson recommended separating them, for garden flowers suffered "some disgrace" if they were intermingled with onions and parsnips.

John Parkinson was the first to mention new introductions which he called "outlandish," but he particularly delighted in those which gave "the beauty and bravery of their colours" earlier than many of England's "owne bred flowers." He listed "Daffodils, Fritillarias, Iacinthes, Saffron-flowers, Lilies, Flowerdeluces, Tulips, Anemones, French Cowslips or Beare's eares, White and Yellow Jasmine, Cyclamen, Muscari, Christmas rose, Oleander, Bellflowers of many kinds, Pyracantha or Prickly Corall."

Bulbs and rhizomes were the most numerous of the new European introductions. John Rea (1676) described the ideal way of planting them: "in the corner of each bed the best Crown Imperials, lilies Martagon, and such tall flowers, in the middle of the bed, great tufts of peonies, and round about them several sorts of cyclamen, the rest with Daffodils, Hyacinths and such. The straight beds are fit for the best tulips, where account may be kept of them. Ranunculus and Anemones also require particular beds — the rest may be set all over with the more ordinary type of tulips, fritilarias, bulbed iris and all other sorts of good roots."

The two John Tradescants, father and son, were England's first true plant explorers. John the elder, gardener to Lord Salisbury and later to Charles I, traveled on the continent under the aegis of the former to buy "rootes, flowers, seedes, trees and plants" (as recorded in documents preserved in Hatfield House, Hertfordshire). Thirteen thousand tulip bulbs were purchased in Holland. Trips to Russia and Algeria enriched his patron's gardens, and his own investment in an expedition to the colony of Virginia enriched his own garden at Lambeth with rare trees such as the tulip tree, the red maple, and the American plane tree. The son, sent to Virginia by his father in 1637 to explore and collect, was responsible for the introduction of the red columbine, the scarlet cardinal flower (*Lobelia cardinalis* or *Americanus*), phlox, bee-balm, lupine, and aster (renamed Michaelmas daisy).

Other seventeenth-century American newcomers to England's gardens were sunflowers, French and African marigolds, marvel-of-Peru or four o'clocks, goldenrod (a little later than Parkinson's time), evening primrose (*Oenothera biennis*), and yucca. Since the garden was still a relatively small area divided into many sections, it is not amiss to visualize further the added beauty of the small fruit trees which always were a part of the whole.

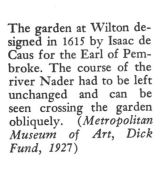

The garden at Wilton designed in 1615 by Isaac de Caus for the Earl of Pembroke. The course of the river Nader had to be left unchanged and can be seen crossing the garden obliquely. (*Metropolitan Museum of Art, Dick Fund, 1927*)

Both in their blossoming and in their fruiting, almonds, apples, apricots, cherries, nectarines, plums, peaches, pears, and quinces would all add color.

The love of flowers is a great leveler of people; cottager, squire, and noble all grew them. From the Elizabethan period to this very day, the cottage has spread its garden before itself like a welcome mat, and proudly shows off its beauty to every passerby. The release from cares and the relaxation of the spirit which envelop one in the garden were ably described by Lawson; he pitied the gentry, who, "tyred with the hearing and judging of litigious Controversies . . . withdrew themselves from the troublesome affaires of their estate . . . into their gardens and orchards . . . wherein they were so much delighted."

Lawson's knowledge was gained through many years of gardening. A "cheife grace" of the garden, he said, was a "brood of Nightingales, who with several notes and tunes, with a strong delightsome voyce, out of a weake body, will beare you company night and day." Nightingales would cleanse the trees of "Caterpillars and all noysome wormes and flyes." The "gentle Robin-red-brest" would help, too, and the "silly Wren in Summer, with her distinct whistle (like a sweet Recorder) to cheere your spirits."

The "outdoor rooms" of Tudor and Elizabethan gardens were furnished in the most appealing way with their green-tapestried and flowery hedges, with beds of flowers for floor coverings and quaint topiary shapes for high-standing furniture. They had an intimacy never regained once the impact of the high Italian Renaissance and the French grand manner reached England. This was in the mid-seventeenth century, by which time the country had settled down after the Cromwellian disturbance and Charles II had been restored. Reflecting foreign influences, English gardens gained greater scope and became more formal, but the fine green lawns easily maintained in the mild, moist climate individualized and enriched them far more than the cold stone adornments of European fashion ever could.

As early as 1615 a superlatively beautiful garden was created for the Earl of Pembroke

241

Plates

147. At Compton Wynyates, Warwickshire, ancient topiary specimens grow in the gardens below the red brick mansion. (*Noel Habgood*)

148. A bluebell wood within Winkworth Arboretum, Surrey. (*By courtesy of the National Trust. Photo: Pamela Booth, F.R.P.S.*)

149. The Palladian bridge at Wilton, built in 1737. (*Author's photo*)

147

242

at Wilton. The place was designed by the Flemish architect Isaac de Caus and was significant for its *parterre de broderie*, the earliest indication of the new Continental influence in England. The French style was to reach a peak of fashion among the *haute monde* after 1660, when Charles II returned from his exile at the French court. While many gardens had been ruined during the eleven-year Commonwealth (they were much too pleasurable for the moral scruples of the Puritans), Pembroke managed to save Wilton by deserting the King's cause, and the original gardens were preserved for over a hundred years.

Wilton was documented in a series of engravings, and full descriptions of the gardens are left us by de Caus himself. Historically these are interesting because there was soon to be a big change in the whole concept of garden design in England. De Caus wrote:

> This Garden, within the enclosure of the new wall is a thowsand foote long and about Foure hundred in breadthe divided in its length into three long squares, the first of which heth ffoure Platts, embroydered; in the midst of which are ffoure fountaynes with statues of marble in their midle. In the second are two Groves with divers walkes, and through those Groves passeth the river Nader having a breadth in this place 44 foote upon which is built the bridge of the breadth of the great walke. In the midst of the aforesayd Groves are two great statues of white marble, of eight ffote high, the one of Bacchus and the other Flora, and on the sides are two covered Arbors of 300 foote long. At the beginning of the third division are on either side of the great walke, two Ponds with Fountaynes and two Collumnes in the midle, casting water all their height which causeth the moveing and turning of two crownes att the top and beyond is a Compartiment of greene with diverse walkes planted with Cherrie trees and in the midle is the Great oval with the Gladiator of brass; the most famous Statue of all that antiquity hath left. On the sydes of this compartiment are three arbours of either side with twining Galleryes. Att the end of the greate walke is a Portico of stone in which are 4 ffigures of white marble. On either side of the sayd portico is an assent leading up to the terrasse upon the steps whereof are sea monsters casting water, and above the sayd portico is a great reserve of water for the grotto.

From this we can detect an Italian influence as well as the French.

Wilton is very different today, for during the eighteenth-century "landscape cult," the entire formal garden was replaced with sweeping lawns, meadows and an informally landscaped riverside. Perhaps the most rewarding of the changes are the magnificent cedars of Lebanon which preside majestically over the lawns.

At Hampton Court, King Charles, with the aid of French gardeners, began imitating what he had admired in the Tuileries. Three great avenues of lime trees were cut into the parks behind the Palace. These avenues radiated out from a semicircle of limes at the end of the long canal or "Long Water," as it was now named. The design formed a typical *patte d'oie* or goose foot. Parliament controlled King Charles's funds for such luxuries and it was not until the reign of William and Mary (from 1689 until her death in 1694 and his in 1702) that this area was fully developed. For the new King Sir Christopher Wren designed the magnificent addition to the palace facing east on the park, which in scale and grandeur rivals Versailles. Immediately in front of the new wing was a large *parterre de broderie* created by George London and Henry Wise, the most eminent garden architects of the period. The parterre probably owed its inspiration to André Mollet's book of garden embroidery designs, published in 1651. With French design at the peak of fashion, King Charles had invited Le Nôtre to come from Paris to work on his royal gardens, but it is not certain whether Le Nôtre did execute the commissions at Saint James's Park, Whitehall Park, Hampton Court, Bushy Hill Park, Greenwich Park, and Chatsworth or whether the designs merely reflect his influence. In 1771 Horace Walpole (who lived within memory of the possible visit) wrote in an essay on gardening that "Le Nôtre came hither on a mission to improve our taste. He planted St. James's and Greenwich parks — no great monuments of his invention." And in the latest exhaustive study made by Helen M. Fox, in her book *André Le Nôtre, Garden Architect to Kings,* Walpole's statement that Le Nôtre did come to London is corroborated. She indicates that he supplied designs to be followed after he left, notably for Chatsworth.

At the center of William III's parterre at Hampton Court was a large circular basin, with a *jet d'eau.* Other smaller basins and jets were essential parts of the design and are well delineated in Jan Kip's early-eighteenth-century view. The parterre became known as the Fountain Garden.

The main lines of this remodeling still exist, although the complicated parterre has been replaced by lawns and rows of yew trees. In joining the new wing to the Tudor buildings, Wren had to follow the natural flat gradient of the land, so that no elevated terrace could be made from which to look down on the patterned garden. Instead, a gravel walk of over two thousand feet ran along the entire east front. The path was lined with tubbed orange trees, which symbolized William's Dutch lineage from the House of Orange. About forty years later George II's consort, Queen Caroline, had the flower gardens made along this broad walk, which today make one of the most spectacular sights at Hampton Court.

William and Mary were keenly interested in horticulture. The Queen had three hothouses and she spent considerable money commissioning plant collectors to bring back "exoticks." Many plants were brought from Virginia, and some came from the Canary Islands. She excused her extravagance by saying, "it employs many hands" and she hoped she would be forgiven. Changes in the palace garden, begun early in William and Mary's reign, stopped during a four-year war with France. They were recommenced under the King's guidance after his Queen died of smallpox, and at the time the new building was nearing completion. The maze and the wilderness belong to this period, and in imitation of Dutch topiary work a circular battlemented fort called Troy Town was fashioned from yews and variegated hollies. Both shrubs also lined the straight walks in the gardens and were clipped alternately into pyramids and globes.

The influences of Dutch "busyness," and French grandeur were strongly felt by all gardeners during this period, and interest in horticulture was steadily on the increase. Daniel Defoe wrote that gentlemen began "to fall in" with the King's interest and "fine gardens and fine houses began to grow up in every corner." An extraordinary example of what became known as a "Dutch garden" still remains at Levens Hall in Westmorland. It is referred to as "Dutch" because it is limited in scale (the Hollanders used their land sparingly) and is crowded with topiary specimens and flower beds. The clipped figures, now grown out of all proportion to the space they occupy, form one of the most delightful collections of topiary art anywhere. The garden plan has scarcely been changed since 1689, and though it is called "Dutch," a Monsieur Beaumont, a French pupil of Le Nôtre who had worked at Hampton Court during James II's short reign, was responsible for it. Other particularly fine examples of topiary work are at Compton Wynyates in Warwickshire, one of the loveliest old houses in England. Seen from the open hillside surrounding the house and garden the topiary garden resembles a giant chess board with the pieces at play. At Hever Castle in Kent there actually are chessmen formed from yew.

The French ideal of spacious and symmetrical gardens captured the fancy of most wealthy landowners in England. Fortunately, many of the impressive estates they developed were depicted in a series of engravings by Léonard Knyff and Jan Kip, known as *Le Nouveau Théâtre de la Grande Bretagne*. Since none of these country seats exists today in its entirety and many of those that partially remain have had their gardens restyled, these engravings form a valuable record of the closing years of the seventeenth century. Almost without exception, a grassy forecourt bisected by a wide walk and defined by grillework fences and imposing gates lay before the immediate entrance to a mansion. A grass parterre was usually adjacent to the house, often with a central water basin and ornamented with *jets d'eau* and statues. Beyond were complicated *parterres de broderie*, and further away, trees planted in regular formation as avenues and *bosquets*. Formal groves of trees, topped and having smoothly shorn sides, now replaced the informal "wilderness" which Bacon had described as a necessary part of his "prince-like" garden. Clearings called "cabinets" usually had statues at the center. Batty Langley, who developed ideas about garden design and published them in a book entitled *New Principles of Gardening* in 1726, decried the custom of planting these woods in "the most remote parts of the garden," so that before one entered them "in the Heat of Summer, when they are most useful, one was obliged to pass thro' the Scorching Heat of the Sun."

Examination of the Kip engravings reveals the many divisions of the garden areas and the rather tiresome repetition of symmetrical designs. One begins to feel that Langley was quite justified in stating that "nothing is more shocking, than a stiff, regular garden; where after we have seen one quarter thereof, the very same is repeated in all the remaining parts, so that we are tired, instead of being further entertained with something new as expected." Langley (not untypical of artists of every century) was critical of the work of other garden designers and complained that their stiff and regular plans "were always stuffed up with trifling flower Knots, Parterres of Cut-work, Embroidery, Wildernesses of Ever-Greens and sometimes of Forest Trees whose walks ever had a niggard Breadth," and that gardens were "crowded with evergreens so that they had more of the aspect of a nursery than a Garden of Pleasure." But in Langley's own designs for ideal gardens he is reluctant to break with tradition even though he attempted to make them in a "more Rural Manner than has been done before."

The trend toward increased naturalness in all forms of art is reflected in the philosophy of the statesman Sir William Temple, who, in 1685, wrote of his liking for "the asymmetrical freedom of Oriental Art, as seen in Chinese painting and garden layout." But

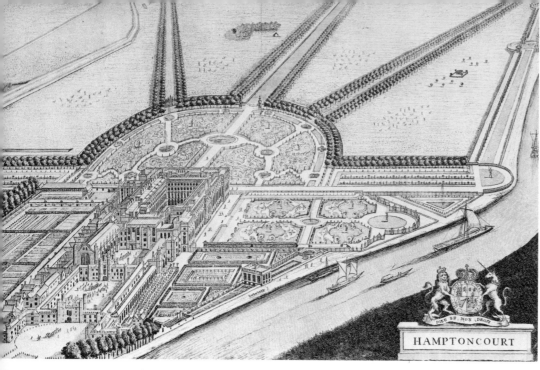

HAMPTONCOURT

(LEFT) Hampton Court at the beginning of the eighteenth century, from *Le Théâtre de la Grande Bretagne*, engraved and published by Léonard Knyff and Jan Kip in 1724. The avenues and canal formed a *patte d'oie*, or goose foot. (*Massachusetts Horticultural Society Library*)

(RIGHT) The engraving of Badminton, Gloucestershire, from the same portfolio of Knyff and Kip, shows severely plain forecourts of lawn and tree-lined avenues. (*New York Public Library*)

being realistic, Sir William thought that such adventures were difficult to achieve by common hands, "whereas in regular figures it is hard to make any great and remarkable faults."

England was due for a change in garden styles, for she had been gardening in prescribed patterns for more than five hundred years. In criticizing topiary work as "vegetable sculpture," essayists provoked a reaction. In *The Spectator* of June 25, 1712, Joseph Addison wrote, "Our British gardeners, instead of humouring Nature, love to deviate from it as much as possible. Our trees rise in Cones, Globes and Pyramids. We see the marks of the scissars upon every Plant and Bush. I do not know whether I am singular in my opinion, but, for my own part, I would rather look upon a tree in all its Luxuriancy and Diffusion of Boughs and Branches, than when it is thus cut and trimmed into a Mathematical Figure; and cannot but fancy that an Orchard in Flower looks infinitely more delightful than all the little Labyrinths of the most finished Parterre."

But perhaps satire had a greater effect on the gardeners than frank disapproval. With tongue in cheek, Alexander Pope published in *The Guardian* a laughable "catalogue of greens to be disposed of by an eminent town gardener";

Adam and Eve in yew; Adam a little shattered by the fall of the tree of Knowledge in the great storm. Eve and the serpent very flourishing.

The Tower of Babel, not yet finished.

St. George in box; his arm scarce long enough, but will be in condition to stick the dragon by next April.

A green dragon of the same, with a tail of ground-ivy for the present.

N.B. These two not to be sold separately.

Edward the Black Prince in cypress.

250

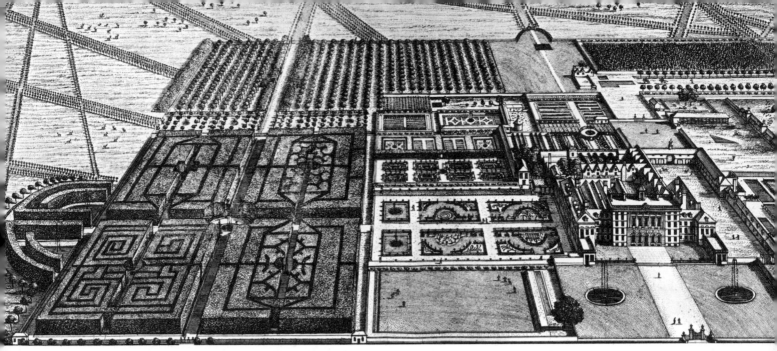

A laurustine bear in blossom, with a juniper hunter in berries.

A pair of giants, stunted, to be sold cheap.

A Queen Elizabeth in phylyraea a little inclining to the green-sickness, but of full growth.

Another Queen Elizabeth in myrtle, which was very forward, but miscarried by being too near a savine.

An old maid of honour in wormwood. A topping Ben Jonson in Laurel.

Divers eminent modern poets in bays, somewhat blighted, to be disposed of, a pennyworth.

A quickset hog, shot up into a porcupine, by being forgot a week in rainy weather.

A lavender pig with sage growing in his belly.

Noah's ark in holly, standing on the mount; the ribes a little damaged for want of water.

A pair of maidenheads in fir, in great forwardness.

(The phylyraea referred to above should read "phillyrea," a genus of evergreen shrubs sometimes called "jasmine-box" or mock privet. Savine was *Juniperus Sabina*; a drug made from the tops of this shrub was the common means of producing an abortion.)

251

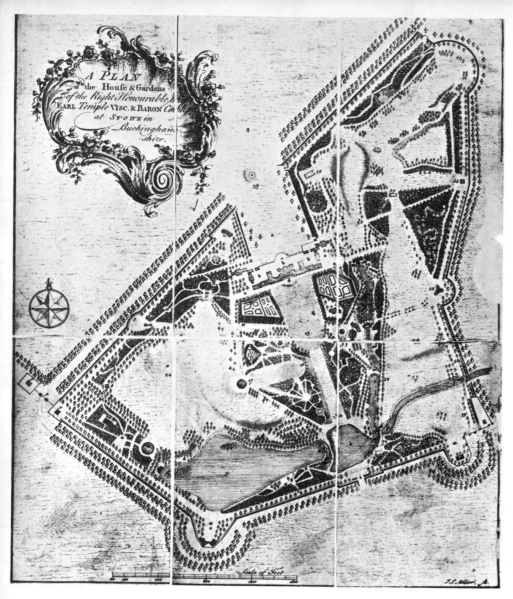

(LEFT) William Kent's plans for Stowe included formal gardens, two irregular lakes, and a belt of trees around the entire park. An engraving of 1773. (*New York Public Library*)

(UPPER RIGHT) Views of Chiswick House and a plan of its grounds, designed by William Kent. The casual winding of the paths seems self-conscious, but it was a bold first step toward informal design. 1736 engraving by Rocque. (*British Museum*)

(BELOW RIGHT) "Capability" Brown removed every remaining trace of formality in Kent's work at Stowe. He retained the belt of trees, added other trees within the grounds, and broke up all regular formations. From *L'Art de Créer les Jardins* by N. Vergnaud, 1839. (*New York Public Library*)

(BELOW) Stowe, as Charles Bridgeman developed it for Lord Cobham, had an ornamental lake large enough for boating. The mansion and Sir John Vanbrugh's Rotunda can be seen at the left of this wash drawing by Jacques Rigaud, made in 1739. (*Metropolitan Museum of Art. Photo: Roche*)

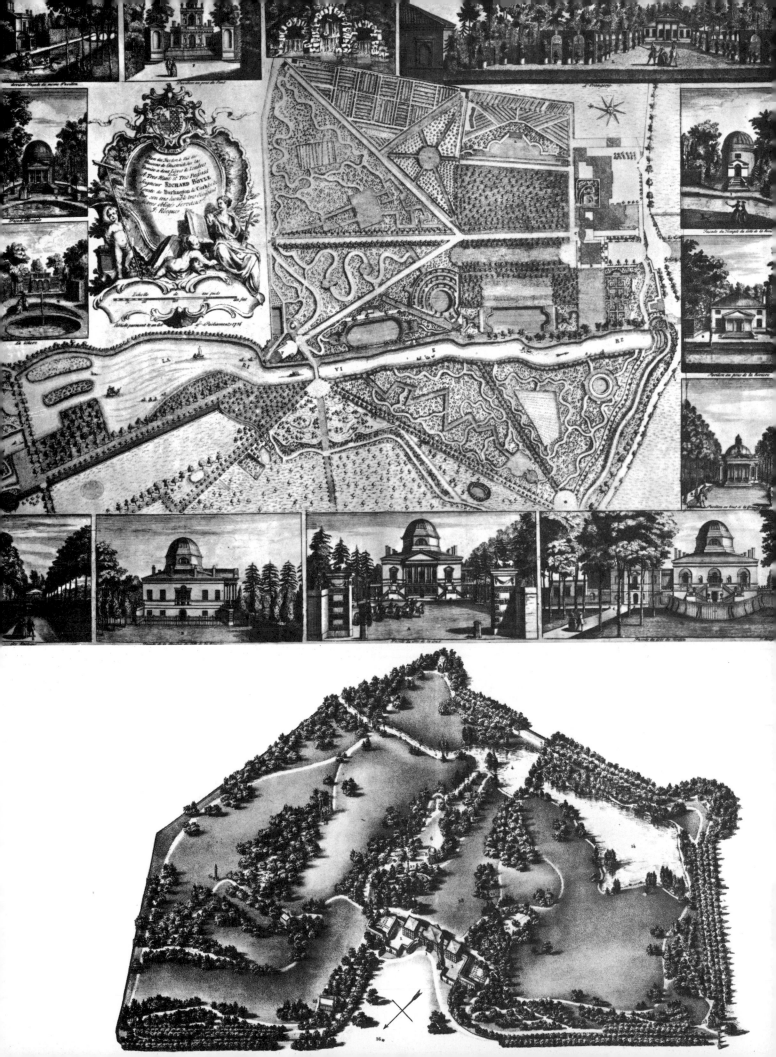

Plates

150. The garden at Warwick Castle has a glorious background of park land planted by "Capability" Brown. The superb cedars of Lebanon, grown to great size, add drama and color contrast, as do the peacocks, which roam freely. (*British Travel Association*)

151. The seventeenth-century "Dutch" garden at Levens Hall in Westmorland has become the most renowned topiary garden in the world. Although rather obscured by the size of the specimens, the plan of the garden remains as it was originally laid out. (*British Travel Association*)

152. The Emperor Fountain at Chatsworth, Derbyshire, thrusts its water two hundred and fifty feet into the air. In the foreground is the Seahorse Fountain. A plentiful water supply from surrounding hills feeds Chatsworth's waterworks. (*British Travel Association*)

153. View of the lake at Blenheim Palace, its island, and the partially submerged bridge. (*Country Life Ltd.*)

154. The lake within the park at Stourhead, Wiltshire. One of the earliest and loveliest remaining examples of the English landscape style of gardening. (*British Travel Association*)

155. The Chinese pagoda in Kew Gardens was designed by Sir William Chambers for George III's mother, the Princes Dowager of Wales. (*British Travel Association*)

150

254

152

153

The garden had been in bondage to the topiarist for centuries but once the excesses were held up to ridicule, clipped yew and box specimens, pleached allées, arbours, and hedges succumbed to the ax and the plow. The new garden practices that evolved conformed to the freer way of living and thinking that came into effect early in the eighteenth century. More than ever before, gentlemen studied the arts, sciences, and horticulture and practiced fine manners in order to mold themselves into what the Earl of Shaftesbury called "men of breeding." The Earl knew Italy well and had obviously been impressed by Cosimo de'Medici's Platonic Academy of "Humanists." In increasing numbers Englishmen traveled to the Continent and came to know the Roman campagna which Nicolas Poussin and Claude Lorrain had painted during the previous century. These idealized landscapes suggested that the raw materials for such beauty were nowhere more available or more beautiful than in the English countryside; therefore the natural elements of the surrounding landscape were composed into vistas, serpentine waters, irregularly shaped open lawns, and groups and glades of trees. But incongruously Italianate classical temples, ruins, and grottoes were added to the English garden scene. The landscape was made pictorial.

The eighteenth century became a golden age for England. It produced great painters, writers, furniture designers, and craftsmen, and also great architects and garden designers. In gardening the period is distinguished by the names of Charles Bridgeman, William Kent, Lancelot ("Capability") Brown, Sir William Chambers, and Humphrey Repton. In an essay called "The History of the Modern Taste in Gardening," Horace Walpole, writing in retrospect about the great revolution in garden design, referred to Bridgeman as the

> fashionable successor to London and Wise. He banished verdant sculpture and did not even revert to the square precision of the foregoing age. He disdained to make every division tally to its opposite, and though he still adhered to strait walks with high clipped hedges, they were only his great lines; the rest he diversified by wildernesses, and with loose groves of oak, though still within surrounding hedges. But the capital stroke . . . was the destruction of walls for boundaries, and the invention of fosses — an attempt then deemed so astonishing, that the common people called them Ha! Ha's! to express their surprize at finding a sudden and unperceived check to their walk. — The contiguous ground of the park without the sunk fence was to be harmonised with the lawn within; and the garden in its turn was to be set free from its prim regularity, that it might assort with the wilder country without. — At that moment appeared Kent, painter enough to taste the charms of landscape, bold and opinionative enough to dare to dictate, and born with a genius to strike out a great system from the twilight of imperfect essays. He leaped the fence, and saw that all nature was a garden, — his ruling principle was that Nature abhors a strait line.

The "fosse" (from the French word for ditch or moat) and the English term "ha-ha" both referred to the ditch cut into a slope and backed up with a brick wall. Invisible at a distance, it extended the landscape and kept grazing animals away from the house.

155 William Kent (1685–1748), whose career as an architect fell between those of Sir

Christopher Wren and Robert Adam, was undoubtedly considered a "man of breeding." In spite of humble origins, he became a painter, interior decorator, furniture designer (a contemporary of Thomas Chippendale), as well as the designer of classic-style mansions and extensive "parks" that surrounded such places as Chiswick House, Stowe, and Rousham. At Chiswick, near London, where the Earl of Burlington had built his Palladian home, Kent was retained in 1729 to landscape it appropriately. His solution was a rather timid attempt to break with precedent. The design included many geometrical areas divided by broad avenues, which, when seen in plan, seem a curious contrast to the several paths which meandered through the woods. Following the recent trend, symmetrically paired parts were not incorporated, topiary work was omitted completely, and tall trees were allowed to retain their natural freedom of form. On the other hand, as a gesture to the past, trimly shorn

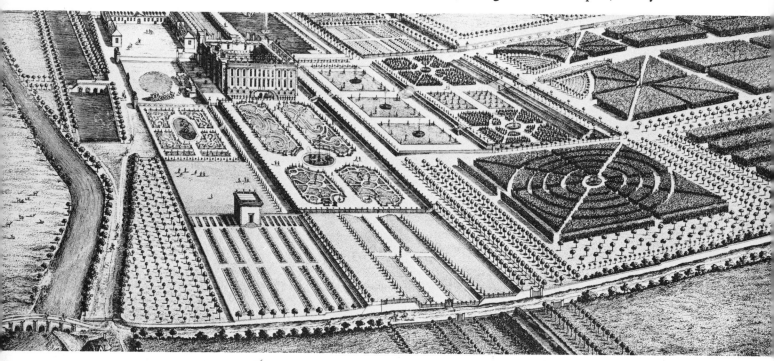

hedges divided the garden. Chiswick House has been fully restored and is now owned by the Ministry of Works. What is left of the original landscaping is well maintained and is open to the public as a park.

The only surviving example of Kent's work — in entirety — is at Rousham, near Oxford. The landscaping was completed late in Kent's career, after he had all but broken with tradition. On the thirty acres of ground above the river Cherwell he remade terraces into grassy slopes and created a number of self-contained landscape "pictures" within the natural contours of the land. In a small wooded valley, pools, cascades, and a grotto became Venus's Vale, and there was a seven-arched Portico of Praeneste, which overlooked the river bank. Although, according to Walpole, Kent's landscapes were "seldom majestic," he managed to achieve a fine interplay of light and shade. "Where objects were wanting to animate his horizon, his taste as an architect could bestow immediate termination." A stone Colossus, a bridge, a temple and an old mill all performed such functions at Rousham; there

(LEFT) Chatsworth House, before it was replanted by "Capability" Brown. This is another engraving of Knyff and Kip, showing the same typical design as at Badminton.

(RIGHT) Batty Langley's designs for an ideal garden showed an attempt to break with tradition and complete symmetry, but seem overcontrived. From his book *New Principles of Gardening*, London, 1728. (*The Pierpont Morgan Library*)

was also a termination, frankly called the "eye catcher" — a fake Gothic ruin on the hillside of an outlying farm! Kent went so far as to plant dead trees — in Kensington Gardens — because they gave "a greater air of truth to the scene." He probably had in his mind's eye Salvator Rosa's rugged and wild painted scenes, which included tumbled rocks, cascades, and torn trees, but he was soon "laughed out of this excess," said Walpole.

Most people agree with Walpole that one of Kent's major achievements in naturalism was his management of water. He banished canals, basins, and fountains and taught "the gentle stream to serpentize seemingly at its pleasure." From then on the word "serpentine" denoted an irregularly shaped lake, the classical example today being the Serpentine in London's Hyde Park. The cult of the irregular or wavy line strongly governed new garden designs. Hogarth's precept of the "Line of Beauty" was a fashionable topic, and an anonymous poet, describing William Shenstone's celebrated landscape garden, Leasowes, wrote in 1756 of "Yon stream that wanders down the dale, / The spiral wood, the wind-

265

ing vale" and also of "The structure of the Cyprian dame,/ And each fair female's beauteous frame," which "Show to the pupils of Design/ The triumphs of the Waving Line."[3]

When William Kent worked for Queen Anne at Hampton Court, he destroyed the parterre fountain garden (Anne said she hated the smell of box) by removing all but the central circular basin. All the rest of the area was turfed. His changes are to be seen today, but at Stowe, where he redid much of Bridgeman's work, his alterations were greatly changed by Brown's.

By the middle of the eighteenth century, England's most discussed garden was that of Stowe, Buckinghamshire, where Lord Cobham extended his park land from twenty-eight acres to five hundred. His lordship kept altering it continuously for almost forty years. Stowe became the most important show place of the Georgian period. Many hundreds of people visited it, for it was customary for people to tour the great estates. Relatives and

(LEFT) Plate from a French volume published by J. G. Grohmann, showing garden embellishments, such as memorials to faithful dogs "which the English love to erect." (*Metropolitan Museum of Art. Photo: Roche*)

(RIGHT) An eighteenth-century view within Kew Gardens. The swan was George III's royal pleasure boat, which brought him up the Thames River from London. Engraving by William Woollett. (*Kennedy Galleries, Inc.*)

friends stayed for weeks; others just came for a walk along the paths of one park, or to picnic on the lawns of another.

Stowe had once had a conventional patterned and enclosed garden, but early in the eighteenth century Charles Bridgeman freed it of such conventions. He removed terraces and boundaries and allowed the trees to grow naturally; he opened up straight avenues and terminated them with classic temples, columns, and obelisks, and designed large glittering areas of water which gave a more French than English effect to the garden. Sir John Vanbrugh, the architect of Blenheim Palace, designed a rotunda and pyramid, and William Kent added a Temple of Venus, a Temple of Concord and Victory (an adaptation of the Maison Carrée at Nîmes), a Temple of Ancient Virtue, and a Temple of British Worthies, which was a series of twelve connected pedimented niches holding busts of famous "gallant countrymen; Heroes, Patriots and Wits." Monuments, bridges, and pavilions also added to the variety, some thirty "eye catchers" in all. Decorations in some of the small buildings ranged from crude frescoes in the Hut or Witch-house (painted by a butler in the family) to the more titillating decorations in the Temple of Venus which showed a heroine of Spenser's *Faerie Queene* reveling among satyrs. Symbolism was enjoyed in the Temple of Ancient Virtue, a classic building with every stone in place, which represented the "flourishing condition of ancient virtue," and the Temple of Modern Virtue, a ruin, described as a "heap of stones which should have composed some regular system of architecture," but which in fact showed "the ruinous state of modern virtue."

Kent's greatest change at Stowe was the division of the largest expanse of water into two irregularly shaped lakes fed by a stream issuing from a grotto in the Elysian Fields. The bigger of the two was dominated by the Temple of Venus, and the smaller one became a focal point along the extensive main vista which swept away from a broad lawn immediately in front of the house.

The final stages in making the grounds of Stowe into a completely idealized natural landscape were executed by "Capability" Brown, whose genius unified the various garden

areas. Brown had formerly worked as a kitchen gardener for Lord Cobham, then as head gardener under Kent, so he had seen the place develop over the years. A comparison of the engraved plans of Stowe as designed by each of the men involved shows how far the landscape style had progressed in copying and improving nature, and well reveals Brown's completely satisfying achievement.

> The World, astonish'd as the Labour grew
> Exclaims, "What cannot Art and Nature do!"

So sang an anonymous poet of the time. Stowe has now become a public school for boys. It is near Buckingham and the grounds and garden buildings may be visited at fixed times.

After the success of Stowe, Brown, who was dubbed "Capability" because he always found "capabilities for improvement" in his clients' estates, soon became the most fashionable landscape gardener in England. The story goes that he once declined a job in Ireland because he "hadn't finished England yet."

Documents show that Brown received over one hundred commissions for work in different parts of the country. He undertook improvements at Warwick Castle, Longleat, Chatsworth, Cliveden, some of the royal gardens and, most notably, Blenheim. Little of his work remains untouched. The nineteenth-century introductions of such trees as the purple beech and such shrubs as the colorful hybrid rhododendrons greatly changed the original aspect of his gardens.

When Blenheim Palace (a gift from Queen Anne to the Duke of Marlborough) was completed in 1722, its south front looked down upon a huge parterre designed by Henry Wise. The grandiose scale of this garden complemented an equally grandiose building. The view from the front of the palace included the top of Vanbrugh's monumental bridge, which spanned a canal connecting two lakes and took in the unique avenue of trees planted to represent the disposition of the troops at the Battle of Blenheim. (The stylized planting of this avenue was subsequently altered by Brown, but in 1905 the ninth Duke had it planted once more in the original manner.) The avenue was terminated by a Column of Victory topped with a lead statue of the Duke. The bridge was criticized for being far too large — it contained thirty-three rooms — and out of scale with the insignificant stretch of water it crossed. "A man without straining could jump over it," Lord Berkeley remarked. However, the experienced eye of "Capability" Brown soon saw that the stream should be dammed to let the water spread out over the old banks and flood the ground-floor rooms. The deeper and wider flow lessened the bridge's apparent height and brought everything into better proportion.

The ornamental water was complemented with cascades upstream and was graced with an island. It is the first sight that greets the visitor after he has passed the archway of the main entrance. Turning a corner on the outskirts of the town of Woodstock, one sees in the distance the turreted palace on its hillside. The hundreds of surrounding acres billow with trees, carefully placed by Brown.

Brown's genius lay not only in visualization but in his ability to translate his ideas into practical reality. He was never thwarted by a difficult problem, even though it meant the lowering of a hillside, the elongation of a slope, or the redirecting of a stream into a depression that seemed made for an irregularly shaped lake. Land had to be drained, roads

(LEFT) A painting from Humphrey Repton's *Observations on the Theory and Practice of Landscape Gardening* which shows a scene at Wentworth, Yorkshire, as it existed before suggested improvements.

(RIGHT) A flap covering part of the painting is turned aside to show the proposed changes. (*Metropolitan Museum of Art. Photo: Roche*)

constructed, "ha-has" made, meadows sown. Lawns swept up to house foundations, and paths wound through the varying scenes of woodland, meadowland, and lakeside, and along the boundary belt of trees which defined each property. Views of terminal features, views looking back toward the house, and views of a countryside freed of hedgerows were all carefully planned. Large trees were transplanted, a few old trees saved and silhouetted, smaller ones grouped in copses; everything was gracefully rounded, cheerfully pastoral, and serene. There was little drama except for the contrast of leafy green trees with the dark of firs and Lebanon cedars. The studied simplicity of Brown's work and of the work of other designers of the period was as artificial as the parterres had been, but the resulting beauty was far more subtle. In his own time, as well as in ours, "Capability" Brown has been reviled as a ruthless destroyer and praised as a great master, but in whatever category we choose to place him he stands as a giant in garden history. Now, two centuries later, the English landscape park of the eighteenth century is a treasured legacy and one of the country's great tourist attractions.

While the famous designers were at work making changes many lesser-known talents and amateur gardeners followed suit. Two enchanting landscape gardens still to be seen are at Wilton (owned by the Earl of Pembroke) and at Stourhead (a National Trust property). Both are in Wiltshire and are open to the public all year. The great de Caus garden at Wilton was changed to the eighteenth-century fashion by its owner-architect, Lord Henry Pembroke. Throughout two centuries of cultivation the magnificent lawns and majestic trees and the meandering river crossed by the Palladian bridge have mellowed into a veritable Arcadia. The splendid triumphal arch, designed by Sir William Chambers as an important focal point on a distant hill, has been moved to the entrance of the estate.

Many connoisseurs consider Stourhead to be the most perfect remaining example of the picturesque landscape park. Certainly it is one of the earliest. Perhaps the only flaw is that it is designed as a self-contained unit, widely separated from its Palladian-style mansion. By damming a river and connecting several small ponds, its owner, Henry Hoare, created a large serpentine lake with a small island at one end. Sparsely wooded hillsides were forested with beeches, firs, and rare trees, and along the path beside the lake three small classic buildings were erected — a Pantheon, a Temple of Flora, and a Temple of the

Plates

156. A herbaceous border at Clare College, Cambridge. (*Country Life Ltd.*)

157. The nineteenth-century parterre garden at Harewood House is bedded out with a variety of flowers according to the season. Although its design and its pebbled areas derive from the seventeenth and eighteenth centuries newer plant materials have endowed it with a Victorian character. (*British Travel Association*)

158. Twin herbaceous borders at Ravelston House, Scotland, display William Robinson's tenets that the flower garden should be planted with an eye to height variations and continuity of bloom and should have a naturalistic setting. (*Scotsman Publications, Ltd.*)

159. Lord Aberconway's gardens at Bodnant, in Denbighshire, Wales, rank among Britain's finest. Three generations have brought to the gardens a rich variety of plant material. This view through a rose arbor shows a lily pond flanked with a perennial flower border. In the woodland below is a superb collection of rhododendrons. (*British Travel Association*)

270

156

157

Sun. There were also a rustic cottage and a grotto of tufa and flint stones, which was built over the springs feeding the lake. It shelters a reclining nymph sculptured in marble. The whole scene is supremely successful and its particular eighteenth-century charm has been further enhanced by the naturalization of hybrid rhododendrons and other flowering shrubs. In the spring the woods are carpeted with daffodils.

The landscape garden style gradually divided itself into two main categories. One school followed Brown's poetic distillation, and the other followed the picturesque and romantic creations of other designers. The latter allowed their scenes to be sprinkled with all kinds of "surprise" elements such as Greek and Roman temples, statues and altars, "Gothick" ruins, grottoes, Chinese pagodas, memorials to animal pets, and hermitages. Some owners even hired "hermits," but they had little luck in keeping them for long, despite the offer of good pay, food, and drink. Such garden fancies seemed absurd to Walpole, who decried this conceit. "It is almost comic," he wrote, "to set aside a quarter of one's garden to be melancholy in." Neither did he like grottoes, which in England's climate, he said, were "recesses only to be looked at transiently." Samuel Johnson, too, was critical of grottoes, which were cool and "probably . . . satisfactory in summer — for toads!" He also suggested that the statue of Venus in one of his friend's garden "be pitched in to the pond to hide her nakedness and to cool her lasciviousness."

After the cult of the classic and the Gothic (such as Horace Walpole's Strawberry Hill) began to wane, the newest inspiration came from China. Traders in the Orient, explorers, and gentlemen voyagers returned to England with *objets d'art* as well as with plants that had taken their fancy, and suddenly everything was *chinoiserie*. Chinese-inspired porcelains and wallpapers and fabrics with Europeanized Chinese designs were all the vogue. At Kew, where a royal pleasure ground in the landscape style had been fashioned by George III's parents (Princess Augusta, and Frederick, Prince of Wales), Sir William Chambers was engaged to make it more picturesque, and he seems to have planned something for everyone's taste: a ruined Roman arch, a mosque with two minarets, several small temples, a Moorish Alhambra, a Chinese pavilion in the menagerie, and, most eye-catching of all, a ten-story pagoda, which still presides over the gardens there. Each up-turned roof tip of the pagoda sported a Chinese dragon ornamented with pieces of glass that glittered in the sun.

Sir William Chambers first went to China when he was in his teens and employed by the Swedish East India Company. Later he studied architecture and, in 1772, as a well-known practitioner, published his *Dissertation on Oriental Gardening*, which was accepted as authoritative and widely read in England. Previously he had published a book of *Designs for Chinese Buildings*, but his better-known *Dissertation* served as a springboard for criticizing garden practices he disliked and campaigning for those he wanted to promote. Even at this late date in the revolt against seventeenth-century formalism he still felt it necessary to have the "Chinese artist" in his book remark to him that the fashioning of colonnades and palaces formed by precisely cut plant materials instead of stone was "purchasing variety at the expense of reason." Chambers' *alter ego* answered that "few objects were more strikingly great than a spacious road planted on each side with lofty trees stretching in a direct line beyond the reach of the eye; and that there were few things more

159

variously entertaining than a winding one," a point of view which happened to be copied directly from Sir William Temple's writing a hundred years earlier! The same "Chinese artist" expressed Sir William's own thinly disguised disapproval of Brown's ideals, remarking that "a little simplicity will go a very long way" and that English gardens "differ very little from common fields, so closely is common nature copied in most of them." Chambers own philosophy concerning the garden came through admirably when he wrote elsewhere that Chinese gardeners were "also attentive to the wealth or indigence of the patron by whom they are employed; to his age, his infirmities, temper, amusements, connections, business and manner of living; as likewise to the season of the year in which the garden is likely to be most frequented by him. . . ."

Chambers also expressed his great interest in those seemingly forgotten denizens of the garden — flowers. Only a few old engravings show flower beds planted in direct relation to the design elements of a garden, at the base of trees, surrounding a pool, or along an arbor. How modern it sounds when Chambers writes that color should never be used at random and that potted plants could fill gaps in the color scheme, with several plants in one hole heightening the effect of color mass. This idea was not new; Louis XV, as mentioned in an earlier chapter, used thousands of potted flowers in the gardens of the Grand Trianon. However, Chambers' observations led fairly directly to the custom followed in the next generation of "bedding out" the garden. Meanwhile his opinions about flowers were little heeded by his fashionable contemporaries, who were trying to outdo one another with landscape improvements.

The rage for the landscape and Anglo-Chinese garden swept Europe. It appealed to many gardeners who were satiated with French grandeur or who found it impossible to achieve Italianate terracing and waterworks. It also appealed to those who were continuously in search of novelty. Marie Antoinette made her charming English park at the Petit Trianon. Also near Paris, there were the *jardins anglais* at Bagatelle and Monceau, and elsewhere, including Germany, princes as well as Romanticists such as Goethe embraced the style wholeheartedly. Many volumes were published containing English ideas for embellishment, such as monuments to pet animals, bridges, false ruins, and shelters.

After Lancelot Brown's death in 1783, Humphrey Repton (1752–1818) became his self-appointed successor. Repton was eminently successful and within twenty years had carried out several hundred commissions. He also prepared red morocco-bound booklets in which his many clever "alterations" were presented in "before" and "after" scenes in water color. These booklets were so attractive that many were preserved in family archives, and some are now in public collections. Following in general the practices of his predecessor, Repton tried to correct some of the mistakes he felt had been made by Brown. Today, however, if we view the parks at Harewood, Longleat, Sheffield, and Holkham, all places which Brown had "improved," it is difficult to distinguish between his and Repton's contributions. In his *Observations on the Theory and Practice of Landscape Gardening* (1803) Repton expressed the opinion that "the baldness and nakedness around a house" produced by lawns that swept up to their foundations was a part of Brown's "mistaken system." He said, "A palace or even an elegant villa, in a grass field appears incongruous." Consequently, he frequently introduced a balustraded garden-terrace before

276

the façade of a mansion as a transitional device. In actuality, the sharp divisions between the house, the terrace garden, and the parkland were so great that no real transition was effected. Within the garden-terrace divisions flowers were allowed to reappear. The parks or "improved landscapes" were now found to be superb backdrops for flower gardens.

Repton's flower gardens were specialized ones. He was horticulturist enough to realize the importance of proper environment for plants, and introduced stones for rock plants and bog earth for American wildings. He also liked the idea of separate gardens for specialized effects; at Woburn, for instance, he planned a rose garden, an American garden, a Chinese garden, and a secluded private garden. Flowers, which for a century had for the most part been relegated to the distant walled kitchen garden, were now allowed to put in an appearance. Once more the pendulum of fashion was ready to swing back.

As new plants continued to be introduced from abroad during the eighteenth century, the Englishman's increasing preoccupations with botany and horticulture resulted in the building of conservatories where exotic specimens could be raised with special care. The addition of a greenhouse to a mansion was as much *de rigueur* as a membership in a scientific society. To rich and poor alike, the newly available trees, shrubs, and flowers which plant explorers brought back from China and the South Pacific, from North America and the West Indies, from Mexico, South America, and South Africa must have been an exciting revelation. Information about new species and their growing habits was disseminated through an increasing number of books and catalogues and through societies and important centers such as the Chelsea Physic Garden, whose curator, Philip Miller, wrote *The Gardener's Dictionary* in 1772.

The gardens at Kew, which George III's mother made into a center for plant research, also played an important part in all this interest, although the gardens were first opened to the public only in the early years of Queen Victoria's reign by William Jackson Hooker, director at that time. For almost two centuries, beginning with the first director, Sir Joseph Banks, who had accompanied Captain Cook on his first voyage to Australia, the scope of the collections has been continuously enlarged by such men as Sir Joseph Hooker, Robert Fortune, and E. H. Wilson. The names of Thomas Drummond, William Kerr, David Douglas, and George Forrest, added to those already mentioned, make but a small listing of all the intrepid and dedicated plant explorers whose names are attached to many of our most loved garden plants.

Aside from exotics for the conservatory, perhaps the greatest botanical interest of the mid-eighteenth century lay in the plants from England's colonies across the Atlantic Ocean. In 1730 the *Catalogus Plantarum* of the Chelsea Society of Gardeners listed eighty-eight trees and shrubs of American origin, but between the years 1734 and 1777 John Bartram of Philadelphia added to this number by sending close to one hundred and fifty different plants and seeds to his fellow enthusiast, Peter Collinson of London. So great were Bartram's efforts that he was appointed, through Collinson's influence, Botanizer Royal for America, with a yearly stipend.

In the closing years of the century rhododendrons, magnolias, camellias, kalmia, and laburnum added color to the new shrubberies. China asters, small flowered chrysanthemums, zinnias, dahlias, phlox, coreopsis, goldenrod, day lilies, and lupine were now avail-

Both "Capability" Brown and Humphrey Repton worked at Longleat, Wiltshire. Repton wrote; "This magnificent park is always open, and parties are permitted to bring their refreshments." Engraving from *Fragments on the Theory and Practice of Landscape Gardening*. 1816. (*Pennsylvania Horticultural Society Library*)

able and two striking new trees were introduced — the weeping willow from China (*Salix babylonica*), and the tulip-poplar, which came from America.

The proof that "what's one man's poison is another's meat or drink" is found in the writings of the journalist and essayist William Cobbett, who discussed the power of rarity in valuing shrubs and flowers. The American rhododendron and kalmia were "amongst the choicest" things in English gardens, while "that accursed stinking thing, with a yellow flower, called the 'PlainWeed,' the torment of the farmer," above all the plants in the world had been "chosen as the most conspicuous ornament of the front of the King of England's grandest palace, that of Hampton Court, where, growing in a rich soil to the height of five or six feet, it, under the name of 'Golden Rod', nods ever the whole length of the edge of a walk, three quarters of a mile long and, perhaps thirty feet wide, the most magnificent perhaps, in Europe. . . . But," he added, "be not too hasty, American, in laughing at John Bull's king; for, I see, as a choice flower in *your* gardens, that still more pernicious European weed, which the French call the *Coquelicot*, and the English, the Corn-Poppy, which stifles the barley, the wheat, and especially the peas, and frequently makes the fields the colour of blood."

An indication of the general interest in gardening during the nineteenth century is shown in the many books published during that time, some on specialized subjects such as city gardening, hothouse gardening, and gardening for ladies. There were many guides as well, such as *The Practical Gardener* and *Practical Gardening*.

In 1804 the London Horticultural Society was formed and later became the important Royal Horticultural Society. Its first experimental garden was in London, but a hundred years later the Society was given an estate at Wisley in Surrey, where the gardens now cover about two hundred acres. In spring each year the Society holds a public exhibition in London called the Chelsea Flower Show.

By the time of Queen Victoria's accession in 1837 an unparalleled eclecticism was apparent throughout the garden world. This had been brought about by the intellectual revolution known as Romanticism and by the industrial revolution, which had wrought drastic economic changes that in turn led to a general deterioration of artistic taste. Romanticists, strongly influenced by the novels of Sir Walter Scott, developed the landscape idea further by emphasizing Gothic design in summerhouses and arbors. Equally popular

278

were rustic garden shelters fashioned from tree roots and branches. Others, primarily interested in new plant materials, employed a fussy style based on the idea of the old parterre. Low-growing flowers were tightly packed into beds which truly resembled carpets spread upon the ground. This carpet-bedding or mosaic-culture is still practiced in public parks and other municipal plantings the world over. However intricate a design, symmetry in form and in color was, and is, the guiding rule. A bed of yellow primroses must be repeated in a corresponding position, or flowers of the same color and blooming time (such as yellow crocuses) must be used.

A great variety of colorful flowering material for "bedding out" was readily available to Victorian gardeners. Among the bulbs were snowdrops, scillas, hyacinths, tulips, and ranunculi. Low-growing perennials included *Phlox subulata*, *Primula vulgaris*, *Dianthus*, *Bellis perennis*, *Ajuga*, heartsease or pansies, forget-me-not, and candytuft. The brightest colors were provided by the annuals — French marigolds, ageratum, lobelia, calceolarias, scarlet sage or red salvia, verbenas, and geraniums. Gray houseleeks and the variegated coleus were chosen for their foliage. In order to maintain the eight months of bloom which it was possible to achieve if plants were rotated frequently, greenhouses had to provide thousands of plants. The small suburban home-owner (and by now there were thousands more around the industrial cities) often placed a single brilliant bed in the middle of a lawn, and for this they chose the showiest plants with the longest period of bloom. Usually these were annuals and the tender tropicals such as cannas, coleus, and wax begonias.

Preoccupation with exciting new plant materials was not the sole reason so many people lost interest in the landscape style of gardening. New philosophies regarding art contributed to the complete reversal of opinion. Whereas the eighteenth-century idealists looked upon the natural landscape and its "improvements" as art, the succeeding generation frowned upon anything which imitated nature realistically. This they said could not possibly be art because it was a deception. C. C. Loudon declared that the designer who produced a scene "in such a natural looking manner that it might be selected for copying by a landscape painter" had "exactly the same pretensions to the character of an artist as a manufacturer of artificial flowers." The geometric garden could never be a facsimile of nature; neither could the landscape that was planted with foreign trees and shrubs instead of indigenous ones. If the latter were used they could be planted in geometrical figures; never were they to "appear to have grown up naturally"!

With two such divergent expressions of garden philosophy as the romanticizing of the landscape and carpet-bedding with flowers, it seemed time for an innovator to effect a compromise. In 1883 William Robinson wrote *The English Flower Garden* — based on the observation, experience, and philosophy of a man who had a deep appreciation of the beauties of the plant world and knew how best to display them. His aim was to blend flowers and colorful shrubs with the landscape, in an informal and often naturalistic manner. He disliked the artificialities of bedded-out gardens — their stiff designs and blatant color, their need for constant replacements, their barren appearance in winter. With emphasis on the hardy perennial flowers, he planned wide borders which gave up to eight months of bloom in the country's generally mild and moist climate. Hedges, fences, or walls provided these borders with backgrounds both for further beautification and for wind protection.

Robinson appreciated the individuality of each member of the plant world and reveled in the form and the color of every specimen. He pointed out that color must never serve merely as crude pigment for the completion of a design, for a plant had other qualities such as height, shape, the type of foliage, the time of flowering, and fragrance. All these factors were taken into consideration when the herbaceous borders were laid out. Ideally, according to Robinson's recommendations, such borders should be between nine and fifteen feet wide in order to give the finest effects of depth and height variation. Today, there is no more glorious sight in the whole world of gardening than England's flowery and undulating perennial borders which edge her matchless green lawns, many of which have been mowed and raked for hundreds of years.

Another innovation was the naturalizing of daffodils and bluebells in the woods. Robinson wrote poetically of planting them in "cloud patterns." Snowdrops, primroses, and columbines were all sown in such surroundings and thenceforth could care for themselves. Azaleas and rhododendron collections were developed and set the pattern for such present-day attractions as Bodnant (in Wales), the Savill gardens in Windsor Great Park, and Leonardslee in Surrey, to name but a few. Naturalistic habitats were also provided in sunny and treeless rock gardens for alpines, among which the brilliant blue *Gentiana acaulis* lifted up its short-stemmed cup. In marshy areas retained for bog plants, clumps of the huge-leaved South American *gunnera* soon flourished. Robinson's valued legacy to future gardeners included the appreciation of every plant's versatile worth to the garden and greater ease of maintenance through the selection of hardy plants and their naturalizing.

William Robinson's famous disciple Gertrude Jekyll, whose several best-selling books and commissioned gardens won her renown and whose own garden at Munstead Wood in Surrey was an important influence, refined the process further. Through choosing appropriate plants she showed how spectacular effects could be obtained within very small areas. She stressed harmony of color and total effect rather than the inclusion of many "beautiful incidents," being against the "parade of conscious effort."[4]

While many people who have a taste for the historic and an interest in garden lore may seek out the authentic or restored gardens of the past, there are few who do not thrill to the beauty of the twentieth-century English flower border, its country cousin the cottage garden, and all the lovely woodland plantings. What can be more enchanting than a glade of yellow daffodils, a haze of bluebells, scarlet rhododendrons *en masse*, or beds of blue delphinium, lilies, or English roses? These surely fulfil Gertrude Jekyll's testament of gardening, which speaks for every gardener of every age: "I hold that the best purpose of a garden is to give delight and to give refreshment of mind, to soothe, to refine and to lift up the heart in a spirit of praise and thankfulness."

And so the English garden style has reverted now to an essentially private, though at times generously shared refuge. This it was in medieval times, this it failed to be during the centuries it went on display, first as a showcase for splendid living, then as a glorification of the landscape.

XI   *American Garden Heritage*

American pioneer life called for stalwart courage and back-breaking work, and the early settlers soon found that the utmost in moral and physical strength was demanded of them to withstand the hardships of the climate, loneliness, and never-ceasing toil, sickness, and death. The local Indian population, too, kept them constantly worried. But these intrepid people looked toward a better future, and their strong religious faith sustained them. The immediate necessities of home building, clearing fields, erecting fences, sowing crops, cultivating, and harvesting left no time for the creation of anything like a pleasure garden until at least a generation later, when communities or plantations were well established and there was a steady flow of newcomers, and labor, from the Old World. Each group that came brought its own garden traditions as well as precious packets of seeds, roots, and cuttings.

In the early seventeenth century two strong colonies were established in New England, the Plymouth Colony of the Pilgrims and the Massachusetts Bay Colony of the Puritans at Salem. They had left England as separatists from the Church. Arriving at the coast of Massachusetts in November, the Pilgrims had to wait out the long cold winter before they could plant anything. By March 7, 1621, when they sowed "garden seeds," most of their plant cuttings carefully brought from England had probably perished. But the seeds held promise, and the Indians, who were inquisitive rather than unfriendly in the beginning, taught the settlers how to raise corn.

Field work was for the men; the dooryard garden a few steps from the kitchen fireplace, the spinning wheel, and the cradle were the responsibilities of the women. These

281

Plates

160. A game of ninepins in a Dutch garden. Painted by Pieter de Hooch about 1660. Little formal gardens such as this were planted behind the houses in Nieuw Amsterdam. (*The James A. DeRothschild Bequest to the National Trust*)

161. The Stephen Fitch House and garden at Old Sturbridge Village, Massachusetts. Useful plants, protected by a board fence, were grown just outside the kitchen door. (*Old Sturbridge Village*)

162. Flower borders beside the long walk at Van Cortlandt Manor, Croton-on-Hudson, were planted by a young bride, Joanna Livingston Van Cortlandt, about 1750. Replanted now with a great variety of eighteenth-century flowers, they recall their earlier renown as "an earthly paradise." The walk connected the manor house with the family-owned ferry house and inn. (*Sleepy Hollow Restorations*)

163. A re-created garden of the mid-eighteenth century at the Mission House in Stockbridge, Massachusetts. A simple picket fence extending from the ends of the house encloses it, and brick paths mark out its symmetrical design. (*Paul E. Genereux*)

164. The pleasure garden of the Powell-Waller House at Williamsburg. Bulbs, roses, flowering shrubs, and small trees provide continuing bloom. The many outbuildings necessary to maintain a typical home indicate that these homes were really plantations in miniature. (*Colonial Williamsburg*)

165. Governor's Palace, Williamsburg. Through the wrought-iron north gates can be seen the garden, in which only trees, shrubs and flowers of colonial days have been planted. (*Colonial Williamsburg*)

166. The holly maze in the palace gardens at Williamsburg, seen from the mount. (*Colonial Williamsburg*)

167. Gay flower beds border the green lawns behind the George Wythe House at Williamsburg. Tree box hedges separate the pleasure area from the kitchen and herb gardens at the right and the dependencies on the left. The central walk terminates at a wooden arbor covered with pleached hornbeam. (*Colonial Williamsburg*)

168. The herb garden at the John Blair House, Williamsburg, gives a very clear idea of a parterre design, adaptable for either flowers or useful plants. Ease of maintenance was assured by the many brick paths. (*Colonial Williamsburg*)

169. A section of the ballroom garden behind the Governor's Palace at Williamsburg. At the right of the long flower beds a pleached alley of beech provides summer shade. (*Colonial Williamsburg*)

170. Standing at the top of the grassy terraces at Middleton Gardens one looks down on the butterfly lakes and rice mill, and beyond to the Ashley River and its bordering marshes. The river provided the most important approach to the plantation, as travel by slave-rowed barge was the usual means of transportation. (*Louis H. Frohman*)

171. West front of Thomas Jefferson's Monticello, with a section of the flower bordered "roundabout walk" in the foreground. (*Louis H. Frohman*)

172. George Mason, author of Virginia's Declaration of Rights, built Gunston Hall between the years 1755 and 1758. It has extensive parterre gardens on two levels and also a view of the Potomac River. (*Board of Regents, Gunston Hall*)

173. The gently terraced formal garden behind the mansion of Mount Pleasant, Fairmount Park, Philadelphia. A central path forms the main axis of a symmetrical plan and is now terminated by the Chinese summerhouse seen at the left. From this point steps formerly led down to the Schuylkill River. (*Philadelphia Museum of Art*)

174. The William Paca garden in Annapolis, Maryland, remarkably restored with the help of archaeologists. Terraces, water conduits, outbuilding foundations, and the outlines of a pond were retrieved from under fifteen feet of debris. A portrait of the eighteenth-century governor, by Charles Wilson Peale, revealed details of a two-story garden pavilion and a Chinese Chippendale bridge. (*M.E. Warren*)

175. Gore Place, at Waltham, Massachusetts, was inspired by the landscape ideals of the English designer Humphrey Repton. Governor Christopher Gore began building his home in 1805, and the parklike grounds were developed over a twenty-two-year period. (*Paul E. Genereux*)

176. The flower garden at the side of the Adams House in Quincy, Massachusetts, has a long history, for the paths and hedges, which form two rectangles, were laid out in 1731 and still define the design of the garden. (*Adams National Historic Site. Photo: Fasch Studio*)

177. In the Moffat-Ladd garden in Portsmouth, New Hampshire, are turf steps, over a hundred years old, which lead to the top level and to the shelter of an old arbor. (*Douglas Armsden*)

161

162

163

170

171

172

173

174

gardens were in the front or at the side of the dwelling, whichever enjoyed more sun, and each plot was enclosed by a simple wooden fence. A door opened directly onto the garden, and paths led to the beds. Within the enclosure all the useful herbs were grown. Seeds and plant divisions were shared with friends, and since roses, peonies, pinks, hollyhocks, lilies, iris, poppies, and pot marigolds (*calendula*) all had important uses, and the less showy perennial herbs added color and a variety of green foliage, these early gardens must have had a great deal of charm and served as constant reminders of the cottage gardens of rural England. Even though these stern Pilgrims frowned upon many pleasures, one could suppose that the small dooryard gardens became "pleasaunces" on warm, sunny days, when the womenfolk could sit on a doorstep and shell a pan of "pease" or churn butter.

The American colonies grew rapidly — in ten years (from 1630 to 1640) fifteen to twenty thousand Puritans emigrated to eastern Massachusetts. In 1628 John Endicott and a small group had settled Salem, and in 1630 John Winthrop, the newly elected governor of the Massachusetts Bay Colony, arrived with eleven shiploads of settlers. Spreading out in groups, they founded Boston and its surrounding towns. Some colonizers "were of the gentry," and the gardens they created were strongly influenced by the formal English manor-house style, with emphasis on symmetry. A central path usually divided the garden area in half. Walls, hedges, or fine fences enclosed the flower beds or knots and small, shaped evergreens adorned them. This tradition was seldom translated into reality until the eighteenth century, but a passage in Governor Winthrop's *History of New England 1630–1649* suggests that he, at least, had something more than a kitchen garden. He invited three French Catholic visitors to "have a private walk" in his garden on "the Lord's Day when all men either come to our meetings, or keep themselves quiet in their houses."

To visualize the gardens of the day much evidence has to be pieced together. The most valuable is the first-hand account of what plants were under cultivation, written by the Englishman John Josselyn, who made two voyages to America. His first trip, made in 1638, lasted a year, but in 1663 he returned for eight years and lived near Boston during most of them. The results of his travels, observations, and recommendations for plants and equipment were published in two small books for colonists, upon which very lives depended; the first book, *New England's Rarities Discovered in Birds, Beasts, Fishes, Serpents and Plants in that Country*, was printed in 1672; two years later this was followed by *An Account of Two Voyages to New England made during the years 1638 to 1663*. Most of the plants mentioned were edible foods and herbs, but in the list of "such Garden Herbs as do thrive there" appear "Marygold, French Mallowes, Fether-few, White Satten [*Lunaria*], Gilly Flowers [pinks], Hollyhocks, English Roses, 'very pleasantly', Dittander [*Dictamnus*] "and Tansie," all of which made colorful additions to any garden.

The Dutch who came to America must have brought with them much horticultural experience, for by the early seventeenth century they were generally acknowledged to be Europe's finest gardeners. Through crop rotation they had learned to produce maximum yields from the soil. They were expert orchardmen and great lovers of flowers, and when their merchant ships returned from faraway places with new "exotics," Dutch

177

artists drew highly detailed paintings of the unknown flowers and botanists published the new knowledge in books.

Where the Dutch settled on Manhattan, on Long Island, and along the Hudson River Valley they soon had orchards and *bouweries* (farms). Word was sent home that emigrants should arrive in New Netherland at spring planting time and that they should bring "domesticated animals" with them on the ships. The records and firsthand descriptions of New Netherland show that orchards were of great importance to the Dutch settlers, as indeed they were everywhere else in the American colonies. Pears, peaches, and cherries grew well, but apples were the key crop. Some apples were kept for eating but most went into the making of cider, the main drink of the colonists and of the country communities they had left behind. Although initial attempts to establish vineyards were made, none ever really succeeded.

In 1629, three years after their purchase of Manhattan from the Indians, a special class of settlers was encouraged by the Dutch under the patroon system whereby manorial estates were established. A grant of sixteen miles along one side of "any navigable river" (usually the Hudson) or of eight miles on facing shores, each extending as far back as "convenient," remained tax exempt for ten years, with the proviso that it be colonized by at least fifty people. The grants excluded Manhattan Island. These holdings became similar to feudal estates, the land being worked by tenant farmers and a few slaves. The basis of a landed aristocracy was then formed and it flourished throughout the Colonial period and into the present century. When the English took over in 1664 the manorial tradition was retained, and ultimately, between New York and Albany, a number of these early estates became the luxurious surroundings of nineteenth-century industrial magnates such as the Vanderbilts.

With a strong tradition of gardening behind them, the Dutch settlers soon started planting a few ornamental flowers, and their eyes were opened to the beauty and interest of native plant materials. From Adriaen van der Donck we have learned the names of some of the most popular flowers and the most common healing herbs. In August 1649 van der Donck had sailed back to Holland as one of a deputation of three carrying a Remonstrance to be presented to the States General. This document censured the West India Company's policy of imposing trade restrictions which "retarded population and restrained enterprice." Although the Remonstrance contained information about the physical conditions experienced in the colony, more details were added in the *Description of New Netherland* (*Beschryvings van Nieuvv-Nederlant*) which he wrote during the three years he remained in Holland to press the complaints. One paragraph translated from his book is pertinent:[1]

> The flowers in general which the Netherlanders have introduced there are white and red roses of different kinds; also peonies and hollyhocks, and those other roses of which there were none before in the country, such as eglantine [the single-flowered sweetbriar rose], several kinds of carnation, also gilliflowers, different varieties of fine tulips, crown imperials [*Fritillaria imperialis*], white lilies [*Lilium candidum*], the little lily Fritillaria [*Fritillaria meleagris* — the checkered lily or

guinea-hen flower], anemones [*Anemone coronaria*; tuberous-rooted], bare dames, violets, marigolds, summer-sots, etc. The lilac has also been introduced and there are various indigenous trees that bear handsome flowers which are unknown here. We also find there some flowers of native growth, as for instance, sunflowers, red and yellow lilies [wood lily — *Lilium Philadelphicum* — and meadow or Canada lily — *Lilium Canadensis*], the Martagon lily, morning-stars, white, red, and yellow lady's slippers, a very lovely flower, several species of bellflowers, etc., to which I have not given particular attention, but enthusiasts[2] would hold them in high estimation and make them widely known.

It is necessary to identify some of these flowers more precisely. For "peonies" the text says *Pejuyne* or *Cornelis Roosen*. In the past, several flowers with double blossoms have been popularly called roses. Some old Dutch books call the peony *Saint Cornelis roos*, referring to several saints of that name whose birthdays were in May and June. Gerard's *Herbal* (published in 1597) mentions the "double red peony with flowers like the great double rose of Province." Because of their straight stems hollyhocks had received the name *stock-rosen* (used in the original text) which means "pole rose." It is still in common use by the Dutch. Like those of the peony, the double flowers were supposed to resemble roses. For this reason the author grouped both flowers with the real roses and went on to mention others "of which there were none before in the country."

There has always been much confusion in the appellation of the clove-scented flowers. The text says *Nagel-bloemen*, which means carnation and which is derived from the word for clove, *kruidnagel*. In the old days the carnation was really the largest-size double pink (*Dianthus caryophyllus*). The Dutch word for gilliflowers was *jenoffelen*, which was sometimes spelled *genoffelen;* the French word *giroflée* and the English words "jilliver" and "gilliflower" are all similar and stem from the Old French word for clove, *gilofre*. They refer to pinks, wallflowers, stocks, and rocket. "Bare dames" refers to *Colchicum autumnale*, sometimes called "naked boys" or "naked ladies." The flowers appear on bare stalks after the spring foliage has died away. The "marigold" was *Calendula officinalis*, or pot marigold, a plant with many herbal uses. For "summer-sots" the text gives *Zomerzotjes*. This was the popular name for *Leucojum aestivum* or snowflakes. They received this name because, unlike the early-spring-flowering snowdrop, in Holland they were foolish enough to wait until early summer to bloom. Gerard's *Herbal* of 1597 says, "In English we may call it the Bulbose violet, or after the Dutch name Somer Sottekens, that is Sommer fooles." The lilac in the text is *Nagelboomtjes*, which literally translated means clove tree. The ordinary lilac (*Syringa vulgaris*) received this name from the Dutch because every floret is shaped like a clove. Of the indigenous trees, one would certainly have been the extremely showy flowering dogwood (*Cornus florida*).

For the Martagon lily the text says *singelen*. The herbal or *kruydtbock* of Rembert Dodoens, published in Antwerp in 1644, uses this word in reference to the Martagon or Turk's-cap lily. *Singelen* therefore would refer to the American Turk's-cap or *Lilium superbum*. "Morning-stars" is a literal translation of *Morgen-sterren*. The name still remains obscure. Dodoens used *morgensterren* to describe the European flower "goat's

Plates

178. The pleasure garden of the Powell-Waller House at Williamsburg. The tulip beds are raised, bordered with box, and edged with brick in typical seventeenth- and eighteenth-century fashion. (*Gottscho-Schleisner, Inc.*)

179. The flower garden at George Washington's Mount Vernon displays the flowers known to eighteenth-century gardeners. The beds, recovered from the overgrowth caused by neglect, have been maintained for over a hundred years. Mount Vernon's existence today is due to the inspiration and zeal of a Charleston lady, Ann Pamela Cunningham, who, during the Civil War years, organized and incorporated an association for its preservation. (*Mount Vernon Ladies' Association*)

180. Harking back to the Victorian era, a round bed of red cannas, red salvia, and coleus brightens a New Jersey summer home. (*Photo: Roche*)

178

beard" (*tragopogon pratensis*). It was too early, however, for this to have become naturalized in America. Morning-glories are not showy wild flowers and would have been included with the bellflowers, so they would be ruled out. The many varieties of the fall-blooming aster or starwort would certainly be a possibility, as would the flowering dogwood, which was actually called "morning star" by the nineteenth-century author William Cobbett. It does seem probable that van der Donck would have had the dogwood in mind when he spoke of the various indigenous flowering trees.

Lady's slippers were referred to in the text as white, red, and yellow *Maritoffles*. *Toffle* is the contraction of the word *pantoffle*, meaning slipper. *Cypripedium Calceolus* (the yellow Lady's slipper of Eurasia) was known in old Dutch as *Cypripedium Calceolus Mariae* and Dodoens called it *Marienschoen*, Mary's shoe. It is therefore easy to see how the American wild cypripedium became known as "Our-Lady's" slipper. The three *maritoffles* mentioned by van der Donck would therefore be *Cypripedium acaule*, the moccasin orchid or pink lady's slipper, *Cypripedium reginae*, the queen slipper orchid or showy lady's slipper, and *Cypripedium pubescens*, the yellow slipper orchid or yellow lady's slipper.

Since the campanulas, which we usually call bellflowers, are neither showy or numerous in the New York area, it is unlikely that van der Donck had them in mind. The term *klocke* which he used could refer to the convolvulaceae, aquilegia, and gentians, all of which have been called *klockebloemen*, or bellflowers, by the Dutch. Wild morning-glories, the red and yellow Eastern columbine, and fringed gentians might all have been meant. The English author Parkinson had previously grouped the red cardinal flower (*Lobelia cardinalis*) with the campanulas or bellflowers, and the Dutch would certainly have noticed and admired it.

Van der Donck's list includes tulips, crown imperials, and anemones, proving that the flower-loving Dutch planted a few things simply for their beauty. Most families probably grew them in kitchen gardens behind their city houses, in their dooryards, or along the paths of the country farms. Wealthier people, however, had little parterre gardens copied from "home." Peter Stuyvesant's city garden undoubtedly was formal; the governor also had a large country farm which was noted for its garden produce, fruit trees, and flowers. It was tended by more than thirty Negro slaves.

An interesting map of Nieuw Amsterdam, known as the Castello Plan, drawn five years after van der Donck's descriptions were published, shows a number of small, formally designed gardens. We can be reasonably sure that at least a few gardens of this nature existed at the time, but doubt has been expressed over the number the map shows. There were numerous empty lots in the city and the Directors in Holland, after receiving the map from Stuyvesant, expressed their opinion that "too great spaces" were without buildings and that the houses were "apparently surrounded by excessively large lots and gardens." Perhaps the map-maker took a few liberties. Any of the small gardens that did exist would have been correctly styled on the map and we can be reasonably sure that they closely resembled the gardens that Pieter de Hooch painted in Holland in the 1600s but without the garden statuary so common in Europe. Written records of the availability of box for border plantings have not been found as early as this, but in all likelihood the first box planted

180

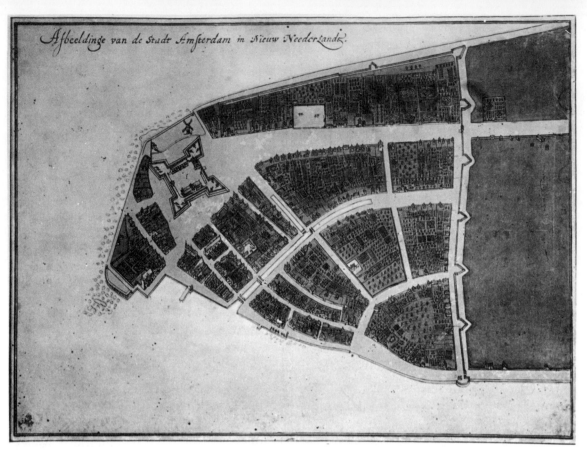

The Castello map of New Amsterdam, 1660, in which small formal gardens are clearly shown. Present-day Wall Street was the northern limit of the town at that period. (*Museum of the City of New York*)

in America was at Sylvester Manor, an English garden begun in 1652 on Shelter Island in Gardiners Bay, between the sheltering arms of Long Island's eastern end.

While the Northern colonies were still struggling with their economy, the Virginians became absorbed in raising tobacco. This industry became so successful that a stable economy was established in Virginia sooner than anywhere else, and with it a very different way of life began to evolve in the South.

It is important to remember that the religious dissenters of New England did not trade with England for many years, and the result was that before the eighteenth century their industrial progress was slow. And further south, the New Netherlands, founded principally as a commercial trading post and not as a new home for Dutch nationals, failed to attract enough people for any marked economic growth. This area was peaceably taken over by the English, who then controlled the entire eastern seaboard. The first colonists in Virginia, who landed at Jamestown in 1607, were "gentlemen" who arrived without womenfolk and without the desire to do menial work. The beginning was as rugged as in New England, but courageous and energetic leaders helped the settlers through the various adversities of killing fevers, combat with Indians, and the terrible so-called "starving time."

The man who eventually did most for the Virginians was John Rolfe, who, realizing the value of an extensive cash crop, tried and discarded the native Indian tobacco and planted seeds of "Spanish tobacco" instead. He acquired these seeds from Curaçao and Trinidad through the help of a sea captain. With their cultivation the colony began to

304

prosper, for tobacco found a ready market in England. The soil was rich, the growing season long. A first purchase of twenty Negro slaves from a Dutch trader provided needed labor. Women, wanted for companionship and home-making, began arriving from England, and they, too, helped in the gardens. With such emphasis on tobacco-growing, a law was passed in 1639 ordering all settlers at Jamestown who owned a hundred acres of land to plant orchards and gardens and to fence them in. These were for sustenance; tobacco fields were for profit.

Before long a pattern of existence was established in the South that lasted until the Civil War. Along the waterways of Tidewater Virginia, the unit of society became the huge plantation, entirely dependent upon slave labor for its existence. These plantations were self-supporting communities with outbuildings including kitchens, dairies, smoke houses, well houses, and "necessaries" (privies), all built near the main house. Farther away were the slave quarters, barns, stables, hen houses, and shops for cobblers, carpenters, and blacksmiths. Most plantations had their own wharves on a river front, from which great hogsheads of tobacco were shipped to England and to which came such imported goods as silks, porcelain, wallpaper, and fine furniture. The garden received its quota of imports also — bulbs, seeds, germander, dwarf box, and garden tools ordered from abroad. However, a great variety of local plant materials were available, and the grounds and gardens of the plantations took on a different aspect from their English counterparts. Native dogwood, redbud, catalpa, and the handsome southern evergreen magnolia (*Magnolia grandiflora*) all yielded blossoms, and the large trees, such as oak, tulip, and sycamore provided welcome shade in the gardens during the hot and humid summers. The design of the gardens retained the English-Dutch geometrical orderliness, dotted with trimmed evergreens. Dwarf and tree box grew well and were popular for borders and hedges, while brick walls and painted fences kept grazing animals out of the decorative knots or parterres.

In 1705, Robert Beverley, brother-in-law of William Byrd II, wrote a book intended to correct the many misconceptions held by the English concerning Virginia, and to attract able gardeners, possibly Huguenots. The English title was *The History and Present State of Virginia*, and we learn from its pages something of the "present state" of gardens. Residing in London, Beverley took the opportunity to berate his fellow Virginians by saying, "A garden is no-where sooner made than there, either for fruits or flowers . . . yett they han't many gardens in that country fit to bear the name of gardens." As a goad, he called his countrymen slothful and indolent. But his writing was not without enthusiasm too: "Have you pleasure in a Garden? All things thrive in it, most surprisingly; you can't walk by a Bed of Flowers, but besides the entertainment of their Beauty, your Eyes will be saluted with the charming colours of the Humming Bird, which reveals among the Flowers. . . . Colonel Byrd, in his garden which is the finest in that Country, has a Summer-House set round with the Indian Honey-Suckle, which all the summer is continually full of sweet Flowers, in which these Birds delight exceedingly." Elsewhere Beverley wrote, "The Inconvenience of heat is made easier by cool Shades, by open Airy rooms, Summer Houses, Arbors and Grottos." Flower beds, arbors, and summerhouses all bespeak the English and Continental style of gardening.

After the beginning of the eighteenth century, when Williamsburg became the capital of the Virginia colony, a number of families had accumulated wealth and gentlemen had enough leisure to occupy themselves with the planning and planting of pleasure gardens, while overseers and estate managers carried some of the burdens of plantation supervision.

As a loyal Royalist colony, Virginia kept in constant touch with the mother country, where an avid interest in horticulture existed. English botanists received plants from all over the world, well-established "physic" or botanical gardens flourished, and a number of informative garden books were published in London. The most popular of these was Philip Miller's *The Gardener's Dictionary*, which became almost a household necessity in the colony. About 1775 it was superseded by John Randolph's *Treatise on Gardening*, a work far more applicable to the needs of Virginians. Robert Furber's *Twelve Months of Flowers*, published in 1770, listed close to two hundred different varieties of flowers. Among them, in this "nursery catalogue," were eleven species with the name "Virginian" attached.

Long before the end of the eighteenth century, England had begun to lose its taste for formality in the garden, but the colonists clung to the earlier traditions. Few changes were made in concept and design, but a greater variety of plant material was used. Gardens literally became flowery. From Mexico to Europe, and back again to America, came the colorful "French" and "African" marigolds. From faraway places, but by way of England, came celosia, globe amaranth, China asters, nasturtiums, and the Oriental poppy. Combined with old favorites such as clove pinks, roses, calendulas, and larkspur, they made gardens more colorful and interesting. Native American plants were coreopsis, gaillardias, black-eyed Susans, blue phlox, summer phlox, and the asters of autumn. American gardeners were happy to receive the spring-flowering bulbs from Europe, and, in turn, English gardeners were entranced with the fall-blooming asters and goldenrod from North America. Both of these plants have been hybridized into greater beauty and are often seen in English gardens today.

An impressive number of plants was exchanged across the Atlantic and newspapers in Baltimore, Philadelphia, and other port cities frequently advertised the sale of bulbs when ships arrived from England and Holland. These exchanges would probably never have come about without the dedication of such plant explorers as John Bartram, Mark Catesby, and John Clayton and the generous and devoted sponsorship of men like Sir Hans Sloane and Peter Collinson of London. Some of their letters tell of the disappointments of receiving plants ruined by salt water, lack of water, or improper packing, but in reading others, we thrill with the exultation felt by Bartram when he wrote to Collinson, " I have now a glorious appearance of carnations from thy seed — the brightest colors that ever eyes beheld."

John Bartram of Philadelphia, farmer turned naturalist and explorer; John Custis of Williamsburg, member of the House of Burgesses, importer of many English plants, and owner of one of the finest gardens of the time; and Peter Collinson of London, wealthy Quaker wool merchant, collector of seeds and plants from all over the world, a true patron in every sense of the word — these three men were truly "brothers of the spade." Bartram and Collinson never met, yet they maintained a close friendship through thirty-eight years of correspondence. Bartram, traveling through Williamsburg on his explorations, was introduced by letter to Custis through their mutual pen friend in England. Collinson and Custis corresponded and exchanged plant specimens for eleven years, and during this period William Byrd II of Westover also sent specimens to Collinson. Byrd's garden was one of Virginia's largest. Its fame reached Collinson's ears, for he wrote to Bartram, "I am told Colonel Byrd has the best garden in Virginia, and a pretty greenhouse well furnished with orange trees. I knew him well when in England; and he was reckoned a very polite ingenious man."

Today Colonial Williamsburg, restored through the vision of the Reverend W. A. R. Goodwin and the generosity of John D. Rockefeller, Jr., forms a living textbook of eighteenth-century American history. It lives not only because of the undying memory of Patrick Henry, Thomas Jefferson, and George Mason, and because its houses, shops, and taverns are well and accurately furnished, but also because the many gardens, laid out and planted in the old ways, invest it with enormous beauty and vitality. The most extensive gardens are at the Governor's Palace, the finest dwelling in the colony. Georgian in feeling, yet with a distinctive Virginian plantation character, the palace was furnished with an elegance suitable to its role as the symbol of royal authority. The gardens that surround it were begun in 1713 under Governor Alexander Spotswood's direction and displayed everything that was traditionally best and most fashionable among the English nobility. In restoring the palace and gardens, the original wall foundations were excavated and every available old record was consulted. Gate openings determined the lines of garden walks, and an old engraving, which came to light in the Bodleian Library at Oxford, clearly showed oval beds in the forecourt and diamond-shaped parterre beds behind the palace. With careful symmetry, the parterre gardens have been laid out on either side of the long walk leading from the rear door of the ballroom to gates beyond. Bordered with box and planted with periwinkle (*Vinca minor*), these beds, combined with interspersed cones of clipped box, form an all-green pattern attractive the year around. Long flower beds lie beyond and twin necessary houses, classically topped with cupolas, are placed in the far corners. The whole area is walled at the sides and fenced at the rear. To the right is a greensward which could be used for lawn bowls, and on the left lie the kitchen gardens, a sloping orchard, and a canal. There is a maze of holly, a worthy rival to the one at Hampton Court, and looking down on it is a tree-shaded mount conveniently protecting an icehouse. Handsome detailing includes wrought-iron gates, lead finials and urns, and wooden settees, all of which appeared in the old inventories of the palace. These gardens and the dwelling itself formed a truly impressive setting for formal entertaining — perhaps too impressive, for the colonists finally dubbed the Governor's residence "palace" after they had been levied for its construction more than once. The money spent on the gardens must have also been criticized, for Governor Spotswood declared in 1718 that "if the Assembly did not care to be at the Expence of the Fish-Pond and Falling Gardens," he would pay for them himself.

The palace grounds and all plantations in general were large enough to allow the outbuildings to be placed in spacious architectural relationship with the house, without intruding on the garden area. In the much smaller town lots, since the prevailing garden style was geometrical, the inclusion of dependencies could also be accomplished with good taste.

There is little of the haphazard in Williamsburg gardens. The town was planned by Sir Francis Nicholson, Governor from 1698 to 1705, when the Jamestown legislators decided to move the capital to a healthier location, then named Middle Plantation and the site of the College of William and Mary. Originally each house lot was half an acre, and by ordinance every house along Duke of Gloucester Street was set back exactly six feet. All lots had to be fenced or walled at the uniform height of four and a half feet, and behind every house was a garden area.

Usually the flower and vegetable gardens were separated, but sometimes they formed a single unit. In the flower gardens there is little basic variation in design; either they are divided by a central path and have crosswalks, or the garden pattern is developed around an oval, circle, rectangle, or square, from which paths radiate. That the cultivation of flowers was fairly general we know from different sources including Robert Beverley's statement that Virginians derived entertainment "from the Beauty of a Bed of Flowers." Dwarf box, which thrives so well in Virginia, has always been the preferred edging for garden beds, since it is so slow-growing that it does not need frequent clipping, nor does it soon crowd the paths. Lawn maintenance was difficult in the hot summers and not much area was given over to grass in the compactly designed gardens.

In the James River area there are still handsome plantation houses that have stood since the early eighteenth century. However, the surrounding lands that once formed part of each estate have shrunk to only a small portion of the original size. In the old days when travel was difficult, people exchanged long social visits. In the same spirit of hospitality visitors are still welcomed into the fine brick houses of Virginia, and many of the gardens are open to the public each April during Virginia Garden Week. Far-sighted owners have preserved such places as Shirley, lived in by the Carter family since 1723; Berkeley, home of the Harrison family, which produced two presidents; Westover, seat of the famous Byrd family; and Brandon, one of the most magnificent of the estates and the one with the oldest land grant. Enough gratitude can never be expressed to the members of the Garden Club of Virginia, who have faithfully re-created gardens such as Stratford, home of the Lees; Kenmore, where George Washington's sister, Betty Lewis, lived: and Gunston Hall, home of George Mason, the author of Virginia's Declaration of Rights and friend and neighbor of George Washington.

The relaxation afforded men's minds by garden planning is nowhere more apparent than in the life of America's first president. Soldier, statesman, and above all a country gentleman, George Washington deeply loved his land. He spent many years developing Mount Vernon, the estate on the Potomac River which he inherited from his half-brother in 1754. After marrying Martha Custis he took up residence there, and for fifteen years, from 1759 until 1775, when he was made Commander-in-Chief of the Continental Army, he had the opportunity to enlarge what he called the "Great House," bring in roads, start planting trees, and lay out the gardens. His diaries and letters give a complete picture of how his plans took shape and of his keen interest in landscaping.

One of the first steps Washington took in improving his inheritance was to order from England Batty Langley's book *New Principles of Gardening, the Laying Out and Planting of Parterres, Groves, Wildernesses, Labyrinths, Avenues, Parks etc; after a more*

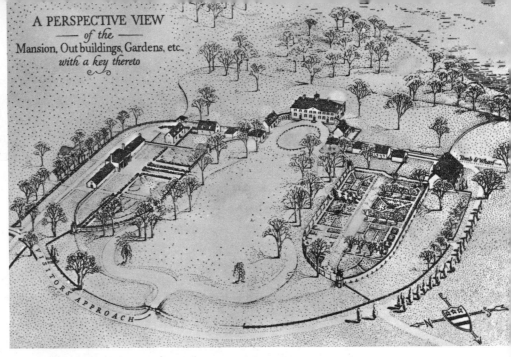

A PERSPECTIVE VIEW
of the
Mansion, Out buildings, Gardens, etc.,
with a key thereto

The careful restoration of Mount Vernon, as it exists today, is due to the inspiration and zeal of a Charleston lady, Ann Pamela Cunningham. (*Mount Vernon Ladies' Association*)

Grand and Rural Manner than has been done before. The pages are filled with information about fruit trees, forest trees, evergreens, and flowering shrubs, and no doubt the book gave many helpful ideas. Early in his planning Washington attempted to hire trained gardeners from abroad who would take care of the greenhouse and the kitchen and flower gardens. Conditions were set forth in a letter addressed to a London firm in 1771:

> Captns. of Ships . . . I know make a practise of engaging Tradesmen of different kinds upon Indenture for four or five years and bring them over from whence I conclude a Gardner may be had in the same way but rather than fail I would give moderate wages. I do not desire any of your fine fellows who will content themselves with Planning of Work, I want a Man that will labour hard, knowing at the same time how to keep a Garden in good Order and Sow Seed in their proper Seasons in ground that he has prepared well for the reception of them.

Washington did not see Mount Vernon from the time he left to attend the Continental Congress in Philadelphia until six years later, when he stopped off on his way to Yorktown. He had left a distant cousin in charge, and in the letters addressed to him during campaigns we become acquainted with new plans and the progress of old ones. His particular interest in trees is revealed in a letter from New York in 1776, stating that he wished trees to be planted "in the room of all dead ones in proper time this Fall." He ordered groves of trees to be started at each end of the house,

> without any order or regularity (but pretty thick as they can at any time be thin'd) and to consist that at the North end, of locusts altogether, and that at the South, of all the clever kind of Trees (especially flowering ones) that can be got, such as Crab apple, Poplar, Dogwood, Sassafras, Laurel, Willow (especially yellow and Weeping Willow) . . . these to be interspersed here and there with ever greens such as Holly, Pine, and Cedar, also Ivy; to these may be added the Wild flowering Shrubs of the larger kind, such as the fringe Tree and several other kinds that might be mentioned.

309

In a later letter, from Newburgh, he expressed the thought: "It is easy to extirpate Trees from any spot but time only can bring them to maturity." A particularly poignant letter tells of great worry over national events, and also concern about his trees. On December 17, 1776 he wrote, "Matters to my view, but this I say in confidence to you, as a friend, wear so unfavourable an aspect (not that I apprehend half so much danger from Howes Army, as from the dissaffection of the three States of New York, Jersey and Pennsylvania) that I would look forward to unfavorable Events." After giving instructions to hide his personal papers in the event that the enemy's fleet came up the Potomac River, he continued, "If I never did, in any of my Letters, desire you to Plant locusts across from the New Garden to the Spinning House . . . I must request it now in this Letter. Let them be tall and strait bodied and about Eight or ten feet to the first Limbs, plant them thick enough for the limbs to Interlock when the Trees are grown, for Instance 15 or 16 feet a part."

These letters show that Mount Vernon was to be developed in the new English manner of ornamental landscaping — lawns sweeping up to the house on both fronts, and formal areas taking their places in the more secluded spots at each side of the bowling green. The "groves, shrubberies and wildernesses" bordering the serpentine drives had direct English antecedents.

After Yorktown, but before Washington became President, the garden plan was completed in a successful blend of the formal and the informal style. In all its details it reveals his fine sense of design coupled with a broad knowledge of plant materials. Both the kitchen and the flower garden were enlarged from their original rectangular shapes and their walls were rebuilt to terminate in small octagonal summerhouses. The orangerie, or greenhouse, was built at one side of the flower garden, and a small botanical garden was set aside for experimentation. The box of the parterre garden was started with a gift of plants from Colonel Henry (Light-Horse Harry) Lee, Jr., of Stratford. Many other gifts came from old friends, and plants were frequently purchased. A shipment of one hundred and ninety-six items came from John Bartram.

Mount Vernon offered release from the pressures of public life only fifteen times during Washington's two terms as President, but he again found tranquillity there for two and a half years before he died. He once wrote "that to be a cultivator of Land has been my favorite amusement," and how well he accomplished this is summed up by a foreign visitor: "The whole plantation, the garden, and the rest, prove well that a man born with natural taste may guess a beauty without having ever seen its model. The General has never left America; but when one sees his house and his home and his garden, it seems as if he had copied the best samples of the grand old homesteads of England."

Thomas Jefferson repeated Washington's sentiments when he wrote to Charles Willson Peale, "No occupation is so delightful to me as the culture of the earth, and no culture comparable to that of the garden. I am still devoted to the garden. But though an old man, I am but a young gardener." Jefferson and Washington developed their homes and gardens under rather similar conditions; both were several times recalled to public life, and any consecutive work in planning and planting was difficult to maintain. But Jefferson, while serving his country in many important capacities, had opportunities for viewing interesting gardens both at home and abroad. During his years as Minister to France (1784–1789) he visited Germany and Italy and spent one April with John Adams, then Minister in London, touring a number of the large English estates. Both men admired and took notes on the landscaped parks of Stowe, Chiswick, and Blenheim.

In a letter to William Hamilton of Philadelphia in July 1806, Jefferson stated his intentions of following the landscape style at Monticello: "The grounds . . . I destine to improve in the style of the English gardens. . . . Their sunless climate has permitted them to adopt what is certainly a beauty of the very first order in landscape. Their canvas is of open ground, variegated with clumps of trees distributed with taste. They need no more of wood than will serve to embrace a lawn or a glade. But under the beaming, constant, and almost vertical sun of Virginia, shade is our Elysium. In the absence of this no beauty of the eye can be enjoyed. . . . The only substitute I have been able to imagine is this: Let your ground be covered with trees of the loftiest stature. Trim up their bodies so high as the constitution and form of the tree will bear, but so as that their tops shall unite and yield dense shade. A wood so open below, will have nearly the appearance of open grounds." He proposed to underplant the trees with thickets of shrubs, particularly evergreens, "red cedar made to grow in a bush, evergreen privet, pyrocanthus, Kalmia, Scotch broom." He added, "Holly would be elegant but it does not grow in my part of the country."

Thomas Jefferson was fortunate in realizing his boyhood dream of building a home at the top of a small, forest-clad mountain on the family lands. In 1768, after the top of the mountain was leveled and roads were brought up, the designing and building of the handsome Palladian-style mansion — Monticello — began. Trees, plants, and shrubs were planted, usually in groups as the naturalistic style dictated. The kitchen garden area was developed as the result of fruit-tree grafting and the introduction of numerous vegetables and berries. When away from home, Jefferson frequently sent shipments to enlarge the plantings. Sometimes a wagon-load of farm produce was sent down to him in Washington and shrubs from a Georgetown nursery filled the wagon on its homeward journey.

A methodical person with an inquisitive mind, Jefferson kept a garden notebook from 1766 to 1824; it has proved an invaluable record for the restoration of his gardens and of many other Colonial gardens as well. The book records eighty-nine trees; sixty-four shrubs; one hundred and thirty-four annuals, perennials, bulbs, and roots; and sixteen roses — all introduced and tried, although some did not take hold. Little in nature escaped his perceptive eye, and no plant sprang up in the woods and fields or in his gardens that he failed to notice. His entries included the simple facts: "Purple hyacinth begins to bloom," "Narcissus and Puckoon [bloodroot] open," "Sowed a bed of forwardest peas and a bed of midling peas," "Both beds of peas up," "forwardest peas come to table," "Blue flower in low grounds vanished" (probably *Mertensia virginica*). He made notes whenever he was at home.

The house at Monticello was about finished when Jefferson assumed the Presidency in 1801. By the middle of his second term, major tree-planting had been accomplished and the place had a look of maturity. Then he started work on the flower-bordered walk which gives Monticello such a distinctive air. No formal parterre or box hedges were ever part of the garden plan, but beds of flowers were placed in the lawns adjoining the house. According to his directions these oval and circular beds were planted with pinks, sweet

William, single carnations, scarlet lychnis, double poppies, cardinal flowers, hyacinths, tulips, double anemones, ranunculus, scarlet Mexican bulbs (probably *Tigridia*), and *Amaryllis formosissima* or Saint James lily (also called *Sprekelia*). These flowers all occur in variations of red and it seems quite possible that he visualized garden beds of this color only. In the back of one of Jefferson's legal notebooks appeared a notation for "The Open Ground on the West — A Shrubbery." He listed nineteen shrubs which grew to a height of about ten feet, native trees, three vines, and the following hardy perennials: "snapdragon, daisy, larkspur, gilliflower, sunflower, lily, mallow, flower de luce, everlasting pea, piony, poppy, pasque flower, goldylock, trollius, anemone, lily of the valley, primrose, periwinkle, violet, flag." It is not clear whether he intended these flowers for the beds near the house or for the long border, but the selection of flowering material provided bloom throughout the gardening season.

Perspective view of Monticello as it exists today. (*Thomas Jefferson Memorial Foundation*)

The "roundabout walk" which encircled the west lawn — a gracefully curving gravel path bordered on each side with narrow bands of flowers — was created for strolling with family or friends. Four years after completion, the continuous beds were separated into ten-foot divisions, each planted with a different flower.

Unfortunately, Monticello was sold after Jefferson's death, in order to pay debts. After long years of neglect it fell into the hands of appreciative and protective owners and subsequently became the property of a foundation set up for its preservation. Today the house, its furnishings, the old trees, and the re-created flower border form one of America's great treasures.

Virginia was not the only colony to develop a plantation culture. Maryland, with its indented shoreline surrounding Chesapeake Bay and its flourishing seaports of Annapolis and Baltimore, had equally fine shipping facilities and fertile land as well. Much of her produce came from fruit orchards. Tobacco also added to her prosperity. Farther south, in the coastal regions of the Carolinas and Georgia, the economy became stabilized, first

312

with the growing and selling of rice and later with indigo, both bringing wealth to their planters. Cotton, grown inland at a higher altitude, became an important money crop in the early nineteenth century.

The cultivation of rice began in South Carolina at the end of the seventeenth century, in the area surrounding what was then called Charles Town. Along the Ashley and Cooper Rivers and the intervening Goose Creek enormous plantations were created by Englishmen with large land grants from the Crown. Many of them were already wealthy; some had been planters in Barbados, and all strove to re-create the pattern of English manor life. A number of French Huguenots also became part of the Carolinian society. Rice was originally grown in land-locked swamps where the water level could be controlled, but soon methods were worked out whereby the marshes along the tidal rivers could be used. Hundreds of slaves were necessary to cultivate this difficult crop.

Of all the beautiful gardens that were once created on these Colonial plantations, only two are left with pre-Revolutionary antecedents — Middleton Place and Magnolia Gardens (formerly known as Drayton Hall). These are still owned by descendants of the original families, and even though the gardens have suffered from wars, hurricanes, and an earthquake they have retained their reputation for beauty. Both gardens are situated on the Ashley River, near Charleston, and both have splendid river views and majestic trees. Through the years they developed differently and today each has its own definite character. Magnolia Gardens is enjoyed for its extensive naturalistic plantings of camellias and azaleas, first set about the grounds in the early 1840s. Informal woodland paths wind past black lakes which reflect the brilliant shrubbery and tall cypresses.

In 1740 Henry Middleton, second in line of an exceptional family of American patriots, began to beautify the extensive property he had acquired through marriage. He built the manor house on a site overlooking the river, then sent to England for a landscape designer. A hundred slaves took about nine years to complete the large, formal plan, which included a flower garden, rayed like the spokes of a wheel, a bowling green, a mount, and a long, narrow reflecting pool or canal. The slope in front of the house was carved into a number of grassy terraces reaching down to two water basins. Although it was necessary to provide falling water for the operation of a rice mill below, it was nevertheless a sure stroke of genius to create this pair of "butterfly lakes," which used the element of water as a link between the wilderness and the formal man-made beauty of the garden. Nostalgia pervades Middleton Place today. There is gray moodiness in the shrouds of Spanish moss which drape its oaks and cypresses. Paths once bordered with rigidly trimmed bushes and trees are now dark, shady walks beneath the old camellias, three of which are originals and the rest descendants of those presented to the second owner, Arthur Middleton, by the French botanist André Michaux. The widespread limbs and massive trunk of the "Middleton oak" proclaim its great age, and there are sad reminders of the two wars which swept over the plantation. One statue remains of the many that once stood in the gardens before British soldiers knocked off the heads during the Revolution. Only one detached wing of the original Tudor-style house is left; all else was destroyed by fire in 1865. The entrance steps of the main dwelling remain, alone and overgrown, mute evidence of Sherman's marauders. On many plantations after the Civil

Plates

181. A view in Cypress Gardens, north of Charleston, South Carolina. (*Gottscho-Schleisner, Inc.*)

182. Typical of innumerable Southern plantations is this live-oak avenue leading to Mulberry Castle, near Charleston, South Carolina. Such tree-lined avenues are frequently all that remain of once beautiful plantings which were destroyed during the Civil War. (*Ronald Allen Reilly*)

183. A twentieth-century California garden designed by Thomas Church. Ease of maintenance is stressed by the introduction of a mowing strip of bricks which outlines the lawn area. (*Rondal Partridge*)

184. A garden invades the living room at Palm Springs, California. The design is by Raymond Loewy. (*Raymond Loewy*)

181

183

184

War all that was left were the magnificent live oaks, which bordered the entrance drives, and which today seem so typical of the old South.

Many other plantation houses suffered the same fate as Middleton Place and live on in name only: Cedar Grove, Oak Forest, The Elms, Tranquil Hill, Bloomfield, and Crowfield (said to have been the most famous and beautiful of all). Modern subdividing has doomed others. But two remain: Mulberry Castle and Dean Hall, now known as Cypress Gardens. Although their gardens were originally designed in the formal European manner, the use of native plant materials gave them a highly individual aspect. Avenues and groves of spreading live oaks provided shade, the shiny broad leaves and robust growth of *Magnolia grandiflora* added elegance, redbuds gave color, yellow jasmine fragrance, and catalpas, dogwoods, and silverbell trees shimmered with a white airiness and grace in strong contrast to the permanent greenery. Today masses of azaleas grow beneath the gray cypress trees and are reflected in the black waterways.

The greatest change in all Southern gardens came toward the end of the eighteenth century when André Michaux arrived from France to collect plant materials in the Carolinas. It was he who introduced the *Camellia japonica*, the *Azalea indica*, crepe myrtle, the pink silk tree (*Albizzia julibrissin*), and the chinaberry. All are now widely grown in Southern gardens, but do not rightfully have a place in any Colonial or pre-Revolutionary scene.

The residents of Charleston have always been garden-minded. As early as 1732 the *South Carolina Gazette* advertised seeds and as the century progressed more and more advertisements told of ships arriving with cargoes of Dutch bulbs, rose bushes, plants, and more seeds, all destined for planting in the small, patterned gardens of the city. Oyster-shell paths traced the designs within their walls, and bricks edged the beds. Lawns were small and summerhouses and arbors common. In the nineteenth century Banksia roses and wisteria were brought from China, and the colorful poinsettia (*Euphorbia pulcherrima*) was introduced by one of Charleston's noted citizens, Joel Poinsett, United States Minister to Mexico. Today some of the most beautiful spring gardens in America are found in Charleston. They lie behind protective walls, but lacy wrought-iron gates permit small and provocative views of them.

In the North, concurrent with the height of the Southern plantation culture of the eighteenth century, port cities like Philadelphia and Boston supported a wealthy class of merchants who were eager to surround themselves with gardens worthy of their social standing. Philadelphia, initially laid out by William Penn with five city parks or public squares, maintained a constant interest in horticulture. Among the botanic gardens established there, John Bartram's was especially noteworthy. In 1784 David Landreth founded the first sizeable seed house in America and newspapers constantly ran advertisements of plant materials for sale. Behind city houses small formal gardens were planted with Quaker simplicity. Larger gardens were attached to the homes of German Quakers who settled Germantown, just outside Philadelphia. But the finest gardens and houses of all were created on fashionable hillsides above the Schuylkill River. These estates followed the prevailing English style, a combination of lawns, trees, shrubs, and parterre gardens. Statues, lead vases (soon to be melted down for bullets), clipped evergreens, *allées*, ponds, grottoes, and fountain jets adorned the gardens, and hothouses protected citrus fruit trees and imported tropical plants. Probably the first lemon trees imported to Philadelphia belonged to Henry Pratt, who bought Robert Morris's estate, The Hills, after the Revolution. Morris, often called "the financier of the American Revolution," lost his money in real-estate speculation and his house was burned during the war, but the fame of the gardens lived on. They were restored and the house was rebuilt and renamed "Lemon Hill" by the new owner. Citizens of Philadelphia called it Pratt's Gardens, for the public was frequently admitted by ticket. Fifty years later, Andrew Jackson Downing wrote that "at one time the garden was the most perfect specimen of the geometric mode in America."

Near Lemon Hill an equally famous home, Mount Pleasant, was built in 1761 by privateer John Macpherson. It was later bought but never lived in by Benedict Arnold. The gardens were high above the river, arranged in a series of three gentle terraces. An old description tells that the terrace nearest to the house was planted with annual flowers in

Lemon Hill on the Schuylkill River, painted by J. A. Woodside in 1807. The southern exposure of the slope made an ideal site for a large conservatory. (*Historical Society of Pennsylvania*)

the box-bordered beds, the middle terrace was for perennials, and the lower terrace was a rose garden. Both house and garden have been restored, in what is now Fairmount Park.

New England's farm folk and those living in small towns clung to their tradition of combination herb and flower gardens, as did the pioneers who pushed into the western parts of New York State, Pennsylvania, and Ohio. But the garden scene changed in Boston, Newport, Salem, Portsmouth, and other prosperous cities as larger and finer houses were built. From the very beginning, New Englanders had found fishing profitable, and in the eighteenth century shipbuilding brought a new flow of wealth through international commerce. Just after the Revolution, when trade abroad was revived, a French traveler, Jacques Pierre Brissot de Warville, writing of Bostonians, said, "Commerce occupies all their ideas, turns all their heads, and absorbs all their speculations."

By the end of the eighteenth century the separation of the kitchen garden from the pleasure garden, or flower garden, was customary, and what is sometimes referred to as "the parlor garden" was frequently created in front or at the side of a house. This garden was made purely for beauty's sake, an adornment for classical, freshly painted houses enclosed by gracefully designed picket fences. As vegetables and herbs were relegated to the rear, flowers and flowering shrubs, lawns, brick paths, and edging plants conforming to an orderly plan became the fashionable rule of the day. In the garden of the Adams House in Quincy, Massachusetts, flowers remained incidental to the planting of fruit trees in the eighteenth century; but in the mid-nineteenth century Charles Francis Adams, son of one President of the United States and grandson of another, laid out flower beds. Magnificent wisteria clings to the chimney and half smothers the stone library building, while an old yellow-wood tree dominates the lower half of the garden.

The growing season in the North was short, and the severe winters precluded the successful growing of box that was possible in the South. Lilac, however, thrived and can be said to be as typical of New England as crepe myrtle is of the South. New Hampshire likes to claim the first American lilacs, for some were planted there by Governor Benning Wentworth in 1750, but John Bartram reported lilacs in Colonel Custis's Williamsburg garden thirteen years earlier. In neither instance were they actually the first, for new evidence has disclosed that the Dutch of New Amsterdam were growing them in 1655.

Two especially imposing Boston estates, forerunners of the many fine houses and gardens created later in the eighteenth century, were those of Thomas Hancock, uncle of John Hancock, and of Andrew Faneuil, the French Huguenot. The Faneuil house was set back from the street and, across a terraced flower garden, commanded a fine view of Boston Common. Wrought-iron railings topped with golden balls, a pagoda-like summerhouse flaunting a gilded grasshopper vane copied from the one on the London Royal Exchange, a hothouse, and extensive grounds attended by professional English gardeners made this a famous show place in the 1730s.

Thomas Hancock's house was also on Beacon Hill; his interest in gardening as well as several of the trials and tribulations of ordering from abroad are disclosed in some very human letters written from Boston to a nurseryman in England. In the summer of 1736, he ordered some fruit trees, requesting the nurseryman to "be Carefull That ye Trees be Took up in ye Right Season, and if these answer my Expectations I shall want more, and it will Ly in my way to Recommend Some Friends to you." The following December he wrote a letter of acknowledgement:

Sir, . . . My Trees and Seeds pr. Capt. Bennett Came Safe to hand and I like them very well. I Return you my hearty Thanks for the Plumb Tree and Tulip Roots you were pleased to make me a Present off, which are very Acceptable to me. I have sent my friend Mr. Wilks a memo to procure for me 2 or 3 Doz. Yew Trees Some Hollys & Jessamin Vines & if you have any Particular, Curious Things not of a high price will Beautifie a flower Garden, Send a Sample with the price of a catalogue of 'em; pray send me a Catalogue of what Fruit you have that are Dwarf Trees and Espaliers. I shall want Some next Fall for a Garden I am going to lay out next Spring. My Gardens all Lye on the South Side of a hill, with the most beautiful Assent to the Top & it is Allowed on all hands the Kingdom of England don't afford so Fine a Prospect as I have both of Land and water. Neither do I intend to Spare any Cost or Pains in making my Gardens Beautiful or Profitable.

If you have any Knowledge of Sir John James he has been on the Spott & is perfectly acquainted with its Situation & I believe has as high an Opinion of it as myself & will give it as Great a Carractor. Let me know also what you'l Take for 100 Small Yew Trees in the Rough, which I'd Frame up here to my own Fancy. If I can Do you any Service here I shall Be Glad & be assured I'll not forgett your Favour....

> Your most Obedt Servant,
> THOMAS HANCOCK.

The following June, in bitter disappointment, he wrote:

Sir, ... I Rec'd your Letter & your Baskett of flowers per Capt. Morris, & Have Desired Francis Wilks Esqu. to pay you £26 for them *Though they are Every one Dead*. The Trees I rec'd Last Year are above half Dead too, — the Hollys all Dead but one, & worse than all is, the Garden Seeds and Flower Seeds which you sold Mr. Wilks for me Charged at £6.4s.2d. Sterling were not worth one farthing. Not one of all the Seeds Came up Except the Asparrow Grass, So that my Garden is Lost for me this Year. I Tryed the Seeds both in Town and Country & all proved alike bad. I spared Mr. Hubbard part of them *and they All Served him the Same*. I think Sir you have not done well by me in this thing, for me to send 1000 Leagues and Lay out my money & be so used & Disappointed is very hard to Bare, & so I doubt not but you will Consider the matter & Send me over Some more the Same Sort of Seeds that are Good & Charge me nothing for them, — if you don't I shall think you have imposed upon me very much, & t'will Discourage me from Sending again for Trees or Seeds from you. I conclude,

> Your Humble Serv't,
> T.H.

P.s *The Tulip Roots you were pleased to make a present off to me are all Dead as well.*

His utter disgust and disappointment are not at all difficult for a gardener to imagine.

It is fortunate for us that it was customary to keep a copy of a business letter even in those days, when it had to be laboriously hand written. Many such documents have turned up in family records and throw light on many obscure and fascinating details regarding architecture, furniture, and gardens. From Hancock's correspondence we learn that dwarf and espaliered fruit trees were grown, that yew trees instead of box were used for topiary specimens (Hancock used the term "framed"), and that his flower garden was a separate entity, intended to be as beautiful as flowers could make it.

Many fine eighteenth-century houses remain in New England today, but many more have disappeared or have been altered or neglected almost beyond repair, as neighborhoods have changed their character. The same has happened to the gardens. Happily, with growing frequency, the Colonial Dames, garden clubs, foundations, and women's committees are assisting with the re-creation of old-style gardens. While certain worth-while houses can be restored, in nearly every case the garden must be re-created. In recent years this has been somewhat easier because eighteenth-century plant materials have been thoroughly researched and are listed in a number of publications.

At the turn of the century, two outstanding estates, partially intact today, were created in Waltham, Massachusetts. Both were inspired by the English landscape style. George Washington, Thomas Jefferson, and John Penn had already experimented successfully in this direction, but it remained for Theodore Lyman and Governor Christopher Gore of Boston to achieve completely "naturalistic" scenes which included water, fields,

The Hermitage, near Nashville, Tennessee, was the home of President Andrew Jackson. The garden, designed in 1819 by an Englishman, William Frost, is planted with spring bulbs and other old favorites. (*Tennessee Conservation Department*)

and skillfully placed trees. Lyman retained the services of an English garden designer, William Bell, who had been trained in Humphrey Repton's theories, and the outstanding mansion and grounds called "The Vale" remained a monument to the combined talents of this gardener, the owner, and the architect Samuel McIntire of Salem. The large white clapboard house was built on a gentle hill overlooking meadows, a deer park, and a pond. The pleasure grounds, developed behind the house, had a wide lawn informally bordered with paths and planted with specimen trees. An early inventory lists over thirty kinds of trees, but today two pines and an impressive purple beech with four trunks are probably the only original ones left. At the back of the lawn a long brick wall joins the greenhouses at one end and a charming white summerhouse with Corinthian columns at the other. Another small garden shelter is incorporated in the wall where it turns a slight angle. Along a stretch facing south, referred to as the peach wall, peach trees were always espaliered, and a perennial flower border, now edged with hundred-year-old box, blooms in front. Hidden behind the wall was the kitchen garden.

At the neighboring country seat, all the elements of Romanticism were again combined — hillside sites, large expanses of lawn, a park, and "every variety of forest tree." Gore Place overlooked its own duck ponds and the Charles River as well. Christopher Gore had stayed in London from 1796 to 1804 as chief member of the commission under Jay's Treaty to settle war claims. Impressed by the English country estates and especially by Repton's landscape ideas, on his return home in 1805 he started work on his large classic-style brick mansion and over the next twenty-two years developed its surroundings into an

English-type park. Recently this historic property was saved from demolition by public-spirited citizens who have brought it back as near to its original state as possible. The grounds are in the process of rehabilitation.

Another fine example of early-nineteenth-century garden art, now carefully maintained by the Ladies' Hermitage Association, was the Hermitage, near Nashville, Tennessee, the home of President Andrew Jackson and his wife, Rachel. The garden was designed for her in 1819 by the Englishman William Frost. An acre in size, its flower beds and borders are planted with spring bulbs and such old favorites as peonies, iris, lilies, roses, snowballs, and crepe myrtles.

During the nineteenth century the story of American gardening differed little from that of gardening in England and France. It might seem that where these two countries led, America followed, but in reality each separately responded to the same influences. There was a strong undercurrent of Romanticism in every form of art and design, and all three countries benefited by the exchange of plant materials. The aim of the Romanticists was to eliminate formulas and exploit the subjective, yet one landscape designer, Andrew Jackson Downing of Newburgh, New York, thought it necessary to lay down a few working rules in his *Treatise on the Theory and Practices of Landscape Gardening adapted to North America; with a view to the Improvement of Country Residences* (1841):

> A taste for rural improvements of every description is advancing silently, but with great rapidity in this country ... while yet in the far west the pioneer constructs his rude hut of logs ... in the older portions of the Union, bordering the Atlantic, we are surrounded by all the luxuries and refinements that belong to an old and long cultivated country. Within the last ten years especially, the evidence of the growing wealth and prosperity of our citizens have [*sic*] become apparent in the great increase of elegant cottage and villa residences on the banks of our noble rivers, along our rich valleys. ... In all the expenditure of means in these improvements, amounting in the aggregate to an immense sum, professional talent is seldom employed in Architecture or Landscape Gardening, but almost every man fancies himself an amateur, and endeavors to plan and arrange his own residence. With but little practical knowledge, and few correct principles for his guidance, it is not surprising that we witness much incongruity and great waste of time and money.

Downing's premise was that the landscape gardener should "aim to separate the accidental and extraneous in nature, and preserve only the spirit or essence." He should "arrange materials so as to awaken emotions of grace, elegance or picturesqueness, joined with unity, harmony and variety, more distinct and forcible than are suggested by natural scenery." According to Downing there were two leading expressions of landscape design, the "graceful school" and the "picturesque school." In the former he sought to create all outlines with graceful curves: undulating ground forms, luxuriant, drooping tree forms, walks and roads stretching out in easy flowing lines, and the edges of brooks and lakes all freely curved. Besides this, perfect order and neatness should reign. "The house should belong to one of the classical modes ... which readily admit of the graceful accompaniment of vases, urns and other harmonious accessories."

The aim of the "picturesque school" was to produce outlines of "a certain spirited irregularity with surfaces comparatively abrupt and broken." The ground could vary between smoothness and sudden changes to "dingles, rocky groups and broken banks." Plant growth was to be bold in character and trees old, irregular, and with rough bark. Pines and larches were appropriate, and "thickets, glades and underwood, as in wild nature" were indispensable. On estates with lakes, the wild romantic spots were to be preserved. The houses were to be built in irregular outlines, as in the Gothic mansion, old English cottage, or Swiss chalet styles. Ornaments, such as baskets for plants, were to be rustic, and so were summerhouses and garden furniture, made of rough-textured bark and branches.

While today we do not attempt to create such artificial quaintness as Downing's picturesque style called for, we can benefit by his principles, which are an important consideration in any artistic medium. He called for unity in the production of the scene, variety in its detailing, and over-all harmony to prevent discord.

In the actual planting of trees Downing was adamant that they be grouped at irregular distances, that they differ in height and have a variety of outline. What he called the "clumping method" — planting trees of the same age and like growth at the same time in a circular form — resulted in clumps "as like to each other as so many puddings turned out of one common mould." He stated that the group was the keynote of the "modern" landscape, just as the avenue or straight line was the key to the old. He further emphasized that groups of trees should serve as a background or frame for the house and lawn, and that single "elegant trees should grow as specimens." Groups of small trees, unusual in form, foliage, or blossoms, were admitted to the lawn also. This advice led to the popularity of purple and copper beech trees, weeping beeches, ginkgo trees, tulip trees, cut-leaf maples and oaks, Japanese maples, and other unusual trees which we still admire on old properties.

Downing considered the flower garden a natural adjunct of the home, but only as a small part in any over-all plan. Three kinds were recognized. One was the "architectural flower garden" consisting of regular beds and walks, with the center dominated by a sundial or fountain. The "irregular flower garden," of varied outline bounded with shrubs — the complete antithesis of the first — was made up of unrelated and differently shaped beds. The third kind of flower garden, "the English type," consisted of curvilinear flower beds making up one whole design, like a parterre garden. He suggested that each section be planted with "highly brilliant" varieties. He then referred to this process as "carpet bedding," and stated that the "mingled" flower garden was the most commonly admired in America "though seldom well effected." This is what most gardeners today attempt — the growing of many different kinds of flowers so that continuous bloom is achieved throughout the growing season. Downing's advice that the "showy plants be repeated in different parts of the garden" and that "the smallest be nearest the walk, those a little taller behind them and the largest at the back," foreshadowed the theory of the herbaceous border, which William Robinson promoted in England in the 1880s.

Even though he advocated many aspects of the English natural style of landscape gardening, Downing never visited England until after the publication of his treatise. The young man's busy career designing Hudson Valley estates was tragically cut short by the explosion of a Hudson River steamboat on which he was traveling. He was only thirty-seven years old when he died, but the work he left behind inspired America's first and probably greatest creator of public parks, Frederick Law Olmsted who, together with Calvert Vaux of England, won the competition for planning New York's Central Park.

The nineteenth century was an exciting period for plant-lovers. Clipper ships trading with China brought back forsythia, kerria, wisteria, and bleeding hearts; fuchsia, dahlias, gloxinias, canna, red salvia (scarlet sage), verbena, and petunias were brought from Mexico and from Central and South American countries, and lobelia and geraniums arrived from Africa. Many of these became favorites in carpet-bedded gardens, sometimes in private ones and very frequently in public or municipal settings. The average home-owner lacked gardeners to raise the many plants needed to maintain a carpet-bedded design and therefore often placed a single round bed of flowers in the center of his front lawn or circular driveway, brightly lit up with tall cannas and scarlet sage. Coleus, neatly alternating in color might encircle it, or any of the "bedding out" plants could border it. Colorful beds like these often relegated the more charming old-fashioned roses and shrubs to the back yard, which was actually where the garden was more lived in and enjoyed. The front was for show.

In keeping with the Victorian taste for excessive ornamentation, mass-produced cast-iron ornaments were strewn about the garden in the late nineteenth century. Basin-like fountains supported by cranes or topped with cupids, urns for red geraniums, vinelike grillework, settees, tables, and chairs were all inexpensive enough for the average man to buy and were therefore more often seen in the gardens than costlier urns, statues, and fountains made of stone. Many a home owner had a cast-iron stag on his lawn.

At the end of the Victorian era there was a compromise between the oversentimental landscape and the overembellished flower garden. The informal gardens, and particularly the English herbaceous border, became popular on both sides of the Atlantic. Few yards were without a mixed flower border, few lawns without the color of flowering shrubs.

In the twentieth century, until World War II, many great gardens were developed on large estates in most sections of the United States. Famous plant collections were made for formal gardens, which usually followed French or Italian models and sometimes English or Spanish. Other estates were designed with series of gardens which might include one of the formal styles as well as a Japanese garden and a natural woodland garden. Most often, however, a large formal house has had an appropriate-sized garden of no particular "style," in which bulbs, perennials, and annuals were grown in straightforward borders.

By the mid-twentieth century, gardening entered a new phase. Social conditions had so changed that the labor needed for the upkeep of even moderate gardens was difficult to find, let alone to pay for. Today, only a very few people can afford to maintain the old order and gardening has largely become a "do it yourself" proposition. Sometimes either a weekly handyman is employed to mow the grass and do some clipping and a little weeding, or the upkeep of the lawns is provided for under contract. As a result, ease of maintenance is the aim of all garden designers and home-owners. In future chronicles the garden design of the latter half of the twentieth century may be said to have been one of economy and great ingenuity, where the utmost is made of a small area, even if it is only a patio, a poolside, or a terrace with a view.

326

XII   *The Gardens of Old China*

Without an appreciation of Chinese painting there can be no understanding of Chinese garden art, for the most important ingredient of any pleasure garden, large or small, has always been a picturesque quality directly derived from painting. It has not remained for professional designers or horticulturists to create gardens. Rather, this has always been left to the poets, monks, and scholars, whose sensitive feelings toward nature found expression in painting first and in garden-making afterward. Poetry, painting, and garden art were closely interrelated, since all three strove to express the beauty of the landscape and the contrasts found in nature.

Because Chinese garden art was introduced to Japan by Buddhist monks some may think the Japanese garden imitative, especially so because of its adherence to rustic nature. The difference lies in the fact that although the Chinese adhered to their traditional combinations of plant materials and rocks and water, they did not resort to strict formulas in their placement, nor did they attach symbolism to each one, like the Japanese. Moreover, the Japanese garden makes a complete picture. The Chinese garden was planned as a series of pictures which one might compare to a scroll painting.

The three founders of the major religions of China, Confucius, Lao-tse, and Buddha, taught men to revere nature and to strive toward an ideal fellowship with it. Since the most striking ornaments of the earth are rocks and mountains, lakes and rivers, these were incorporated into the garden from the very beginning, and since continuity of cultural ideas and customs has always been a characteristic of the Oriental mind, we find that the Chinese always continued to represent them. Unfortunately another custom precluded the preservation of many of the fine old gardens. Among those of high birth, or within the imperial family, the next in line never remained in a home where death had claimed his predecessor. He moved on to another and the old fell into disuse.

Rocks, stones, and mountains have been looked upon as the skeletons of the earth, and rivers have been compared to its arteries. All were greatly venerated. The Chinese ideograph for "garden" is a combination of the two words "land" and "water," while the word for landscape painting is *shan shui*, or "mountain-water" picture, indicating that these were the two essentials. Custom dictated the seeking out of rocks of fantastic shapes, smoothly water-worn and irregularly pierced, the most prized ones being procured from old lake and river beds. These were built up into simulated cliffs or lined the banks of garden streams. Sometimes they were formed into grottoes and very frequently individual ones were set up to be admired in the round, as the European would admire statuary.

As far back as the Han Dynasty (207 B.C.–220 A.D.) there are records of garden rocks, mountains, and artificial hills, and even hunting parks similar in intent to those of ancient Persia. But it was during the great and enlightened Sung Period (960–1280 A.D.), which brought the art of landscape painting to a high degree of development, that the garden emerged as a complete art form. Of significant influence was the eleventh-century poem by the statesman Hsi-Ma-Kuang, describing and extolling his own "hermitage," to which he welcomed his friends. He described a large estate with many kinds of pavilions, with ponds, waterfalls, islands, meadows, and groves of trees. Its grottoes, river, and streams, its hilltop pavilions, stands of pines, and forest of bamboo, as well as its weeping willows, inspired painters and garden designers.

More than two centuries later, from Marco Polo, the Western world received, somewhat dubiously, the first information about Cathay and about the great Kublai Khan and his vast palace and its surroundings at Cambaluc (Khanbalik), situated near the Pei River, not far from the site of the modern city of Peking. His descriptions indicate that the tradition of elevations, pavilions, and lakes in garden areas was well established by then. "Within bow-shot" of the palace walls there was an "artificial green mount of earth . . . clothed with the most beautiful evergreen trees"[1] and surmounted with an ornamental green pavilion. In Marco Polo's words:

> Whenever the Khan receives information of a handsome tree growing in any place he causes it to be dug up, with all its roots and the earth about them, and however large and heavy it may be, he has it transported by means of elephants to this mount and adds it to the verdant collection. From this perpetual verdure it has acquired the appellation of the Green Mount. . . . The view of this altogether — the mount itself, the trees, and the buildings form a delightful and at the same time a wonderful scene. . . . Equally within the precincts of the city, there is a large and deep excavation, . . . the earth from which supplied the material for raising the mount. It is furnished with water by a small rivulet and has the appearance of a fish-pond but is used for watering the cattle.

The Venetian traveler told of other water-filled excavations and canals which lay between the Mongolian Emperor's palace and that of his son Chingis and which had furnished earth to increase the size of the mount. These were all stocked with fish, swans, and aquatic birds. We learn too that the Khan believed, on the advice of his astrologers, that "those who plant trees are rewarded with long life." Therefore, where possible, roads in his kingdom were closely tree-lined for shade in summer and for marking the way through the snows of winter.

As the Emperor's administrator, Marco Polo traveled throughout the provinces, and in his memoirs vividly described the "noble and magnificent city of Kin-sai" (later Hangchow), the ancient capital of southern China, which was added to the Khan's holdings in 1279. Here were "houses and mansions of great size, with gardens" and a very fine palace belonging to the King. The city lay beside the famed Western Lake, which was extolled by all who saw it. It was mountain-rimmed, and its waters were crystal clear. A center of culture, Hangchow long remained noted for the beauty of its large homes, which were garden-houses in every sense of the word. The description of the King's palace reveals a complex of ten courts, each surrounded by fifty apartments with their respective gardens and interconnecting covered passageways and colonnades. These were in addition to the large cloister occupied by the King and Queen; they formed "the residence of a thousand young women, whom the King retained in his service. . . . Other divisions of this seraglio were laid out in groves, areas of water, animal enclosures, and beautiful gardens stored with fruit trees [peaches and a variety of pear noted for the great size of its fruit]. No male person was allowed to join the parties the king organized with some of his damsels to course with dogs and hunt," for "when fatigued with these exercises" they retired to groves, shed their dresses, and swam sportively in the nude "whilst the king remained a spectator of the exhibition." Sometimes these same damsels served a repast afterward in the groves. Marco Polo pointed out that by consuming "his time amidst the enervating charms of his women and in profound ignorance of whatever related to martial concerns . . . this king enabled the Great Khan to deprive him of his splendid possessions and to expel him with ignominy from his throne."

It is thought-provoking to read the graphic descriptions of thirteenth-century Chinese life and customs which Marco Polo dictated for posterity, as a glance into European history of that period makes one realize that, except in the Moslem world, life in the West was still being lived within the fortress-like walls of castles or within the meagerness of peasants' farm huts. In China the enjoyment of the pleasure garden, a "made" landscape of rocks, trees, and water, had for several centuries been a part of life for all people of substance. Kingly precincts quite naturally were on a grander scale, vast in area, imposing in detail, but they had private areas akin to those of the aristocrats and wealthy city merchants in which gardens were an integral part of the architectural complex, sheltered by walls, corridors, and pavilions.

Until the seventeenth century the hidden and mysterious beauty of Cathay lay unrevealed to other Western eyes, with the exception of Arab traders. British ships finally reached the China coast in 1637 and in the following century Sir William Chambers, at the time a young man, lived and traveled in China for a few years, using his sketchbook to record his impressions. Some of these were later translated into reality at Kew Gardens.

A few Jesuit missionaries followed close on the heels of the seventeenth-century explorers, and finally in 1743 we have the superbly written account by Father Attiret[4] of

Plates

185. A mountain landscape such as this was the ideal scene which the Chinese tried to represent in their own garden areas. Ming period painting. (*Freer Gallery of Art, Washington*)

186. The most charming garden features of an eighteenth-century Chinese dwelling are revealed in this scroll painting. At the left a large-leaved banana-plantain makes a decorative foil for an upright stone. A rose trellis displays the blooms of *Rosa chinensis* or of *Rosa Banksiae*, and beyond, graceful willow trees lean over a stream. A pavilion, built over the water, looks down upon blos-soming lotuses. "Ladies with Fans," copy after Chou Fang. (*Metropolitan Museum of Art, Kennedy Fund, 1913*)

187. View of the imperial summer palace, painted by an early-twentieth-century artist. (*Metropolitan Museum of Art, Gift of Franklin Jasper Walls*)

188. "Harp Player in a Pavilion," sixteenth-century painting by the artist Ch'in Ying. The beauty of a tree peony growing beneath the pine tree seems to be the object for contemplation. (*Museum of Fine Arts, Boston*)

185

the gardens of the Manchu Emperor Ch'ien Lung which surrounded the summer palace ten miles outside of Peking. Father Attiret, who "was employ'd by that Emperor to Paint the Apartments in those Gardens," sent a lengthy letter back to France accurately detailing all their parts. First he described his two-thousand-mile journey to Peking, the first part by boat, during which "by the Rules of good-breeding" he and his compatriots were never allowed to go ashore or even look out windows, and the last stage over land, when they were carried in "a sort of Cage, which they were pleas'd to call a Litter." In this they were shut up all day long and their curiosity concerning the country remained quite unsatisfied. However, once at the court, they had an almost unparalleled opportunity to see the emperor's splendid surroundings, for, in the missionary's own words, "of all the Europeans that are here, none ever enter'd this Inclosure, except the Clock-makers and Painters, whose Employments make it necessary that they should be admitted everywhere." The enclosure he spoke of was *Yuen-ming-Yuen*, the "Garden of Gardens." A second, the "Garden of Perpetual Spring," was for the use of the Emperor's mother and her court. The princes and grandees lived in still other "pleasure places."

Father Attiret declared, "There is but one Man here; and that is the Emperor. All Pleasures are made for him alone. This charming Place is scarce ever seen by anybody but himself, his Women, and his Eunuchs. The Princes and other chief Men of the Country, are rarely admitted farther than the Audience-Chambers." The painters were conducted to the places they were decorating under "a large guard of Eunuchs" and were "obliged to go quick, and without any Noise, and huddle and steal along softly, as if going upon some Piece of Mischief." It was in this manner that bit by bit all parts of the garden and the apartments were seen. He compared their combined extent to that of the entire French city of Dijon, whence he had come. Vast courts, plantations of trees, and flower gardens separated the many parts of the palace. There were some two hundred pleasure houses with roofs "cover'd with varnished Tiles of different Colours; Red, Yellow, Blue, Green, Purple" and artificial hills, twenty to sixty feet high, surrounded huge lakes on which magnificent boats were poled.

> All the Risings and Hills are sprinkled with Trees; and particularly with Flowering-trees, which are here very common. The Sides of the Canals, or lesser Streams, are not faced, (as they are with us), with smooth Stone, and in a strait Line; but look rude and rustic, with different Pieces of Rock, some of which jut out, and others recede inwards; and are placed with so much Art, that you would take it to be the Work of Nature. In some Parts the Water is wide, in others narrow; here it serpentizes, and there spreads away, as if it was really push'd off by the Hills and Rocks. The Banks are sprinkled with Flowers; which rise up even thro' the Hollows in the Rock-work, as if they had been produced there naturally. They have a great Variety of them, for every Season of the Year.
>
> Beyond these Streams there are always Walks, or rather, Paths, pav'd with small Stones; which lead from one Valley to another. These Paths too are irregular; and sometimes wind along the Banks of the Water, and at others run out wide from them. . . .

I have already told you, that these little Streams, or Rivers, are carried on to supply several larger Pieces of Water, and Lakes. One of these Lakes is very near Five Miles round; and they call it a Meer, or Sea. This is one of the most beautiful Parts in the whole Pleasure-ground. On the Banks, are several Pieces of Building separated from each other by the Rivulets, and artificial Hills above mentioned. . . .

The Banks of this charming Water are infinitely varied: there are no two Parts of it alike. Here you see Keys of smooth Stone; with Porticoes, Walks, and Paths, running down to them from the Palaces that surround the Lake; there, others of Rock-work; that fall into Steps, contrived with the greatest Art that can

"Enjoyment of the Chrysanthemum Flowers," painted by Hua Yen in 1753. The ninth lunar month was dedicated to the chrysanthemum in China, and during that period special festivities were held to view the blossoms. (*City Art Museum, Saint Louis*)

be conceived: here, natural Terraces with winding Steps at each End, to go up to the Palaces that are built upon them; and above these, other Terraces, and other Palaces, that rise higher and higher, and form a sort of Amphitheatre. There again a Grove of Flowering-trees presents itself to your Eye; and a little farther, you see a Spread of wild Forest-trees, and such as grow only on the most barren Mountains: then, perhaps, vast Timber-trees with their Under-wood; then, Trees from all foreign Countries; and then, some all blooming with Flowers, and others all laden with Fruits of different Kinds. . . .

To let you see the Beauty of this charming Spot in its greatest perfection, I should wish to have you transported hither when the Lake is all cover'd with

(OPPOSITE) A pagoda and willows by a stream. Illustration from *The Pictorial News*, 1870. (*The Montclair Art Museum. Photo: Roche*)

The principles of *yin* and *yang*, the dualism of opposites, are revealed here in the contrasts of mountain and water, represented by the eroded stones (right background) and the pool, while the erect

growth of the banana-plantain and the gnarled old pine tree are the antitheses of each other and could be compared to youth and old age. (*Freer Gallery of Art, Washington*)

Boats; either gilt, or varnish'd: as it is sometimes, for taking the Air; sometimes, for Fishing; and sometimes, for Justs, and Combats, and other Diversions, upon the Water: but above all, on some fine Night, when the Fire-works are play'd off there; at which time they have Illuminations in all the Palaces, all the Boats, and almost on every Tree. The *Chinese* exceed us extremely in their Fire-works: and I have never seen any thing of that Kind, either in *France* or *Italy*, that can bear any Comparison with theirs.

Added to all this lavish beauty was the series of European gardens which one of Father Attiret's compatriots, Father Michel Benoit, designed for the Emperor in association with another European court painter, Father Giuseppe Castiglione. Since these gardens are not mentioned by Attiret, they presumably came into being soon after he wrote his letter. They were short-lived, for as the Emperor aged he seldom visited them. Their complicated waterworks soon fell into disrepair and were abandoned, and in 1860 they were virtually destroyed by British and French soldiers.

The most charming aspect of the Chinese imperial gardens was that even in their immensity they retained intimacy, for sections were hidden behind hills and all was not revealed at once. This quality was common to all large, privately owned estates which had areas outside the family compounds. The architectural beauty of colorful tiled pavilions and of the simple rustic ones was matched in diversity only by the views and sensations to be enjoyed. These were planned for the varying atmospheric beauties of day and night, for different seasonal effects, for the appreciation of certain blooms, and for the admiration of representational scenes in nature. The drooping willow tree, groves of bamboos, and gnarled pine trees took their places near the "mountains," "lakes," and streams of the arranged landscape. Flowers and the small flowering trees found their places in the more intimate enclosures of the home.

The Chinese family dwelling of one story raised on a high platform was a complex of many-angled courtyards. In their private recesses there were verandas overlooking gardens and rectangular pools or canals. There were foot bridges and high walls of stone or stucco. On the walls flickered the shadows of leaves and branches and through artistically shaped apertures and circular moon gates little vistas could be enjoyed. There was a variety of shapes in the window grilles — flowers, butterflies, bats, fans, vases, gourds, and fruits such as the peach. Further decoration was provided by the rich color of red lacquer and gold ornamentation, which were in striking contrast to the black-tiled roofs. The enclosed garden had no lawn but was sometimes mosaicked with pebbles or paved with stones. Harmony and intimacy with nature prevailed. Flowers were enjoyed, but in a very special way. Flower beds rarely existed, other than raised ones for the revered tree peony (*Paeonia suffruticosa*), the "king of flowers." Chrysanthemums were brought in pots to the courtyard so that their cycle of bloom could be fully appreciated. For women with bound feet, and for the philosopher who studied the ways of life in the unfolding of blossoms — growth, perfection and decline — this was quiet contentment. Roses grew against trellises, wisteria draped itself over walls, and fragrant jasmine flourished. In the pools lotuses raised their pink heads and chalice-like leaves above the mud and, to the Buddhist, symbolized

Pagoda, moon gate, pavilions, and zigzag foot bridge all look down upon a water scene. Pines and flamboyant rock forms, suggestive of mountains, complete the idealized scene. Illustration from *The Pictorial News*, 1870. (*Montclair Art Museum*)

purity. The flowery magnolias and the plum, peach, and pomegranate trees were a part of the permanent planting. Pine, juniper, and cedar were the evergreens, with small or dwarfed ones used in small places. A type of banana called plantain (*Musa paradisiaca*) was especially favored, and bamboo was ever-present. All of these were constantly represented in Chinese painting. Many had symbolical meanings, and certain groupings such as the pine, plum, and bamboo, the "three friends of the cold season," were significant. The peach tree signified immortality, the pine and the bamboo longevity, the banana-plantain, abundance. China, well-named "the flowery kingdom," was very generously endowed with a vast array of flora, but only those with significant symbolism or with cer-

341

tain associations were admitted to the garden. By the manner and time of their planting both good and evil spirits had to be propitiated.

Even within the courtyard gardens an attempt was made to reproduce scenes in nature. Always there had to be the fanciful rock shapes representing mountains. To a Westerner's eyes they appear grotesque and unreal but the fact that they were considered to be a necessity in a garden is evidenced by even a cursory view of Chinese painting and illustration. Such stones in combination with an irregularly shaped pine tree and even a small piece of water could conjure up a remote and wild country scene and at the same time reveal the Taoist concern with the unity of opposites called *Yin* and *Yang*.

Large or small, the old Chinese gardens retained an air of intimacy. They were never monumental, they were never symmetrical. These were the qualities that impressed the Europeans and brought fresh inspiration to their eighteenth-century designs.

189. (OPPOSITE) A lily pond in the gardens of the Summer Palace, Peking (*Magnum*)

XIII

The Gardens of Japan

In the Far East the garden has been looked upon as a barometer of a nation's prosperity, for epochs of peace and abundance have produced gardens of great scale and beauty. In Japan, however, it has never been thought of merely as a product of luxury and material wealth, but rather as a part of that yearning for nature ever present in the innate character of her people. This intense love of nature has been so strong that long ago the garden became a necessity of life, both for its physical beauty and for its mental and spiritual uplift. No house has been considered complete without its surrounding garden, and domestic architecture has provided open-sided rooms from which to view them. Sliding screens of rice paper have subtly silhouetted the delicacy and constant variation of swaying foliage.

The Japanese peoples' intimacy with nature is revealed in many ways. Their love of gardens is so strong that even a narrow passageway is treated as one and the most meager bit of land in front of a home is given up to the growing of a pine tree or a clump of bamboo. Nature is also appreciated through a variety of art forms which make use of plant materials brought indoors. Perfectly scaled miniature landscapes are often planted in boxes or trays, the larger ones at the entrance, the smaller ones taking their places within the *tokonoma* or alcove. Stones, moss, sand, and water all play a part in their design. The art of bonsai, or the cultivation of dwarf trees, is so highly developed that trees are not only stunted to live in small pots for generations, but are made to assume the shape and dignity

Based on a monograph by Jiro Harada of the Imperial Household Museum, Tokyo, published as *Gardens of Japan* by Studio Ltd., London, 1928.

190. (OPPOSITE) The landscape garden of the Ginkakuji or Silver Pavilion, Kyoto. (*Martin Hürlimann*) 345

Plates

191. The garden of the Silver Pavilion, Kyoto, is the best preserved of all those laid out in the latter half of the fifteenth century when Zen Buddhism exerted the greatest influence on landscape gardening. (*Japan National Tourist Organization*)

192. Rock Garden of Ryoanji Temple, Kyoto. Just sixty square yards in size, this rectangular plot of ground with only clean white sand and fifteen rocks in it is a garden in which all superfluities have been eliminated; it is a manifestation of Zen Buddhism. (*Japan National Tourist Organization*)

193. Planted four centuries ago when the Golden Pavilion of Kinkakuji was built, this "pine ship" still flourishes within its garden, reflecting the skill, patience, and veneration of its caretakers. (*Underwood and Underwood*)

194. Detail of the Rock Garden of the Ryoanji Temple. It is up to the observer to interpret what he sees. (*Japan National Tourist Organization*)

195. The garden of the Samboin Temple at Daigo, in the southeastern suburbs of Kyoto, was laid out in 1589 and planned particularly to be viewed from the rooms opening on it. The more than seven hundred stones carefully arranged throughout the garden are among its outstanding features. (*Japan National Tourist Organization*)

196. The celebrated Rikugien Garden in Tokyo dates from the late seventeenth century. A typical landscape garden of feudal days, it includes a large pond around which various scenic seaside resorts in Japan are represented symbolically. (*Japan National Tourist Organization*)

197. One of Japan's most beautiful lake gardens is that of the Golden Pavilion or Kinkakuji in Kyoto. Built as a villa in 1397 and later used as a temple, the pavilion burned to ashes in 1950 but was completely reconstructed five years later. (*Japan National Tourist Organization*)

198. The Japanese greatly admire snow scenery and plan special snowfall effects. Legged lanterns with broad, flat caps are designed to catch the snow and hold it, and are called "snow lanterns." The one shown here is in Kenroku Park, Kanazawa. (*Japan National Tourist Organization*)

199. Another scene in the Kenroku Park, Kanazawa, showing a similar lantern. (*Japan National Tourist Organization*)

200. Massive stones form a bridge in Rikugien Garden, Tokyo. They are staggered to prevent the stroller from hurrying. (*Japan National Tourist Organization*)

201. In typical Japanese fashion the lantern in this garden of an inn is partially concealed by tree branches. (*Japan National Tourist Organization*)

202. The Suizenji Garden at Kanazawa is a "hill and pond" garden laid out in the seventeenth century, with a replica of Mount Fuji. Like other gardens of large size, it is referred to as a "stroll-in" garden. (*Japan National Tourist Organization*)

203. Ritsukin Park of Kagawa is a large water garden whose artistry is displayed against a natural background. (*Japan National Tourist Organization*)

192

193

194

195

198

199

200

201

202

of ancient trees according to their species. The art of flower arranging, *ikebana*, has been developed into an aesthetic science during so many centuries that it has become an essential part of everyday life, taught in girls' schools and in private homes by masters. All the decorative arts also express a reverence for nature and we see its many moods and motifs revealed in scroll paintings, prints, textiles, and ceramics.

HISTORY

It seems likely that the art of garden-making, like many other things, was imported from China, either directly or by way of Korea. Gardens of ancient Nippon exist only in literature; according to what we are told, there seems always to have been a lake with an island and bridges. In fact the garden was originally called *shima*, or island. Old writings tell of literary parties held along the winding streams of gardens, after the custom of ancient China, and of the cherry trees, plums, pines, and willows planted in imperial gardens. Since it was customary to change the seat of the imperial court upon the death of each emperor, no definite style emerged until in 710 A.D., when the capital was established in Nara, where seven successive emperors ruled. Each of the historic gardens there had ponds with islands.

At the end of the eighth century the capital was shifted to Kyoto, and here in long succession many large and extravagant gardens came into being. For the first time we read of ponds fed by waterfalls, of water rushing through rocks shaded by pine trees, and of the various kinds of flowers that adorned the gardens — chrysanthemums, orchids, wisteria, and *Lespedeza bicolor*. During that period, a formal and symmetrical style of architecture prevailed and the main garden, always laid out on the south side of a house, invariably contained hills, and a pond with an island. Of the two bridges that connected the island with the garden one was arched to allow the passage of boats.

The period between 1186 and 1335 was one in which a militaristic spirit retarded the progress of art and culture, but with its austere mode of living coupled with the introduction of Zen Buddhism the people learned the value of simplicity. Buddhist names were given to different rocks in the garden, and various principles of the religion were attached to the rules governing its make-up. Religion became a means of enforcing aesthetic rules. Not only Buddhism, but what the Japanese called the *in-yo*, or passive and active principles in nature according to the Chinese philosophers, were inculcated in garden design. Always, too, certain superstitions, which still influence the gardeners of today, became closely connected with garden construction. In short, religious doctrines and philosophic principles expressed by symbols, as well as popular superstitions, were woven into the garden. The laws of direction, of harmony, of five elements, and the principles of cause and effect, of active and passive, of light and shadow, of male and female, or of the nine spirits of the Buddhist pantheon, are still strongly insisted on in determining the general plan of a garden or in the grouping of stones.

During the fourteenth, fifteenth, and sixteenth centuries there was a renaissance of the arts in Kyoto, due to the supremacy of the art-conscious Ashikaga clan. With the development of painting, flower arranging, the No drama, and other pastimes came the popularization of the garden. Certain improvements were effected. Hitherto gardens were so constructed as to be admired primarily from outside a house but now changes in domestic architecture allowed them to be enjoyed from within as well, thus opening a new era in their development. Priests returning from China after studying the Zen form of Buddhism molded the thoughts of the people into a subjective mood. This rather than the objective attitude became the motive power in creating the garden. Gardens thus became alive with individuality. The influence of Zen was irresistible in all branches of art. It found an artistic expression in the tea ceremony, or *chanoyu*, the esoteric cult "founded upon the adoration of beauty in the routine of everyday life." It infused everything with the quality of *shibumi*, that unassuming presence of a refined taste hidden underneath a commonplace appearance. *Chanoyu* required the garden to be different from the formal kind, and the aesthetic priests — "tea men" — and connoisseurs devised new forms and developed a style which revolutionalized the Japanese garden. Some gardens reproduced famous scenes in China or Japan in miniature. With great ingenuity the designers sometimes planned the garden and planted trees to give the visual appearance of extending far beyond its confines, stretching to distant hills. At other times they designed it to form a seclusion from the world and created a sylvan solitude conducive to retrospection. One famous master, Rikyu, planted a grove of trees to obstruct the open view of the sea from his garden. But when a guest stooped at the water basin to wash his hands and rinse his mouth preparatory to entering the *chaseki*, where the tea ceremony was held, he caught an unexpected glimpse of the shimmering sea through the trees — a glimpse of Infinity that suddenly revealed the relationship of the dipperful of water lifted from the basin to the vast expanse of the sea, and of himself to the universe.

Several gardens preserved to the present day are attributed to the famous Zen priest Muso Kokushi, who died in 1351. It was he who designed the garden of Ginkakuji in Kyoto, home of the Silver Pavilion, and the gardens of Tenryiji and Saihoji. The latter was famous for its pond, which was shaped like the Chinese character for the word "heart."

Another famous name is that of Soami, who, in the fifteenth century, created the justly celebrated rock gardens of Ryoanji and Daisen-in, both of which are attached to monasteries in the suburbs of Kyoto.

It is interesting to observe that gardens of this period often took ideas from the black monochrome landscape paintings on silk then in vogue, for the painters themselves were often garden designers. Furthermore, it was during the fifteenth century that the three styles of elaboration — *shin*, *gyo*, and *so* (finished, intermediary, and rough), to be explained more fully later — came into being, in gardening as in other branches of art.

The last quarter of the sixteenth century, the Momoyama Period, marks the time in the development of Japanese art when all foreign influence was cast off. It was characterized on the one hand by gorgeous luxuriance, bold and free in conception, and on the other by the quiet refinement of *shibumi*. The former was a reaction to constant turmoil and bloodshed, the latter the reflection of tea-ceremony ideals, and in both the people found peace and satisfaction. A number of famous gardens were created in Kyoto and its environs during this time. Some were attached to Buddhist monasteries and others to the castles of the shoguns and the palaces of the emperors. Splendid still are the gardens of Samboin of the Daigoji temple in the southeastern suburbs of Kyoto, the dry garden of

356

Nishi Hongwanji, originally a part of Fushimi Castle, and Chijaku. Legend attributes the construction of Chijaku to the great *chanoyu* master and originator of the tea ceremony, Sen-no Rikyu. Also considered to be a masterpiece is the celebrated garden of the Katsura detached palace. It is said to have been undertaken by the master Kobori Enshu on three conditions: no limitation as to time of completion, no interference, and no limit on expenditure.

In 1603 the Tokugawa shogunate was established in Edo, which is now called Tokyo, and here the *daimyos*, or feudal lords, built many mansions with spacious gardens. Even among the common people the garden became a great fashion. *Chanoyu* was still highly regarded, but one noticeable change during the years that followed was that the actual design and execution of gardens gradually passed from the hands of "tea men" and priests to those of professionals, called *niwashi*, or gardeners, who dealt in materials such as rocks, stone lanterns, and trees.

The Zen Buddhist gardens gradually ran to artificialities, vainly copying the outer forms of past masters without reflecting an understanding of their inner meanings, and so finally ended in stereotyped formulas. As a reaction, though lacking widespread influence, the literary men's garden found expression in the seventeenth century. Simpler tea ritual and a vogue for Chinese literature brought it into being.

In 1868, with the surrender of the three-hundred-year-old Tokugawa shogunate to the imperial house, Edo, renamed Tokyo, became the seat of the imperial regime. At the same time the abolition of the feudal system came about and every phase of national life was affected, dooming many celebrated gardens to neglect or sacrifice. In their stead rose such buildings as military schools, a naval college, an arsenal, the Imperial University. But during the period of prosperity which later followed, the people vied with each other in creating spacious and costly gardens or in remodeling or improving old ones. By the proclamation of 1873 the establishment of parks was encouraged throughout the country, with Tokyo setting the first example. In the catastrophes of the twentieth century, the earthquake and fire of 1923 and the bombings of World War II, tens of thousands of people sought refuge in her great parks and gardens. In the first disaster, with all the trees burned to the ground, many lives were saved by the ponds and in no few instances the gardens checked the havoc of sweeping conflagration. Terrible destruction took place with the World War II bombings, but Tokyo, rebuilt and in keeping with her heritage, has provided open green areas for places of peace and rest and the appreciation of nature.

GARDEN STYLES

Gardens of Nippon have long been classified into two general types: *tsuki-yama* (artificial hills) and *hira-niwa* (level gardens). As the names signify, the former consists of hills and ponds, while the latter is a flat piece of ground made to represent a valley or a moor. Needless to say, the two are not always separable: the former, if it is of a considerable size, concedes a part of itself to the latter. For many centuries the main garden on the south side of a nobleman's house was invariably in the *tsuki-yama* style, but for the treatment of spaces between different buildings the *hira-niwa* style was necessarily resorted to.

Thus, the two types developed side by side until the necessity arose to choose one or the other for a limited space of ground. Since the fifteenth century, when the tea ceremony came into vogue, the *hira-niwa* or level garden has progressed into a distinct type known as the *chaseki* garden.

As in calligraphy, painting, flower arranging, and other branches of Japanese art, both general types have been rendered in three forms of *shin*, *gyo*, and *so*. Applied to gardening, the differentiation comes chiefly from the degree of elaboration. The *shin* is the most elaborate and formal, the *gyo* is intermediary and semiformal, and *so* is abbreviated and informal. By a careful comparison of the accompanying diagrams one may see the abbreviations and at the same time conceive of the infinite number of stages of abbreviation possible.

Four main styles of gardens have developed from the two general types: the dry rock garden, the water garden, the literary men's garden, and the tea garden. In the *kare-sansui*, or dry landscape, rocks are put together to form a waterfall and its basin, and the shape of a winding stream and a pond are worked out in every detail. Instead of water, gravel and sand are skillfully strewn to suggest it. This scheme can be applied to both hill and level gardens. In old temple compounds many a famous garden still exists which contains merely rocks and sand, and on occasion, a few trees and shrubs.

A rare example is that of the Ryoanji Temple stone garden, where, enclosed by low walls on three sides, there are simply fifteen rocks of varying sizes grouped on a flat piece of ground covered with sand. Not a single tree or shrub is used, but the trees outside the walls and distant views beyond serve as a fitting background for this idealized garden. Similarly, in the gardens of Shinjuan and of Daitokuji, there are fifteen rocks in the favorite groups of seven, five, and three, but these gardens make use of low-growing shrubs and moss. Each is a narrow strip of ground bordered on the farther side by a low hedge which serves to connect the narrow garden with distant scenery. The famous garden of Daisen-in is another dry landscape. Constructed with many appropriately shaped rocks to suggest a waterfall, hills, streams and a pond with a boat, it contains not a drop of water.

The garden that consists mainly of water is called either *sen-tei* (water garden) or *rin-sen* (forest water). Many of these have been made in varying sizes, all over the country. Some are small and laid out so as to be enjoyed in a single view from a house, but larger ones in which to stroll are provided with paths that encircle the lakes and also have bridges and boats. Endless details as to the placing of rocks or planting of trees must be carefully thought out in order that different parts of the garden may be admired from varying angles. One of the largest is the one at Shiba, formerly of the imperial detached palace, but now given to the city of Tokyo. Its pond is connected with the sea.

The literary men's style or *bunjin-zukuri* suggests the simple taste of men of letters in contrast to that of the exponents of the ritual of the tea cult. A simpler method of tea preparation, an interest in Chinese literature and in *nanga*, the Southern school of painting, all played a part in this simplification of garden style. In a simple, quiet, leisurely way its devotees sought to enjoy tranquillity, finding beauty in such things as the evening glow on a grove of crimson maples, a few blossoms of plum by the window at snowy dawn, or a dove on a pine in the morning mist. Materials were chosen and arranged to conform to such

358

ideas, and the garden was necessarily simple and small. Though it became fashionable in the latter half of the seventeenth century, its influence was not especially far-reaching, the chief cause of its decline being its lack of variety and its inadaptability for large gardens. For a limited space, such as an enclosure in front of a room or for one corner of a spacious garden, it is still used. It may be but a group of palms or a clump of bamboo planted with a rock or two, with a few flowering plants to give variation in different seasons.

The *chaniwa*, or tea garden, which conforms to the requirements of the Zen cult of *chanoyu*, is the fourth distinct type of Japanese garden. In reality it is essentially a garden path to and from the *chaseki*, or teahouse, and is regarded as the passage to self-illumination. The entrance is an opening so low that it necessitates bending over, which signifies humility. A *chaniwa* is small, often partitioned off from the rest of the garden, frequently has a waiting shelter outside, and always has a well, stone basin, and lantern. In former times there was a sword rack. It should never be ornate and it must not be artificial. It must look rustic and natural. More than that, it must be planned to arouse sensations in harmony with the spirit of the tea ceremony and conducive to meditation, the purpose of the ceremony being to impress upon the mind the virtues of modesty, politeness, restraint, and sensibility. Once inside the *chaniwa*, the Japanese feels a detachment from the world, away from the hustle and bustle of life. Here a certain poetic atmosphere is induced, for the designers have felt that the tea garden should express sentiments suggested by such verses as "The lonely precincts of a secluded mountain shrine with the red leaves of autumn scattered around," and "A pale evening moon, a bit of the sea, through a cluster of trees." Yet so affected did the insistence on wild naturalness become that there could be no variation in the number of plants, stones, lanterns, water basins, or even the nails in the woodwork.

Within the tea garden evergreen trees are generally used and flowering plants are greatly restricted in order to enhance the appreciation of a spray of flowers thrust in a vase awaiting the guests in the *chaseki*. An infinite care is taken to grow moss on the ground and on stones, in order to invest the garden with *sabi*, or patina, which is highly valued in all things connected with *chanoyu*. No matter what their type, there is no doubt that all Japanese gardens have been greatly influenced by the tea garden.

THE MAKE-UP OF THE GARDEN

Though few Occidentals can comprehend the symbolism within the Japanese garden, they can at least appreciate the ingenuity shown in the simulation of certain natural effects and the picturesque way in which garden accessories such as stones, bridges, lanterns, wells, and pavilions are arranged. These objects are all integral parts of the garden scene and are never placed haphazardly, for each has a significance which is readily apparent to the trained Japanese eye.

Waterfalls are so greatly admired in Japan that thousands of people make pilgrimages to them each summer. Therefore, the waterfall dominates nearly every landscape garden. Located far from the main house, it is generally made to fall from a valley between two mountains with a background of dense forest. Ten different forms of falls are recognized: "glide falling," "linen-falling" (a thin sheet), "thread falling" (thin lines), "uneven falling"

The following illustrations were taken from *Tsukiyama Teizo-Den* (*The Making of Hill Gardens*), published between 1818 and 1830 but written in the sixteenth century by Soami. They were republished with notes by Jiro Harada in *The Gardens of Japan*.

(TOP LEFT) *Shin* style of hill garden. A: The main hill. B: A companion hill to A, with the cascade between them. C: A lower hill — a spur with a depression for a hamlet. D: A low rounded hill near the foreground. E: A distant peak in mountain scenery. I: Guardian Stone. II: Cliff Stone, employed as companion to the Guardian Stone for the cascade. III: Worshiping Stone. IV: Perfect View Stone, or Stone of Two Deities. V: Waiting Stone, arranged in relation to the highest water level. VI: Cave Stone, similar in character to the Guardian Stone, which it sometimes replaces. VII: Pedestal Stone at the parting of stepping stones. VIII: Moon Shadow Stone, implying the mystery of distance. IX: Seat of Honor Stone. X: Upper and lower Idling Stones. 1: Tree of Upright Spirit, or the Principal Tree. 2: View-Perfecting Tree. 3: Tree of Solitude. 4: Cascade-Screening Tree. 5: Tree of the Setting Sun, to intercept glare. 6: Distancing Pine, suggesting a faraway forest. 7: Stretching Pine. a: Veranda. b: *Chozubachi*, stone water basin. c: Sleeve fence. d: Stone lantern. e: Garden well. f: Shrine.

(CENTER LEFT) *Gyo* style of hill garden. I: Guardian Stone. II: Cliff Stone. III, IV: Cascade Stones. V: Water Tray Stone. VI: Abbreviation of Hill D, in *Shin* style. VII:

Bridge-Edge Stone. VIII: Seat of Honor Stone. IX: Perfect View Stone, or Stone of Two Deities. X: Worshiping Stone. XI: Cave Stone. XII: Moon Shadow Stone. XIII: Stone lantern in snow-viewing style. XIV: Stone lantern in *Kasuga* style. XV: Water basin as "Waiting Stone.

(BOTTOM LEFT) *So* style of hill garden. I: Guardian Stone. II: Waiting Stone. III: Hill Stone. IV: Worshiping Stone. V: Evening Sun Stone. VI: Moon Shadow Stone. VII: Seat of Honor Stone.

(TOP RIGHT) *Shin* style of flat garden. I: Guardian Stone. II: Seat of Honor Stone. III: Hill Stone. IV: Perfect View Stone. V: Moon Shadow Stone. VI: Parting Stone. VII: Label Stones. VIII: Garden well. IX: Worshiping Stone. X: Fence. XI: Tree of Evening Sun. XII: Tree of Solitude. XIII: Stone of Two Deities. XIV: Solitude Stone. XV: Stone water basin. XVI: Island Stone.

(CENTER RIGHT) *Gyo* style of flat garden. I: Guardian Stone. II: Hill Stone. III: Moon Shadow Stone. IV: Worshiping Stone. V: Cave Stone. VI: Garden well. VII: Solitude Stone. VIII: Pedestal Stone. IX: Label Stones. X: Stone of Two Deities. XI: Seat of Honor Stone.

(BOTTOM RIGHT) *So* style of flat garden. I: Guardian Stone. II: Worshiping Stone. III: Perfect View Stone. IV: Garden well. V: Stone of Two Deities.

(more on one side than another), "left and right falling" (divided in the middle), "straight falling," "side falling" (water leaps out from one side), "vis-à-vis falling" (gushes from two sides to meet), "detached falling" (water shoots out from the fall), and "repeated falling" (several levels). Even when there is no water available, a rocky bed is made to give an appearance of a fall that has dried up, as sometimes happens in nature during the dry season. Always the idea must be conveyed that there is a stream in the valley behind, by which the waterfall is fed. There must also be a basin with rocks into which the water can plunge. When possible the cascade is so located that the beauty of the sunshine and moonbeam upon it may be appreciated.

In the level garden a spring is often devised to issue from moss-covered rocks and form the origin of a stream that winds through the garden from the east toward the south and then passes out through the west. It must never flow directly through the center, cutting the garden in two. When the stream is intended to convey the idea of a large river, naturalness is achieved by placing a group of big rocks at the bend for the water to dash against. For a small, quiet stream posts instead of stones preserve the bank where it bends. In order to introduce the sound of a gushing stream, the spring is narrowed at one point to a gorge by using rocks on either side and placing a rock in the middle to divide the flow. Whirlpools may be created by obstructing the water flow with rocks and by placing others diagonally across to turn the course of the water. In shallow places stepping stones are often artistically arranged.

Lakes and ponds play such a very important part in garden design that since earlier times they have been the subject of careful study. Some are meant to appear as big as an ocean; others represent rivers, lakes, or swamps. With the aid of trees and plants they are curved so as not to let their full extent be seen from any one position. In the construction of the banks, some parts are arranged with rocks, others with posts — for which chestnut is considered the most durable — and still others with turf coming to the edge of the water. In certain places stone steps lead down to the water. Small ponds are often made to be admired in a dried-up state. Rocks, pebbles, and sand form the bed of the dry watercourse, and plants are used along the banks.

Garden hills are generally formed from the earth dug to make ponds. In an ordinary hill garden, three or four in varying sizes are considered more effective than a solitary one or a great many. They are carefully placed to serve as backgrounds for cascades and as heights from which to enjoy the view of the garden or the surrounding scenery. Since Mount Fuji is looked upon as the ideally shaped mountain, it is not unusual to see its form reproduced in a garden.

Garden lakes usually have islands if size permits, and they vary in form and character. Some represent rock formations with crags from which pieces have fallen into the water below; some are shaped like mountains rising from the water; others represent forested islands or ebb-tide islands half immersed in water. Two islands are always designated as the Host's Island and the Guest's Island, and not infrequently a special isle named *horai-jima* (Elysian isle) is formed in the shape of a tortoise with stones for the head, four legs, and tail. It is always planted with pine trees and signifies longevity. Since this island is supposed to be in mid-ocean, it is never connected to the bank with any bridge.

362

A wide variety of bridges adds picturesqueness to the garden. They are of stone, wood, or wattle covered with earth. The wooden bridge has the greatest number of variations, for it may have a balustrade, be curved or level, be suspended or constructed on piles, be of logs or of planks. Bridges provide places from which to view the garden scene, considered just as necessary as the providing of spans across water. The zigzag plank bridge of eight sections generally used in iris ponds is actually just a viewing platform which enables one to admire the flowers at close range.

Natural stones, valued for their size, shape, texture, and color, play a very important part in the make-up of the garden and are sought after in faraway places. Those that come from the mountains are placed in such a way that they simulate precipices and crags, while those found on the seashore are given places by the garden lakes. According to their shapes stones are classified into five varieties: "statue," "low-vertical," "flat," "recumbent," and "arching" stones. Sexes have been attributed to some of the forms and they are generally combined in contrasting pairs. In a large elaborate garden there may be as many as one hundred and thirty-eight principal rocks having special names, each with its own function to perform, in addition to a large number of others of secondary importance. Absolutely necessary in even the smallest garden are the "guardian" stone, "stone of worship," and "stone of two deities."

Stepping stones combining beauty with use were devised by the tea masters in the *chanoyu* gardens. They have always been placed with studied irregularity for aesthetic reasons and, of equal importance, to force the visitor to walk slowly through the garden in order that all its facets may be appreciated. Always the stepping stones lead to definite places — the *chanoyu* room, a well, or a stone lantern — but the paths may divide or be laid out in unusual patterns such as that of wild geese in flight.

In the dry landscape, sand, which symbolizes water, is indispensable, and an infinite variety of markings with the rake have been devised to simulate the flow of water. Sand is also thought to instill a sense of freshness and cleanness. In feudal times a fresh supply was kept on hand in some gardens to scatter on a path before the emperor or shogun.

The scarcity of flowers and the preponderance of evergreens is very significant in most of the gardens of Nippon. The deciduous trees welcomed in the garden are those whose trunks and branches are beautiful even when stripped of their leaves, also those with a subtle gradation of seasonal coloring. As with stones, the origin of trees should be respected. None should be planted in positions at variance with their natural habit of growth. Pine trees are the great favorite, no garden being really complete without them. A beautifully shaped pine is generally used in a prominent position both for its dignity of masculine power and its symbolism of longevity. With great artistry trees and shrubs are planted so that they partially hide a cascade mouth, break the monotony of a waterfall, or screen the light from a stone lantern. Tree branches extend in front of bridges and over walls and cast shade on arbors and gateways. Planted behind water basins, their charm is reflected. For the mere enjoyment of the music of raindrops, big-leafed palms are sometimes planted near a house, though because of their ragged unsightliness they are kept out of sight of main rooms. In planting trees in groups, gardeners generally balance three against one, one against two, five against two, etc. Moon reflections upon water must never be obscured because of tree heights, and plantings should not be thick enough to obstruct the passage of the wind. Balancing one group against another, poising one space against another, uniting straight lines with curves, following the rhythm created by the masses, spaces, and lines to a climax fulfills the laws of nature by showing unity and harmony and the relationship of one thing with another.

Wells and water basins have practical as well as decorative uses and are both essential elements of the tea garden in particular. In dry gardens wells and basin drains are often treated as the source of a stream. Stone lanterns, perhaps the most striking garden features, are also requirements of the tea garden. Whether lighted or not, they symbolize light dispelling darkness. Stone pagodas add exotic beauty to some scenes, and full-sized ones of wood which reproduce old shrines or temples are to be found in the more spacious gardens. Placed on heights, they are thought to aid in the peaceful meditation upon unworldly things.

Arbors and summerhouses serve as resting places where one may enjoy solitude or the beauty of the garden. They are built over the water's edge, in wooded ravines, or close by cascades, where the heat of summer may be washed away by the sound of falling water. The *chaseki*, or teahouse, is generally located in a secluded spot, and there may be more than one, built in different styles in different parts of the garden.

Garden gateways and fences show such fascinating variety that it is impossible to describe them all. The garden entrance is usually a roofed gateway with swinging doors. Fences may enclose all or a part of the garden, or short sections called *sode-gaki*, or sleeve fences, may be used to screen off one part from another. They strongly resemble the sleeve of a kimono, not only in its shape, but in its coquettish use as well. Together with the stone water basin, they perform the important function of connecting the garden with the architecture, blending nature with man's art.

It may be said that the Japanese garden is created not merely as a place of beauty but as a place of peace and rest, a fitting abode in which the soul can find nourishment.

XIV

Old-Time Garden Maintenance

A GARDEN NEEDS TOOLS FOR CULTIVATING AND WATERING

" 'Tis not sufficient for a Flower Gardner to take the precaution of providing himself with the necessary Instruments and Tools, without he likewise takes care to keep 'em Bright, and free from Rust, and have 'em mended, set, or dress'd, when, by much using, they are blunted, broke or spoiled."

— FRANCIS GENTIL, 1706

"Watring of the Beddes ought be done in the morning soone after the Sunne rising and at the evening when the Sunne possesseth a weake force upon the Earth. . . . By watering at the hote time of the day as at noone, the water then made hote by heate of the Sunne would so burne the yong and tender rootes of the plantes. . . . If the gardener bee forced to use Well water, . . . or some deepe pit, he ought then to lette the same drawen up stand for two or three dayes togither, or at the least for certayne houres in the open aire, to be warmed of the sunne, least the same . . . sprinkled forth on the beddes both raw and colde, may feeble and kil the tender yong plants coming up. . . . To the water standing in the Sonne, if the owner or gardener mixt a reasonable quantity of dung, thys mixture no doubt will be to great purpose, for as much as the same gently watered or sprinkled abrode, procureth a proper nourishmente to the tender plantes and yong herbes coming up."

— THOMAS HYLL, *The Gardener's Labyrinth*, 1577

EIGHTEENTH-CENTURY TOOLS

1. Spade. "The first instrument the Gardner takes in his Hand. It is chiefly used by Apprentices."
2. Shovel. "Used for throwing earth out of a Trench or Ditch, to throw rakings into a Wheel-barrow or Dosser."
3. Rakes. "This Tool, is in the Gardner's Trade, a Symbol of Neatness."
4. Rakers. "A necessary tool for keeping a Garden clean of Weeds."
5. Displanter. "Used for transplanting, and for taking up all Flowers, that the Gardner is obliged to transport from the place where they were sowed to another."
6. Pruning Knife. "So necessary, that a Gardner ought always to have one in his Pocket."
7. Dibbles. "For planting small Flowers that have Roots and for planting Bulbes."
8. Watering Pot. "It imitates the Rain, falling from the Heavens."
9. Beetle. "This serves to smooth the Walks; and hinders most effectively the growing of Weeds upon 'em."
10. Flower Basket. "A Gardner that cultivates Flowers ought to have Baskets by him, to gather the Flowers in upon occasion. This sort of Baskets, shew a Gardiner's Neatness, and the genteel way of his Profession."
11. Sieve. " 'Tis by this that the Earth is reduced almost to Dust."
12. Saw. "For cutting the Branches which can't be lopped with a knife."
13. Transplanter. "Used for raising together with the Earth, plants for transplanting."
14. Garden Pots. "To put Flowers in, that grow better so than in full Earth, such as Pinks, Bears-Ears, Tube-roses etc. These may be either of plain Earth, or of Dutch Ware, the former for the Plants last mentioned; and the latter, which are much larger, for holding Jessamins, and Clove-Gilly-flowers."
15. Plainer, or Rabot. "Tho' you run the Rake never so often along the Walks and Paths — it will still leave some roughness; which is easily rectified with this instrument."
16. *Pailassons*, or Panniers of Straw. "Very necessary to keep out the Frost."
17. Mallet. "Used with a chizzel for lopping Branches, that can't be so neatly taken off with the force of one's hands."
18. Wheelbarrow. "To carry the Stones and Rakings of a Garden to Places appointed to receive 'em; or, to carry Earth, or Mold, to improve such Grounds as are hungry."
19. Handbarrow. "To carry into the Green-house, Trees or Shrubs, set in Boxes. . . . 'Tis like wise of use for carrying Dung upon the Beds."
20. Caterpillar Shears. "For removing Caterpillars which would otherwise destroy all. . . . They clip, or cut the end of the Branch upon which the Tuft of Caterpillars is lodg'd."
21. Garden Shears. "For trimming the Box, Yews, and other Trees and Shrubs that serve to embellish a Garden."
22. Double Ladder. "For trimming the upper part of an Arbour, or high Bower."
23. Pickax. "For raising the Plants that adorn the Borders . . . or for giving some small Culture to Trees or Shrubs."
24. Rolling Stone. "For smoothing Walks after they are raked."
25. Hook. "A Gardner that has Rows of Greens to dress, can't trim 'em well without a Hook, which is used after a certain particular manner, that a young Gardner quickly learns."
26. Glass Bell. "A Florist can't be without this unless he has a mind to run the risk of losing his Plants, . . . such as are sown in Beds immediately after the end of Winter."
27. Straw Bell. "Proper for covering Plants newly transplanted, in order to guard them from the Heat of the Sun, which might annoy them at first."
28. Garden Fork. "For spreading and disposing the Dung upon the Beds."
29. Trowel. "By the help of which a Flower Gardner takes up Plants with the Earth about them."
30. Hurdle. "For passing the Earth through. . . . Of great use for separating the good Earth from the Stones."

— Plate from *Le Jardinier Fleuriste*, by le Sieur L. Liger d'Auxerre, 1787

—Text from *Le Jardinier Solitaire* (*The Solitary or Carthusian Gard'ner*), by Francis Gentil, London, 1706

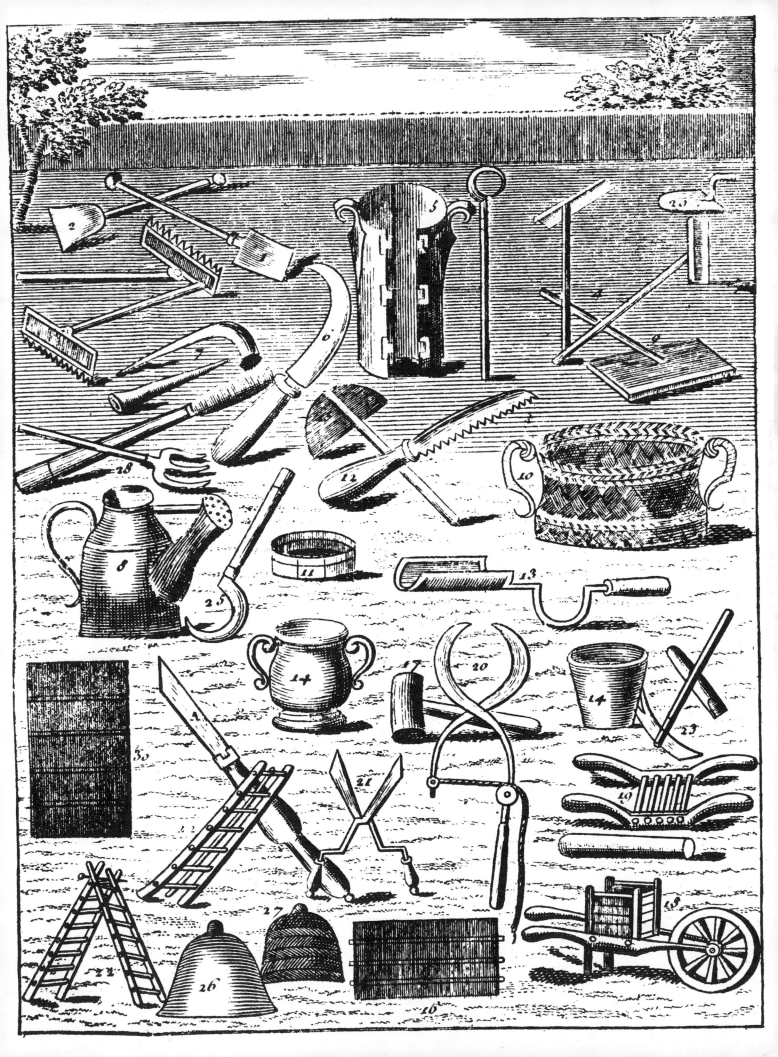

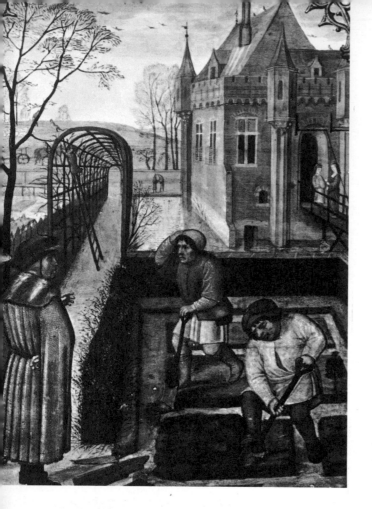

(ABOVE LEFT) Spring gardening activities within the walls of a moated castle. The master and overseer watch the first spading of the season. 1495. (*The Pierpont Morgan Library*)

(ABOVE RIGHT) "Through cunning, with dibble, rake, mattock and spade
      By line and by levell, trim garden is made."
            — THOMAS TUSSER, *A Hundred Good Points of Husbandrie*, 1557
Illustration from Thomas Hyll's *The Gardener's Labyrinth*, 1577 (*New York Public Library*)

(OPPOSITE ABOVE) A seventeenth-century Gobelin tapestry in the Pitti Palace showing child gardeners cultivating a flower garden. Spades, rakes and a hoe are all in use. (*Alinari*)

(OPPOSITE BELOW) The busy activity of a spring day is depicted by Pieter Brueghel, the Elder. Spading, raking, seeding, planting, watering, and pruning are being done by the gardeners while merry-makers in the background dine under a tree pavilion. (*Metropolitan Museum of Art*)

368

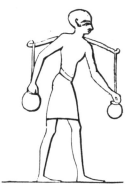

(LEFT) Bringing buckets of water to the garden from a nearby well has been the simplest and oldest way of watering.

(RIGHT) The ancient Egyptians watered with pots borne on wooden shoulder yokes. They also used the *shaduf*, which consisted of a leather bucket suspended from a pole, similar to a well-sweep. From Georges Perrot and Charles Chipiez, *History of Art in Ancient Egypt*; London: Chapman and Hall, 1883.

A sixteenth-century watering device, made of perforated earthenware, made use of the principle of the siphon. Thomas Hyll wrote about it in *The Gardener's Labyrinth*, 1577. "The common watering potte for the garden beds with us, hath a narrow necke, bigge belly, somewhat large bottome, and full of little holes, with a proper hole formed on the head, to take in the water, which filled full and the thumbe layde on the hole to keep in the aire may in such wise be carried in handsome manner." Sixteenth-century Flemish engraving. (*Metropolitan Museum of Art*)

Puncheons or tubs, on wheels, could be trundled through the garden to distribute water. Eighteenth-century engraving by Salomon Kleiner. (*Metropolitan Museum of Art. Photo: Roche*)

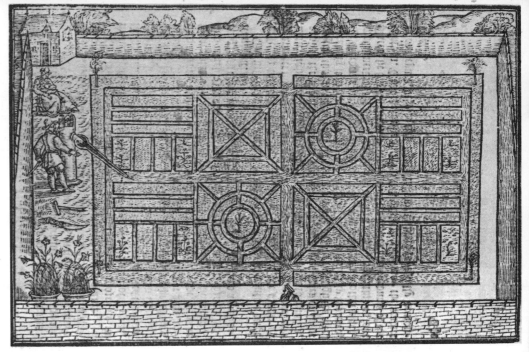

A system of irrigation troughs could distribute water to all parts of a garden.

A watering cart which could "be used to advantage in watering the lawns, ... to preserve the greenness as well as laying the dust of walks. Also for watering the vegetable garden." Figures 1 and 2 show how the sprinkler could be used either lengthwise or crosswise. Figure 3 shows a single wooden sprinkler which could be aimed in a particular direction. Engraving by J. G. Grohmann, 1796. (*Metropolitan Museum of Art. Photo: Roche*)

The "great Squirt of Tin" took "mighty strength to handle" and "looked like a small cannon." Water could be thrown in "great droppes" like a fountain or sprinkler. Three illustrations from Thomas Hyll's *Gardener's Labyrinth*, 1577. (*The Pierpont Morgan Library*)

A copper watering pot with "bigge bellie, narrow necke and stronge handle" was commonly used in the eighteenth century, as can be seen in tapestry (ABOVE LEFT) and engraving (ABOVE RIGHT). French tapestry, "March." (*Metropolitan Museum of Art*). French engraving. (*Pierpont Morgan Library*)

THE FORMAL GARDEN HAS ALWAYS NEEDED PRUNING AND CLIPPING

Hedge shears were long and kept sharp. Movable platforms sometimes eased the chore of clipping. Engravings by Salomon Kleiner, 1730. (BELOW AND OPPOSITE BELOW) (*Metropolitan Museum of Art. Photo: Roche*)

Trimming the hedges in a seventeenth-century Flemish garden. Engraving, "Odoratus," by Abraham Bosse. (BELOW LEFT) (*New York Public Library*)

Knives have been used for centuries for pruning and cutting shrubs, vines, and small trees. One of a series of Gobelin tapestries depicting child gardeners during the four seasons, in the collections of the Pitti Palace, Florence. (BELOW RIGHT) (*Alinari*)

(LEFT) The wheelbarrow has been one of man's most useful inventions. It has transported people, merchandise, and produce and had a hundred different uses in the garden. (*New York Public Library*)

(BELOW) During the seventeenth and eighteenth centuries Europeans customarily followed the Italian practice of placing orange and lemon trees in tubs or terracotta jardinieres about the garden. After the winter spent inside orangeries, or conservatories, they were wheeled to their places in the patterned garden. Engraving by Salomon Kleiner, 1730. (*Metropolitan Museum of Art. Photo: Roche*)

(OPPOSITE) A movable and decorative pulley for lifting trees out of tubs when they were to be planted in the ground. From Volckamer. *Nurnbergische Hesperides*, 1708. (*New York Public Library*)

WHEELS HAVE MADE THE GARDENER'S LIFE EASIER

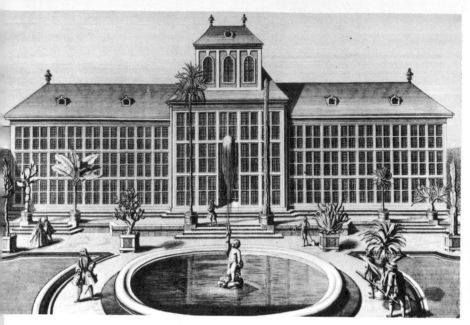

With eighteenth-century interest in "exotics," or plants from other parts of the world, the old orangerie gave way to the conservatory. The glass area provided greater sun heat. Heat from stoves also protected tropical plants in such collections as the unusual one owned by the Prince of Schwarzenberg. Engraving by Salomon Kleiner, 1730. (*Metropolitan Museum of Art. Photo: Roche*)

(BELOW) Bell-shaped glass cloches gave frost protection to plants set out in the very early spring. Illustration from *The Gentleman and Gardener's Kalendar*, 1718, by Richard Bradley. (*Massachusetts Horticultural Society Library*)

GARDENS AND THEIR PLANTS NEED WINTER PROTECTION AND HEAT FOR FORCING

Late-seventeenth-century Dutch "stove" for protecting orange trees in winter. Charcoal was burned in preference to wood. Illustration from *Den Nederlantsen Hovenier*, 1696. (*New York Public Library*)

(LEFT) Cold frames protected tender plants. Those weathering the winter could be mulched with straw. Gobelin tapestry, eighteenth century. (*Alinari*)

(BELOW) Humphrey Repton's proposed forcing garden for Woburn Abbey. Illustrated in his *Fragments on the Theory and Practice of Landscape Gardening*. (*Pennsylvania Horticultural Society Library*)

THERE ARE PESTS IN A GARDEN

To banish moles "take white Hellebore, and the Root of Palma Christi, bruise and pound, mix with Barley-meal and Egg, dilute with Wine and Milk, make a Paste and divide into several Pieces and put in the Mole-holes." Some people "take a thick piece of Wood, well arm'd with great long nails, and narrowly watching the moment of the Earth's heaving, thrust down the Log of a sudden which so stuns the Mole, that 'tis easily taken up with a Spade."

To get rid of caterpillars, "cut Tufts of 'em off Trees, at the break of Day, . . . they being then gather'd into Knots thro' the Cold of the Night."

(LEFT) Detail from an engraving by Hendrik and Daniel van Damme, 1730. (*Metropolitan Museum of Art. Photo: Roche*)

(OPPOSITE) After a lawn was scythed the grass clippings were swept up with twig brooms called besoms. A print showing the garden at Carlton House in Pall Mall, which belonged to George III's mother, the Princess Dowager of Wales. Engraved by William Woollett in 1760.

Seek for snails "by Break of Day, or after Rain, that being the time when they come out of the Earth to feed, and are easily squashed."

To destroy ants, "Burn empty Snail shells with Storax wood and throw ashes on the ant hill — which will presently oblige the little inhabitants to remove, . . . or use origanum in Powder with Brimstone."

"Dogs and Cats ought not to be suffer'd in a Flower Garden. Your Dogs do, by their continual leaping, leave ugly Marks or Impressions upon the Surface of the Ground, . . . and the Cats scattering their Ordure all about, and then scraping the Earth to cover it, grub up many Plants."

— LE SIEUR LOUIS LIGER D'AUXERRE, *The Compleat Florist*, 1706

A FINE GREEN LAWN

"Nothing is more pleasant to the eye than green grass kept finely shorn," as Francis Bacon wrote in his *Essay on Gardening*, and it is in England that the skill of making and maintaining the lawn has been perfected. Pampered by the climate, the fine grass lawn has been one of her greatest contributions to garden beauty. In Tudor times turf was cut from pastures to use for small plots, walks, or wide borders beside garden paths. In preparation, stones were removed and boiling water was poured on the site to kill any weeds. When the turf was planted it was pounded into place with a flat wooden tool called a "turf beater" or "beetle."

During the seventeenth century the popularity of bowling called for a greater extent of grass and a smoother lawn of compact growth. Often camomile and white clover were mixed with hay seed to provide it. Camomile was started by "sets" which made runners, and therefore grew better if walked upon, or if rolled, for this pushed them firmly into the soil.

Eighteenth-century gardeners developed much more extensive lawn areas and maintained their beauty through the constant use of the scythe and the roller. Rollers were of wood, stone, and iron.

It was not until the nineteenth century that improved grass seeds were developed by nurserymen. That century also produced the mechanical lawn mower.

(BELOW) There must be "frequent use of the gritstone in sharpening the scythe."
— JOHN PAPWORTH, *Hints on Ornamental Gardening*
Detail from an engraving by William Woollett, 1757. (*Metropolitan Museum of Art. Photo: Roche*)

(OPPOSITE) "The occasional use of a heavy roller, after rain will tend to smooth over inequalities in the ground. The surface should be kept as smooth as possible." "To free the surface from worm casts etc., it is common practice to roll the previous evening as much as may be mown the next day." —ANDREW JACKSON DOWNING, *A Treatise on the Theory and Practice of Landscape Gardening.* Detail from an engraving by William Woollett, 1757. (*Metropolitan Museum of Art. Photo: Roche*)

The first lawn mower was patented in England in the year 1830 by Edwin Budding, who worked as an engineer in a textile factory. After studying a machine which sheared the nap off cloth, he applied the principle to a machine for cutting grass. J. R. and A. Ransome started manufacturing it in 1832. (*Ransomes, Sims & Jefferies Ltd.*)

EPILOGUE

"The Gardner had not need be an idle, or lazie Lubber, for so your Orchard . . . will not prosper. There will ever be something to doe. Weeds are alwaies growing. The great mother of all living Creatures, the Earth, is full of seed in her bowels, and any stirring gives them heat of Sun, and being laid neere of day, they grow: Mowles worke daily. . . . Winter herbes at all times will grow (except in extreme frost). In Winter your young trees and hearbs would be lightned of snow, and your Allyes cleansed: drifts of snow will let Deere, Hares, and Conyes, and other noysome beasts over your walls and hedges, into your Orchard. When Summer cloathes your borders with green and peckled colours, your Gardner must dresse his hedges, and antike workes: watch his Bees, and hive them: distill his Roses and other herbes. Now begins Summer Fruit to ripe, and crave your hand to pull them. . . . No man is sufficient for these things. If there is a Garden to keepe, you must needs allow him good helpe, to end his labours which are endless."
— WILLIAM LAWSON, *A New Orchard and Garden, London,* 1618

NOTES

I. In the Time of the Pharaohs

[1]Nina M. Davies and Allan H. Gardiner, *Ancient Egyptian Paintings* (Chicago: University of Chicago Press, 1936).

[2]Richard A. Parker, "The Late Demotic Gardening Agreement," *Journal of Egyptian Archeology*, Vol. 26, 1941.

V. The Gardens of Islam: Persia

[1]Arthur Urbane Dilley, *The Garden of Paradise Rug and the Holy Carpet of the Mosque at Ardebil*, probably printed in 1924.

VII. The Italian Renaissance

[1]Trans. by John Addington Symonds, *The Renaissance in Italy* (London: Smith, Elder and Co., 1875–1886).

[2]Michel de Montaigne, *Complete Works, Essays, Travel Journal, Letters*, trans. by Donald M. Frame (Stanford: Stanford University Press, 1957).

[3]Edith Wharton, *Italian Villas and Their Gardens* (New York: The Century Co., 1904).

[4]A copy is available in the Print Room, Metropolitan Museum of Art, New York.

VIII. French Grandeur

[1]Jacques Androuet Du Cerceau, *Des Plus Excellents Bâtiments de France* (Paris: 1576–1607).

[2]The Duc de Saint-Simon, who lived at the Court of Versailles, wrote lengthy *Memoirs* which reveal much concerning the last twenty years of Louis XIV's reign.

[3]From the official history of André Félibien, architect and historian.

[4]Helen M. Fox, *André Le Nôtre, Garden Architect to Kings* (New York: Crown Publishers, 1962).

X. English Traditions

[1]Mollie Sands, *Gardens of Hampton Court*, (London: Evans Bros., 1950).

[2]Francis Bacon, "Of Gardens," *Essays*.

[3]J. Dodsley, *Works in Verse and Prose of William Shenstone, Esq.*, Vol. II (London: 1791).

[4]Gertrude Jekyll, *Home and Garden* (London: Longmans Green & Co., 1900).

XI. American Garden Heritage

[1]The author gratefully acknowledges the assistance of Cita van Santen, Dutch horticulturist of The Hague, Holland, who undertook this translation.

[2]The text uses the word *senderlinge*, which is close to *zendelingen*, meaning "missionaries." In this sense it has no religious connotation but refers to a person who spreads information. "Enthusiast" has been substituted as a synonym.

GLOSSARY

Eg	Egyptian	J	Japanese
E	English	P	Persian and Mogul
F	French	R	Roman
I	Italian	S	Spanish

ALLÉE (F): Long avenue bordered by trees.

AQUARIUS (R): Servant in charge of private fountains.

ATRIUM (R): Entrance hall of a dwelling; had an opening in the ceiling and a pool in the floor.

BAGH (P): Pleasure garden and dwelling.

BERCEAU (F): Arched trelliswork forming a covered walk. A support for greenery.

BERSO (I): Same as above.

BONSAI (J): Cultivation of dwarf trees.

BOSCO (I): Grove of trees.

BOSQUET (F): Same as above.

BRODERIE (F): Elaborate curvilinear design of dwarf box, similar in effect to embroidery.

CHABUTRA (P): Small outdoor platform or throne.

CHANIWA (J): Tea garden.

CHANOYU (J): Tea ceremony.

CHASEKI (J): Place where the tea ceremony is held.

CLAIRVOYÉE (E and F): Window-like aperture cut through a hedge or wall.

CRYPTOPORTICUS (R): A columned and roofed ambulatory for use in bad weather.

DIAETA (R): An entire apartment containing everything necessary for daily living.

GESTATIO (R): Garden area used either for horseback riding or for riding in a vehicle.

GIARDINO SEGRETO (I): Small, enclosed private garden.

GLORIETA (S): Garden bower of clipped trees, usually cypress.

GYO (J): Semiformal style.

HA-HA (E): Ditch, usually walled, to prevent animals from intruding on turfed or garden areas.

HIRA-NIWA (J): Level garden.

IKEBANA (J): Art of flower arrangement.

KARE-SANSUI (J): Dry landscape.

NIWASHI (J): Nurserymen.

NYMPHAEUM (R): Pleasure pavilion embellished with water.

PARTERRE (F): Patterned garden, its design usually worked in low-growing evergreens, its compartments filled with flowers, turf, and/or colored earths.

PATTE D'OIE (F): Goose-foot arrangement of three avenues radiating from a curved center.

PERGOLA (E): An open-work, pillared archway, usually covering a walk or passageway, over which plants such as vines are trained to climb.

PERISTYLE (R): Inner court of dwelling, open to sky.

PISCINA (R): Fish pool.

PLEACHED ALLEY (E): Arched walkway, or one lined both sides with "walls" of interlacing trees specially trained and pruned.

PRATO (I): Flat grassy area used for games or tilting.

RAGNAIA (I): Thicket or grove suitable for netting birds.

RICAMI (I): Plant embroidery. *See* BRODERIE.

ROCAILLE (F): Rockwork, with stucco, as used in grottoes.

SAVINA (R): Pool.

SEN-TEI (J): Water garden.

SHADUF (Eg): Pole-and-bucket water-raising device similar to a well-sweep. Used for irrigation purposes.

SHIMA (J): Ancient word for island, or garden.

SHIN (J): Formal style.

SO (J): Informal style.

STANZONE (I): Conservatory especially meant for wintering lemon and orange trees.

TOKONOMA (J): Alcove for display of art objects. A flower arrangement is usually included.

TOPIARUS (R): Gardener.

TORII (J): Shinto gateway.

TRICLINIUM (R): Dining area, usually with three reclining places around a table and the fourth side open, for ease of service.

TSUKI-YAMA (J): Artificial hill garden.

VASCA (I): Pond, reservoir, or water basin.

VIRIDARIUM (R): Peristyle in which there was a garden pool.

XYSTUS (T): Garden terrace surrounded on three sides by colonnades; this area might be paved or planted.